Graham and Dodd's

Security Analysis

Fifth Edition (Abridged)

Other Financial and Investment Titles from McGraw-Hill

Bauman/Komarynsky/Siska Goytre
INVESTMENT SECURITIES PROGRAM GUIDE USING THE HP-12C

Cottle/Murray/Block
SECURITY ANALYSIS, Fifth Edition

Finnerty
CORPORATE FINANCIAL ANALYSIS

Gianturco
THE STOCK MARKET INVESTOR'S COMPUTER GUIDE

Greenwald
THE CONCISE McGRAW-HILL DICTIONARY OF ECONOMICS

Ibbotson/Brinson
INVESTMENT MARKETS

Rock
THE MERGERS AND ACQUISITIONS HANDBOOK

For more information about other McGraw-Hill materials, call 1-800-2-MCGRAW in the United States. In other countries, call your nearest McGraw-Hill office.

Graham and Dodd's
Security Analysis

Fifth Edition

Abridged Edition for the Institute of Chartered Financial Analysts

Sidney Cottle

President, FRS Associates
Coauthor of *Security Analysis*, Fourth Edition

Roger F. Murray

S. Sloan Colt Professor Emeritus of Banking
and Finance
Columbia University Graduate School of Business

Frank E. Block

Member of Financial Accounting Standards Board,
1979–1985 (retired)
Past President of FAF and ICFA

With the collaboration of
Martin L. Leibowitz

Managing Director, Bond Portfolio Analysis Group
Salomon Brothers, Inc.

McGraw-Hill Book Company

**New York St. Louis San Francisco Auckland
Bogotá Hamburg London Madrid Mexico
Milan Montreal New Delhi Panama
Paris São Paulo Singapore
Sydney Tokyo Toronto**

Library of Congress Cataloging in Publication Data

Graham, Benjamin, date.
  [Security analysis]
  Graham and Dodd's security analysis. — 5th ed., abridged ed. for
the Institute of Chartered Financial Analysts / Sidney Cottle,
Roger F. Murray, Frank E. Block; with the collaboration of
Martin L. Leibowitz.

    p. cm.
    Includes bibliographical references and index.
    ISBN 0-07-013237-2
    1. Investment analysis.   2. Securities — United States.   I. Dodd,
David L. (David Le Fevre), date.   II. Cottle, Sidney.
III. Murray, Roger F.   IV. Block, Frank E.   V. Title.   VI. Title:
Security analysis.
HG4529.G7 1988b
332.63'2 — dc 19   88-13556
                                                              CIP

This is an abridgment of *Security Analysis,* Fifth Edition, by Sidney
Cottle, Roger F. Murray, and Frank E. Block. This edition has
been published specially for the Institute of Chartered Financial
Analysts.

1234567890 DOC/DOC 89321098

ISBN 0-07-013237-2

*The editors for this book were Martha Jewett and Caroline Levine,
the designer was Naomi Auerbach, and the production supervisor was
Dianne Walber. This book was set in Baskerville. It was composed by the
McGraw-Hill Book Company Professional & Reference Division
Composition unit.*

*For more information about other McGraw-Hill materials,
call 1-800-2-MCGRAW in the United States. In other
countries, call your nearest McGraw-Hill office.*

Contents

Part 1. Financial Analysis and Approach

1. Economic Analysis   3

Part 2. Analysis of Financial Statements

2. Overview of Financial Statement Analysis   23

3. Analysis of the Income Statement   39

4. Effect of Reserves, Contingencies, and Valuation Accounts on the Income Statement   57

5. Inventory Valuation and Cost of Goods Sold   85

6. Effect of Depreciation and Amortization on Taxes and Income   101

7. Analysis of the Funds Flow Statement   127

8. Results of Subsidiaries, Affiliates, and Foreign Operations   153

9. Effects of Income Taxes   165

10. Balance Sheet Analysis   183

11. Asset Values in Balance Sheet Analysis   205

12. Ratio Analysis   223

13. Key Ratios in Company Comparisons   255

14. Ratios in Industry Analysis   273

Index   291

PART 1

Financial Analysis and Approach

1

Economic Analysis

Return expectations for the stock and bond markets and sales, cost, and profit projections for industries and nearly all companies necessarily embody economic assumptions. It is the exceptional case for which this is not true.[1]

Economic forecasts need to be considered in terms of the individual analyst's requirements and must be viewed from the standpoint of both their usage and their preparation. Accordingly, this chapter:

- Describes the nature of economic forecasts required by the security analyst

- Discusses the need for longer-term (secular) forecasts as well as near-term (cyclical) forecasts and explains the conceptual differences between the two

- Points out the need to understand the interrelationships among macroeconomic variables and to develop linkages between these variables and the performance of capital markets, economic sectors, industries, and companies

- Provides a discussion of projection methodology and illustrations of key underlying assumptions

Economic assumptions may be explicit or implicit. For an investment organization, explicit forecasts are necessary for effective communication throughout the organization. Individual investors may assimilate

[1]Several exceptional cases are noted at the end of this chapter.

from review of a series of forecasts an implicit and intuitive set that is satisfactory for their purposes.

In all instances, investors using such forecasts should have clearly in mind the time span (or spans) for which they want projections and the key cyclical or secular assumptions underlying the forecasts used.

Economic Forecasts in Perspective

Economic forecasts provide essential underpinning for stock and bond market, industry, and company projections. The outlook for stock and bond markets depends on the outlook for such basic economic factors as:

- The growth rate for real GNP and GNP in current dollars
- The supply of funds coming principally from business and personal saving, including pension funds[2]
- The demand for funds arising from financing expenditures by consumers, business, and governments
- The inflation rate and anticipated inflationary pressures
- Corporate profits

Similarly, the outlook for industries and companies depends on the outlook for those economic factors that affect demand for their products and the cost of labor, material, and capital. The accuracy and consistency of analysts' projections for industry and company sales, expenses, and earnings lie in the closer knitting of economic and security analysis. This requires establishing internally consistent economic projections on which all other forecasts should depend.

Large organizations with in-house economists develop their own forecasts. In the process, they examine the projections of others (such as brokerage houses and banks) and frequently subscribe to one or more forecasting services, such as Data Resources, Inc., Chase Econometrics, and the Wharton Econometric Model. Computer access to these models allows for testing of alternative assumptions and otherwise modifying the "standard" projections produced by the forecasting services.

Small investment organizations and individual investors typically rely on external forecasts as provided by brokerage houses and subscription

---

[2]For several years, some state and local governments have had an operating surplus, which is also a source of gross savings. Foreign capital inflows are an additional source of funds.

services as mentioned above. These smaller organizations are less likely to have computer access to an econometric model and will rely primarily on the memoranda and reports issued at regular intervals (quarterly or more frequently).

Cyclical and Secular Forecasts

Investment decisions should be based on longer-term as well as near-term projections. Indeed, institutional investment decisions are increasingly made on a longer-term basis.[3]

On the one hand, investment theory tells us that the worth of a common stock is the present value of its entire future earnings or dividend stream. However, the uncertainty of projections rises as futurity is lengthened and the present value of distant earnings or dividends is small. Therefore, explicit long-term projections are impractical.

On the other hand, the earning power or dividend-paying capacity of an enterprise and thus the central tendency in its price cannot be judged adequately on the basis of a one- or two-year outlook. The normal current price level, longer-term growth, stability of earnings, and the dividend payout ratio of the typical company cannot be effectively appraised in terms of what may happen in the next year. Likewise, it would be purely coincidental if the future growth rate of industries, the stock market, or the total economy were meaningfully indicated by the near-term outlook. Undue emphasis on the near-term can produce distorted investment decisions.

The conceptual differences between near-term cyclical predictions and longer-term secular projections are as pronounced as the differences in the projection spans. These differences must be understood because they involve substantially different appraisals of the future.

Near-Term Forecasts

In general, near-term projections comprise the next four to eight quarters and are typically designated as "forecasts" by business economists. These projections represent definitive estimates of what will happen in a given time frame. They are predictions of the specific level

---

[3]Unfortunately, too frequently investors pressure for gains in short-term (quarter-by-quarter) profitability. This places undue emphasis on near-term forecasts and may prove disadvantageous in the long run.

and nature of economic activity on a quarter-by-quarter basis, and thus they map out the cyclical path that the economy is expected to follow.

Quarterly Demand Forecasts.   Near-term forecasts are primarily "demand" forecasts.[4] The level of business activity in the short run is determined more by changes in income and expenditures than by changes in capacity. Accordingly, although careful consideration must be given to the relationship of demand to the nation's existing output capacity (whether little or substantial "slack" exists in the economy), demand rather than capacity can change significantly over the near term.[5]

Putting aside such major disruptive events as war, severe droughts, or an oil embargo, economic change in the near term is almost entirely the result of changes in the incomes and expenditures of individuals, the level of corporate profits and business expenditures, and monetary and fiscal policy designed to influence incomes and expenditures. Accordingly, near-term forecasts are primarily the result of economic forces; that is, forces generated within the economic system itself. For this reason, economic models are particularly vital to near-term forecasts.

Economic Models.   These models are derived from extensive systematic analysis of the past behavior of key economic variables and delineate in general terms the behavior patterns and interrelationships within the economic system of households, businesses, governments, and foreigners—the principal classes of economic units. Whether they are preparing a set of mathematical (econometric) forecasts with extensive sectoral detail or only simplified judgmental forecasts, economists develop models systematically within a given conceptual framework.

The practical use of models lies in answering such questions as the following: What are the implications of a reduction of income taxes on the level and pattern of personal consumption expenditures? What effect on business plant and equipment expenditures can be expected from an increase in the investment tax credit? What will be the impact of a significant increase in federal expenditures on aggregate demand? What will an increase in the gasoline tax do to fuel consumption?

---

[4]See Geoffrey H. Moore, *Business Cycles, Inflation, and Forecasting*, National Bureau of Economic Research, Studies on Business Cycles, no. 24, 1980.

[5]However, it is to be recognized that, as a result of economic recovery, accelerated depreciation, and tax reduction, considerable capacity was added in 1983 and 1984.

Articles and books dealing with the methods and techniques of near-term economic forecasting exist in profusion.[6] An overall knowledge of the workings of the economy is essential in analyzing industries and companies as well as in reaching effective investment decisions.

Longer-Term Projections

Longer-term predictions are frequently referred to as "projections."[7] No consensus exists as to the length of the longer term, since the projection span beyond the next two years cannot be forecast as confidently as the near term. For in-depth analysis and a comprehensive set of projections, the optimum longer-term span is considered to be 5 to 10 years. A period much shorter than 5 years is unduly affected by cyclical forces; whereas for the longer span, projections are considered more in terms of secular forces and structural changes. An interval much longer than 10 years raises an increasing number of uncertainties, particularly in regard to social, political, and technological change.

Use of a five-year span is suggested in most instances. Because the U.S. and world economies are highly dynamic, an in-depth analysis is more manageable when restricted to five years. Furthermore, the duration of the business cycle in the postwar period (measured from trough to trough) has averaged between four and five years.[8] Thus, a five-year projection span covers the typical business cycle and is also a reasonable period for measuring the investment performance of security analysts and portfolio managers.

Our suggestion that in-depth analysis of secular growth be limited to five years is not meant to confine an organization's horizon. Also needed is a notional (less specific) longer-term idea of the social, political, and economic environment in the form of a skeletal set of projections

[6]For example, see L. Klein and R. M. Young, *An Introduction to Econometric Forecasting and Forecasting Models*, Lexington Books, Lexington, Mass., 1980. Also, a comprehensive collection of 32 papers on the many aspects of forecasting by an impressive list of practitioners is contained in *Methods and Techniques of Business Forecasting*, edited by W. F. Butler, R. A. Kavesh, and R. B. Platt, Prentice-Hall, Englewood Cliffs, N.J., 1974. A summary discussion by two of the editors, Kavesh and Platt, entitled, "Economic Forecasting," is in S. N. Levine, ed., *Financial Analyst's Handbook I*, Dow-Jones-Irwin, Homewood, Ill., 1975, pp. 928–943. Related subjects exist in Part V of the *Handbook*: "Economic Analysis and Timing." Another comprehensive undertaking is a two-volume study by B. G. Hickman, ed., *Econometric Models of Cyclical Behavior*, Studies in Income & Wealth, no. 36, National Bureau of Economic Research, Columbia University Press, New York, 1972.

[7]The terms *forecasts* and *projections* are used interchangeably. The context indicates whether the predictions are for the near or longer term.

[8]For the 1945–1981 span, the average duration was 60 months. If the two extremes (34 and 117 months) are eliminated, the average is 53 months (based on a National Bureau of Economic Research reprint from the *Business Conditions Digest*, July 1982, p. 105).

covering such key variables as the growth rate for real GNP, inflation, GNP in current dollars, and corporate profits. Forecasts beyond five years primarily indicate whether the investment environment will be significantly different from that expected on a secular basis, develop consistency in industry and company projections by security analysts, and provide inputs for the "steady state" or "terminal" stage of a dividend discount model. These projections are more directional than dimensional. For example, inflation was probably the most disruptive economic force experienced by investors from the late 1960s to the early 1980s. It adversely affected economic activity, reduced corporate profits, drove interest rates up and stock prices down, and distorted relative returns in the capital markets. Indeed, for a portion of the 1970s, the return on Treasury bills exceeded the return on both stocks and bonds. Thus, when investing in long-term assets such as stocks or bonds, one must evaluate the economic and investment climate beyond that expected for the next five years.

Secular Average Projections.   Longer-term projections ordinarily take the form of annual rather than quarterly forecasts and are primarily secular rather than cyclical. They should not predict either the actual level of activity for each year over the five-year span or the actual change from one year to the next. Instead, longer-term projections abstract from cyclical variations and represent basic trends and levels in the economy that underlie cyclical swings. Fluctuations in demand cause cyclical oscillations around the trend.

Long-term projections provide specific estimates for a particular future (terminal) year that is ordinarily considered to be a midcycle or representative "average" year. The level of employment and nature of activity in the initial year are also assumed to be those of an average year. The terminal year is thus basically the culmination of forecasts of expected *average* annual changes for the intervening span of years. Use of this averaging concept, which relies on good and poor years offsetting one another, makes secular projections less reliable as the projection span is shortened. This is another reason why longer-term projections should not cover a span less than five years.

Supply Projections.   Longer-term projections of real GNP (output in physical terms, inflation adjusted) are primarily "supply" forecasts. Accordingly, they give particular attention to demographics—the increase in population, age distribution, and growth in the labor force. Capital formation, innovation, and increased productivity (output per worker-hour) are also important. Thus longer-term projections take as their point of departure estimates of growth in the nation's output potential—the average annual increase in the volume of goods and services (output in constant dollars) that the United States could produce if operating at a stipulated level of employment.

These initial estimates are then modified for the expected growth and nature of demand over the projection span to provide "best guess" estimates. Experience establishes that, in their most useful form, these modified projections consider a number of factors in addition to the secular forces of growth and structural change in the economy:

- The relationship of the current and expected near-term level of economic activity to the nation's output potential
- Expected government economic policy, including monetary and fiscal policy
- International political and economic developments
- The nature and amplitude of business cycles over the projection span; the severity of recessions
- The probability of rampant inflation

Resolution of these issues is highly uncertain; however, their consideration is essential to preparing longer-term projections for the economy and security markets.

Conditional and Interdisciplinary.   Longer-term projections are much more conditional than near-term predictions. They are affected substantially more by noneconomic factors. Over a span of years, social, political, technological, and international forces can critically affect both the demand for goods and services and the ability to produce them. Accordingly, effective longer-term economic forecasts are interdisciplinary undertakings to a surprising extent.

Importance of Longer-Term Projections.   The primary importance of these longer-term projections does not lie in the specific numbers generated, which principally represent orders of magnitude. Rather, it lies in the research findings and reasoning on which the numbers are based and in the benchmarks and relationships they establish. It would be coincidence if the projections were an exact anticipation of the future; nevertheless, explicit forecasts are necessary for the mental discipline, logic, and cross-checks required in drawing definitive conclusions.[9]

---

[9]The discipline and key considerations in making a longer-term forecast are effectively set forth by W. S. Gray III in "Developing a Long-Term Outlook for the U.S. Economy and Stock Market," *Financial Analysts Journal*, July–August 1979, pp. 29–39.

In-depth estimates of the longer-term future provide critical insights into the underlying growth and structural changes in the economy that cannot be seen from near-term forecasts. They also provide essential perspective in judging the near term. It is unlikely that the initial year will actually be at midcycle (an average or equilibrium year). The longer-term (secular) projection will thus provide a benchmark for judging the extent of the current departure from the secular trend.[10]

Long-term projections provide security analysts with information to estimate the growth rates of both industries and companies. Longer-term growth in earnings is the major determinant of the multiplier of investment-quality common stocks. Therefore, it is regrettable that so much research effort is devoted to forecasting the next four to eight quarters and that only limited—albeit increasing—effort is devoted to the longer term.

Linkage between Economic and Security Analysis

Linkage with Near-Term Forecasts

There are well-established methodologies for forecasting the near-term outlook for the economy or analyzing the past experience of companies and predicting the future. However, the greatest difficulty exists and the least has been accomplished in tailoring economic forecasts to provide maximum assistance to security analysts.

Finding Stable Relationships.   The challenge is to find reasonably stable relationships between specific macroeconomic variables and such factors as industry and company sales, costs, and profits. Although such a task is not easy, security analysts can increase their judgment factor and reach more effective investment decisions by consistently considering a given set of macroeconomic variables.

Institutions should review and discuss quarterly the economic projections of such macroeconomic variables as real GNP, inflation, nominal GNP, and selected expenditure components. The significance of individual variables will change from time to time, and the amount of attention devoted at a specific time to any one will vary.

---

[10]As a result, the current returns from investment asset classes will probably differ from forecast equilibrium returns.

Judging Risk of Forecasts. The risk (likelihood of being wrong) involved in any set of forecasts must be judged. This estimation should take place at all levels in the hierarchy of forecasts, beginning with the outlook for the economy, progressing through the securities markets, sectors, and industries, and terminating with the outlook for individual issues. Accordingly, the probabilities associated with the economic projections adopted as the "most probable" forecast should be assessed.

Two approaches can be employed in subjectively estimating such probabilities. One is to develop alternative scenarios that bracket a range of reason and indicate more optimistic and more pessimistic possibilities than the most probable forecast.

The other approach is to use as a base either a consensus forecast obtained from external sources or the output of a comprehensive model (such as Data Resources' model). This base set of projections can then be modified to the extent that an organization has strongly differing opinions. The probabilities assigned in this case can be judged not only by appraising the degree of conviction held relative to the modifications of the control model but also by examining the range of forecasts prevailing among other forecasters, such as several Wall Street economists.

A summary of key macroeconomic variables in a set of near-term forecasts is provided in the following pages, together with examples illustrating the relationship of sales for two industries to a major economic variable.

Key Macroeconomic Variables Identified. The mass of data pertaining to the U.S. economy can be segregated into two principal categories—income and expenditure (the latter is the so-called product category). The overall level of economic activity is considered in terms of its major expenditure components and is illustrated in Table 1.1.

The summary of key macroeconomic variables provides the minimum amount of information needed in terms of expenditures. How much further disaggregation is required will depend on the depth of analysis within an organization. For example, personal consumption expenditures for nondurable goods can be further disaggregated in terms of clothing and shoes, food, fuel oil and coal, gasoline and oil, and other expenditures.

Table 1.1 shows that the realized increase in expenditures from 1984 to 1985 was significantly different from one major component to another. For instance, among personal consumption expenditures, the rate of increase for services was substantially more than that for nondurable goods. In similar fashion, the increase in business expenditures for investment in structures exceeded that for any other component. These and other obvious differences in sectoral expenditures carried important implications for the growth in sales and profits of industries and companies in 1985.

Table 1.1. Summary of GNP and Major Expenditure Components Percentage Change between 1984 and 1985

	Year (in billions of dollars)		Percent change
	1984	1985	
GNP (1982 dollars)	3,489.9	3,585.2	2.7
GNP deflator (1982 = 100)	107.9	111.5	3.3
GNP (current dollars)	3,765.0	3,998.1	6.2
Personal consumption expenditures	2,428.2	2,600.5	7.1
Durable goods	331.2	359.3	8.5
Nondurable goods	870.1	905.1	4.0
Services	1,227.0	1,336.1	8.9
Gross private domestic investment	662.1	661.1	(0.2)
Fixed investment	598.0	650.0	8.7
Nonresidential (business)	416.5	458.2	10.0
Structures	139.3	154.8	11.1
Producers durable equipment	277.3	303.4	9.4
Residential	181.4	191.8	5.7
Change in business inventories	64.1	11.1	(82.6)
Net exports of goods and services	−58.7	−78.9	
Exports	382.7	369.8	(3.4)
Imports	441.4	448.6	1.6
Government purchases of goods & services	733.4	815.4	11.2
Federal	311.3	354.1	13.7
National defense	235.0	259.4	10.4
Nondefense	76.2	94.7	24.3
State and local	422.2	461.3	9.3

SOURCE: U.S. Department of Commerce, *Survey of Current Business,* December 1986, tables 1.1, 1.2, and 7.4, pp. 3, 13.

Retail Store Sales and Nondurable Goods Expenditures. The next step is to examine the relationship between particular industries and an expenditure component. Table 5.2 illustrates the close relationship between retail store sales and personal consumption expenditures for nondurable goods. Although the 10-year span saw little cyclical fluctuation, no year was far from the period average of 14.6 percent. Thus, a reliable forecast of this major economic variable would have helped a security analyst responsible for the retail trade sector.

Table 1.2. Relation of Retail Store Sales to
Personal Consumption Expenditures for
Nondurable Goods, 1976–1985

Year	Personal consumption expenditures (in billions of dollars)	Retail store sales (in billions of dollars)	Retail sales as percent of personal consumption expenditures
1976	452.0	63.6	14.1
1977	490.4	68.7	14.0
1978	541.8	75.8	14.0
1979	613.2	82.0	13.4
1980	681.4	95.5	14.0
1981	740.6	105.9	14.3
1982	771.0	108.3	14.0
1983	817.0	125.2	15.3
1984	872.4	139.8	16.0
1985	912.5	153.4	16.8

SOURCES: Council of Economic Advisors, *Economic Report of the President 1986*, p. 252. Industry data compiled from *The Value Line Investment Survey*, Retail Store Industry studies.

Toiletries and Cosmetics Sales and Nondurable Good Expenditures. An even closer relationship (both relative and absolute) exists between toiletries and cosmetics industry sales and personal consumption expenditures. The range of cyclical fluctuation over the 10-year average of 1.4 percent was within plus or minus 0.1 percent. Sales as a percentage of personal consumption expenditures for nondurable goods are shown in Table 1.3.

Table 1.3. Sales as Percentage of
Personal Consumption Expenditures
for Nondurable Goods, 1976–1985
(Toiletries and Cosmetics)

Year	Percent	Year	Percent
1976	1.3	1981	1.5
1977	1.3	1982	1.5
1978	1.4	1983	1.4
1979	1.5	1984	1.4
1980	1.5	1985	1.4

SOURCES: Council of Economic Advisors, *Economic Report of the President 1986*, p. 252. Industry data compiled from *The Value Line Investment Survey*, Toiletries/Cosmetics Industry studies.

Linkage with Longer-Term Projections

There are numerous approaches to developing secular projections. The following pages summarize one approach providing a definitive analytical framework for the considerations entailed. This summary gives a set of illustrative assumptions for the key macro variables that underlie longer-term projections for the U.S. economy. This summary is not intended to indicate a preference for a specific method.

First Causes. Domestic, social, political, and international forces are first causes underlying economic developments. Their complex interaction creates both the climate within which business operates and the position of the United States in major international markets. Analysis of these first causes provides the foundation for specific estimates of the economy.

A purely national approach to economics is a fragmentary concept no longer valid in this expanding world market and evolving system of internationalized production. Analysts must consider the world political outlook, the interdependence of nations, and the increasing importance of other nations besides the "superpowers."

Analysts must also identify social forces expected to dominate in the United States over the projection span and appraise the major changes expected to result from these forces. These include changes occurring in values held by Americans as the result of age, education, employment, and affluence. They also entail growing recognition of the power of interest groups and collective action, the extent of federal government involvement, and the impact of changing occupations on people's income and expenditure patterns.

Longer-term estimates should be trend or secular projections representing average ("normal") annual growth rates from an estimated current midcycle year to a midcycle year five years hence. Both the initial and terminal years are estimated to be average from the standpoint of composition of GNP as well as price level.

Key Trend Projections. Since trend projections are based on the growth in supply or output capability of the economy, critical assumptions must be made about the following:

- Trend growth rate in the labor force. This rate is a measure of the increase in the supply of labor. It is a function of the age, sex distribution, and participation rate (percentage of those of working age seeking employment) of the population.

- Trend rate of increase in productivity (output per worker-hour). This increase is determined by such key factors as the amount of business fixed investment (capital-labor ratio), technological progress, shifts in the proportions employed in different occupations, and the age, education, and level of experience of the work force.

- Average unemployment rate for the projection span. Given the supply capability of the economy, this rate is the primary determinant of the level of GNP in real terms (the volume of output).

- Trend growth rate in real GNP. This rate measures the increase in the nation's output potential—in the supply capability of the economy—and is principally the sum of growth in the labor force (giving consideration to the employment rate) and the increase in productivity.

- Average annual inflation rate for the period. This assumption makes it possible to convert GNP in real terms to nominal terms (output valued at market prices).

Two sets of projections will serve as examples: Example 1 is for the five-year span 1984 to 1989 and was developed by a financial institution. Example 2 is a set of assumptions and projections for the five-year span from 1973 to 1978 and was prepared in 1974 by FRS Associates. Each example is generally representative of prevalent assumptions and projections held at the time the projections were made. Example 2 demonstrates the extent to which outcomes depart from expectations in longer-term projections and, through comparison with the forecasts in example 1, illustrates the extent to which expectations can change in a 10-year period.

Example 1. This illustrative set of key projections by a financial institution are for the period 1984 through 1989:

Trend growth rate in labor force	1.3%
Trend rate of increase in productivity	1.5
Trend growth rate in real GNP (1.013 × 1.015)	2.8
Increase in inflation (GNP deflator)	5.0
Trend growth rate in nominal GNP (1.028 × 1.05)	7.9

The above real GNP estimate assumes an average unemployment rate of 7 percent for the five-year span. One must estimate that level of output (real GNP) which, in the last year for which actual data are available, is consistent with 7 percent unemployment. This estimation is usually accomplished by deriving a production function that considers the size of the employed labor force, capital stock, productivity, and so forth.

With real GNP estimated for the base or initial year, the trend values for GNP over the next five years can be calculated using the growth rate established above. The value for real GNP in 1984 was estimated at $3395 billion (by coincidence approximately the actual of $3490 billion). Using a growth rate of 2.8 percent, the trend value for real GNP in 1989 would be $3898 billion ($1.028^5 \times \$3395$).

Real GNP for 1989 can be readily translated into nominal GNP by accepting the GNP deflator in 1984 and then increasing it at a stipulated rate. In this instance, it is an estimated compound rate of 5 percent. In 1984 the deflator stood at 107.9 with 1982 equalling 100. Compounded at 5 percent ($1.05^5 \times 107.9 = 137.7$), nominal GNP in 1989 would be $1.377 \times \$3898$, or $5368 billion.

Example 2. Table 1.4 summarizes the key FRS economic projections for the 1973 to 1978 span, sets forth the supporting logic as stated in 1974, and cites the subsequent actual experience.

Two points are to be stressed. First, although most of the foregoing projections were directionally correct, the margin of error in the individual economic variables producing nominal GNP was substantial. Actual and estimated nominal GNP were close only because of offsetting errors in the projections. Second, as shown in Table 1.5 a tabulation of the estimates prepared in 1974 and 1984—over the 10-year span marked changes have occurred in prevalent expectations about the longer-term performance of the economy.

Given the margins of error, should longer-term economic projections be avoided? Not at all. They are essential to the analytical and decision-making process and must be made. The error factor, however, does require that some concept of the degree of uncertainty surrounding any given set of projections is needed.

Leads and Lags

In most instances, a change in GNP or some specific economic variable will not bring a coincidental and proportional response in the sales and profits of an industry or company. There will be inevitable leads and lags. For example, the dynamics of the inventory cycle are well known.

A pronounced slowdown in consumer spending will cause inventories to become excessive and thus have a compounding impact on retail sales and profits and, in turn, on the manufacture of consumer goods and, with a lag effect, on the raw material producer.

Table 1.4. Economic Secular Projections for the 1973–1978 Span and Actual Results

Projected average	Actual average
Trend growth rate in labor force: The labor force will continue to increase at a rapid rate. The 1.7 percent annual increase over the span will exceed the 1947–1973 average of 1.5 percent, but will be below the 1968–73 average of 2 percent.	2.7 percent (the expected deceleration in the number of women entering the labor force did not take place)
Average unemployment rate: The continued addition of young people and women to the labor force (due to high job turnover rates) will result in an unemployment rate of 4.5 percent over the span rather than the 4 percent used earlier by the government.	7.0 percent (much higher than projected)
Rate of increase in productivity (output per worker-hour): The rate will be 2.2 percent per year for the total economy. Fewer workers shifting out of agriculture, the short supply and high price of energy, and increased investment to improve the environment will deter increases in aggregate productivity.	1.2 percent (due to sluggish growth of the economy)
Trend growth rate in real GNP: The growth in real GNP will be 3.9 percent per year. This span will have a more rapid increase in the labor force and a slower increase in productivity. Because actual output in 1973 was slightly below the high employment potential, the growth rate from actual output in 1973 to the high employment estimate in 1978 will be 4.2 percent per year.	2.8 percent (well below the estimated potential)
Average annual inflation rate: The average inflation will be 6.1 percent, as measured by the GNP deflator—significantly above the 1968–1973 average of 4.7 percent. The deflator will continue to be affected by the momentum of the present rate of inflation, as substantially increased costs work their way through the nation's entire pricing system and wage-rate structure.	7.3 percent (even higher than projected)
Average annual GNP—current dollars (market value of the nation's output of goods and services): The average GNP will be 10.2 percent per year.	10.3 percent (the proximity of the projection to actual outcome is due to the higher inflation rate, because the level of economic activity was less than expected)

Table 1.5. Comparison of 1974 and 1984 Estimates

	Five-year rate of increase (%)	
	1974 projections	1984 projections
Labor force	1.7	1.3
Productivity	2.2	1.5
Real GNP	3.9	2.8
Inflation	6.1	5.0
Nominal GNP	10.2	7.9
Level of unemployment	4.5	7.0

However, it is possible to construct an internally consistent set of macroeconomic projections that provide the security analyst with an essential guide to the future. These projections make possible a level of comparability for company forecasts that otherwise could not be attained.

Exceptional Cases

In stressing the significance of finding linkages between the growth and profitability of industries and companies and economic factors, we do not imply that in most instances there will be a consistent and readily discernible relationship waiting to be discovered. Too many potential variables exist to permit tight correlations in most instances. It is equally important to recognize those industries and companies whose fortunes have little or no meaningful relationship to macroeconomic variables. In these instances, the analyst's assignment shifts to identifying the nonexistence of linkages and to preparing different and independent bases for predictions of the future. The following examples in which noneconomic factors dominate illustrate our point.

Technological Factors

The explosive demand in the early 1980s for computer software programs was not the critical factor in appraising a company in this field. Rather, what was critical was the company's capacity to deliver the most cost-efficient software package and to integrate new features providing competitive equality or advantage. In the case of personal computers, the critical factor was the capacity to be first and become the industry standard, to have a product easily understood by novice users, or to be promoted by heroic advertising. The program itself could be far from perfection.

The demand for defense electronics is derived essentially from new-product development and by the nation's defense posture and, to this extent, is relatively independent of the economic environment.

The market for individual drugs and for whole courses of medical treatment depends on the results of clinical tests and Federal Drug Administration (FDA) approval rather than on economic demand factors.

Regulatory Factors

Despite a probable substantial potential for cellular radio communication services, the granting of licenses will be the critical determinant of company growth, and thus this industry is dominated by regulatory considerations. Some other examples include electric utility companies that have abandoned large nuclear power projects. These companies will find their earnings determined less by the demand for electrical power than by the extent to which they are allowed to recover huge costs through rate adjustments. Another example is financial institutions whose future growth will be significantly affected by whether they are permitted to continue broadening their range of services. Finally, deregulation in the air transport industry has intensified competition and has caused both a shakeout and some industry consolidation.

Political and International Factors

The price of copper may be more influenced by Chilean balance-of-payment problems than by the level of world economic growth—this assessment of the copper industry must consider political and international factors. At the time when world petroleum prices were set more by the OPEC cartel than by free-market forces, world business conditions were not the primary determinant of prices. (Business conditions subsequently have had a substantial impact on the cartel and prices.)

Another example is health care: the federal government policies on cost containment of health services may be more relevant to the industry than the surging social demand for health care.

Global excess capacity caused by worldwide political interference, governmental subsidies, and protectionism have created critical conditions in an increasing number of industries (such as autos, steel, computers, semiconductors, heavy equipment, textiles, and chemicals). Such conditions can dwarf the value of economic correlations based solely on U.S. economic data.

PART 2

Analysis of Financial Statements

2
Overview of Financial Statement Analysis

A major activity of security analysis is the analysis of financial statements. This analysis includes two steps: First, the financial statements must be adjusted to reflect an analyst's viewpoint, that is, the analyst changes the published numbers, eliminates some assets and liabilities, creates new ones, alters the allocation of expenses to time periods, and, in effect, creates a new set of financial statements. Second, the analyst processes the new information by the calculation of averages, ratios, trends, equations, and other statistical treatment.

The Accounting Environment

The Accounting Revolution

The dramatic way in which generally accepted accounting principles (GAAP) and accounting standard-setting have changed over the past quarter century in the United States has been called "an accounting revolution."[1] The rules have been expanded from a few thin pamphlets

[1] William H. Beaver, *Financial Reporting: An Accounting Revolution.* Englewood Cliffs, New Jersey: Prentice-Hall, 1981.

to a massive 2000 pages of opinions, standards, and other pronouncements. There are other new authoritative publications, such as the many industry *Audit Guides* issued by the Auditing Standards Board and the *Statements of Position* on industry and transaction accounting issued by the Accounting Standards Executive Committee of the American Institute of Certified Public Accountants (AICPA). The accounting standard-setting structure has evolved from a part-time, largely volunteer committee of the AICPA to a full-time independent Financial Accounting Standards Board (FASB) sponsored jointly by the AICPA, the Financial Executives Institute, the Financial Analysts Federation, the National Association of Accountants, the American Association of Accountants, and the Securities Industry Association.

The Authority of the Financial Accounting Standards Board

The FASB's authority is derived not from its independence but from recognition by outside organizations. In and of itself, the board has no powers. However, the ethics rules of the AICPA,[2] recognition and acceptance by the Securities and Exchange Commission[3] which is empowered by Congress to set accounting standards for registrant companies, and recognition by the various state licensing bodies that admit certified public accountants (CPAs) to public practice give the FASB its power to make effective accounting rules. In addition, the board's power is ensured by the general acceptance of FASB-established standards by preparers, users, accountants, regulatory bodies, governments, courts, and foreign accounting standard-setting bodies.

Better Rules and Worse Compliance

The improvements arising from the pronouncements of the Accounting Principles Board (APB) and the FASB include the elimination of many accounting alternatives for economically similar transactions, thereby enhancing the comparability of accounting figures among companies

---

[2]American Institute of Certified Public Accountants, *AICPA Professional Standards*, Rule 203, New York, N.Y. This ethics rule forbids departures from an accounting principle which has been established by the FASB or its predecessor, the Accounting Principles Board, unless the auditor is able to demonstrate clearly that following GAAP would result in misleading financial statements. The departures must be clearly explained and the auditor must stand ready to defend his departure.

[3]Securities and Exchange Commission, *Accounting Series Release 150*, December 20, 1973, Washington, D.C. In this release the Commission states that the standards and practices promulgated by the FASB in its statements and interpretations will be considered as having authoritative support, and those to the contrary to have no such support.

and industries, ensuring greater consistency of accounting through time so that trends and variability can be identified, and providing a codified set of definitions and concepts underlying U.S. accounting.

At the same time, the inflation that began in the early 1970s significantly harmed the corporate capital structure. Inflation requires more capital to produce the same physical volume of goods or units of service. This capital could not be obtained by retained earnings alone, and dilutive effects made sale of stock at depressed prices even more unattractive than borrowing at high interest rates. The logic was that the high interest costs were tax deductible (even 18 percent interest costs only 11.88 percent after a 34 percent tax deduction!), and the debt could be refunded later when rates declined. This view led to an increase in the ratio of debt to equity, which increases the risk of corporations. Additional financial leverage occurred because the new debt was issued at high interest rates and therefore interest claimed a larger share of operating income and cash flows.

The inflation put pressure on true profit margins—that is, margins after deducting inventory profits and the current cost of depreciation. Thus, a shortfall of cash flows made the balance sheet risk even more apparent, which led many investors to become more risk averse. Investors sought companies having lower rather than higher risks, which put some pressure on managements to improve at least the appearance of the balance sheet if not the underlying risk. Company managers also were putting pressure on portfolio managers to produce near-term investment performance in pension portfolios, and they were focusing heavily on quarterly measurements. The focus on immediate pension fund investment results led portfolio managers to seek companies that had favorable short-term earnings results, leading both company financial officers and investment managers to complain that the other was forcing an unrealistic time horizon on them.[4] This situation is now changing, particularly as corporate financial officers become more sophisticated in measuring the investment performance of their portfolios and accept that valid judgments of performance require longer periods. Perhaps this will relieve some of the pressures on the companies to report near-term earnings. These pressures were thought by many to have fostered the increase in transactions designed to achieve accounting results that are not justified by the economic substance. The "front ending" of earnings, removing debt from the balance sheet and writing up or down assets, has become something of a problem that mars the overall picture of accounting rules that are steadily improving.

In 1984 the FASB set up the Emerging Issues Task Force to identify questionable transactions and to suggest the appropriate accounting for them.

[4]"The Folly of Inflating Quarterly Profits," *New York Times*, Mar. 2, 1986, pp. 2, 8.

The Committee was formed partly because of SEC concerns whether the accounting community was addressing abusive transactions promptly enough to keep them from spreading.

Adjustments by the Analyst

Implicit versus Explicit Adjustments

The security analyst has two avenues to follow in making adjustments to accounting information. The explicit approach changes the actual numbers in the income statement and balance sheet. The alternative approach makes an implicit adjustment to the earnings multiplier or to the discount rate used to value the security. Since the explicit adjustments can be made with considerable accuracy and the implicit adjustments are simply "Kentucky windage," analysts should make the explicit changes whenever possible. The situation is analogous to processing low-grade ore: Accounting includes estimates and allocations which are not very accurate, but analysts can increase the information content of accounting. The cumulative effect of a number of small explicit adjustments can make the information more accurate and complete. Thus the information content, like the few ounces of gold in several tons of ore, must be extracted to the fullest extent.

Mandatory, Situational, and Judgmental Classes of Adjustments

Analyst adjustments break down into three classifications:

1. *Mandatory adjustments.*   Standard rules, to be applied in every case, for example, the adjustment of all previous per-share figures for a stock split .

2. *Situational adjustments.*   Those made only when appropriate or specific conditions exist—intangibles that are salable or bring in income stay on the balance sheet; all others are removed .

3. *Judgmental adjustments.*   Those applied by the analyst through a combination of experience, common sense, and observation of the practices of other analysts considered to be knowledgeable and experienced

Why Make Adjustments at All?

Presenting economic reality is impossible, through accounting or any other process. Economics is not an exact science; rather it is a social science in which value judgments play a major role. It would be wonderful if accounting were one of the exact sciences that observes all variables, measures them with whatever degree of accuracy is needed, and presents a final number that all would agree was "economic reality." Unfortunately, it is not even possible for two persons to agree on what economic reality is. Economic activity manifests itself in many ways that are not subject to scientific observation and measurement. Accounting cannot observe directly the economic effects of a competitor going bankrupt or an expanded training program. Good management is an asset and bad management a liability, but accounting has no way to put reliable numbers on the balance sheet to reflect such values. Accounting takes a commonsense approach to such problems—it simply measures what it *can* observe and measure, which is mostly exchange transactions in which the company was a party.

The analyst may be able to capture a more faithful picture of reality by adding to or adjusting this information in ways not permitted by accounting rules. Analysts make adjustments to accounting information for a variety of reasons. Perhaps the most important is to adjust the numbers to reflect the analysts' notions of income and capital maintenance, where those notions disagree with the notions used in accounting.

For some transactions, accounting borrows from economics certain simplifying assumptions which most analysts reject: for example, the assumption of perfect, interchangeable, frictionless, costless markets in which participants happily exchange their goods at fair (rather than advantageous) prices, the assumption that markets are always rational or that changes in interest rate differentials fully explain changes in the relative prices of foreign currencies. The analyst may be able to compensate to reflect different beliefs about such matters.

Security analysis is not restricted by the rules of accounting and therefore can use a more flexible approach in dealing with the accounting numbers and the facts garnered from nonaccounting sources. Where accounting allows alternatives for the same transaction or where management judgments allow different presentations for the same facts, the analyst can compensate for these differences, thereby improving comparability, accuracy, and completeness. Analysts can remove the effects of transactions that are narrowly within the rules of accounting but outside the boundaries of economic substance or of common sense.

Analysis requires the ability to discriminate, to separate the ordinary from the unusual, and to detect change. These require disaggregation, enhancement, and reconstruction of accounting information to prepare it for further processing.

Income and Capital Maintenance Notions

Perspectives on Earnings

Economists' Views. One cannot determine income or "earnings" unless one also determines that the original capital has been maintained. This notion was well expressed by J. R. Hicks in a discussion of a series of income and capital maintenance notions.[5]

E1. Well-Offness. Hicks's first definition of income was the amount that one could consume and still be as well off at the end of the period as at the beginning.

E2. Ability to Consume. Hicks also expressed income in expectational terms suggesting that income was the amount one could consume and still expect to continue consuming that much in the future.

E3. Real Consumption. A third notion of income emphasized goods and services in real rather than nominal terms.

E4. Social Welfare Utility Added. Hicks also multiplied his number of definitions by two when he mentioned that the amounts ideally should be adjusted for the utility of the goods and services that the income could buy. He pointed out that utility was impossible to quantify. Hicks's conclusion was that these notions are all useful but fragile, and, with tongue in cheek, he admonished economists to avoid discussions of income whenever possible.

Accountants' Views. Capital maintenance has been the subject of much debate among accountants over the years.

A1. Financial Capital. The objective of financial capital maintenance is to maintain the amount of net worth on the balance sheet. This is a pure *net asset* view that looks to the carrying amounts of assets less liabilities, with some favoring current costs and others historical. Since the balance sheet excludes the assets and liabilities that cannot be measured, this capital-maintenance notion is incomplete.

A2. Physical Capital. Accounting also has considered various physical-capital maintenance notions, generally expressing the idea in terms of

[5]John Richard Hicks, *Value and Capital*, 2d ed., Oxford, Clarendon Press, 1950, pp. 171–188.

either replacement costs or of operating capability, that is, the ability to produce a fixed amount of goods or services.

A3. Distributable Income. The physical-capital maintenance notion can be adjusted to produce an income number known as "distributable income," which is akin to Hicks's first definition of the amount that can be consumed without being worse off at the end of the period.

A4. Purchasing Power. Accounting also offers methods to express each of those forms of capital maintenance in real terms rather than in nominal terms, in general, by adjusting for changes in the general price level (but not, of course, for changes in utility).

Security Analysts' Views.   Security analysts also have thoughts about capital maintenance and counterpart income ideas.

S1. Investor Wealth.   Some believe that a company does not really earn money unless it maintains the market value of the common stock, and thus their approach does not measure the company's operating performance. It measures investor wealth, hardly a matter to include in the company's accounts.

S2. Earning Power.   A second view is that a company earns income only after it has maintained the previously existing earning power.

S3. Expected Dividends.   A third income notion used by security analysts is the excess income after the company has maintained the expected future dividend stream.

S4. Distributable Income.   Some analysts favor the "distributable income" notion developed in Great Britain. That is the amount a company could distribute after making necessary capital expenditures, providing for working capital needs, and using available borrowing capacity.

S5. Liquidating Value.   Still another concept is an asset value notion that requires maintaining the liquidating value of the company before any increment of earnings can exist. This is the accountants' net asset view rather than an investment value approach.

Which Income Notion Should Analysts Use?

All of the notions mentioned are useful in that they help us think about the performance of a corporation. For an *ongoing* firm, the S2 and S3 security analyst income notions of maintaining earning power and maintaining the expected future stream of dividends are best because they lead most directly to the pricing of securities. In the case of mergers, buy-out candidates, bankruptcies, and other asset-oriented analyses, the liquidating value income notion is often very useful.

Asset Values and Investment Values

An important distinction is found in the security analysts' S2 and S3 notions of income when compared with the notions used by accountants. Most accounting income notions use *asset values* (although some values may be out of date). It is implicit that the asset values minus the liabilities (or the value of the liabilities) will provide a net worth number that "represents" the value of the firm. That number is likely to tell the approximate amount at which assets could be sold and the liabilities settled, one by one.

The analyst is looking for another value—investment value. Investment value is concerned not with what the assets could be sold for but with what they can be *used* for—what they will generate in future earnings that can be paid out as dividends or added to the company's growth. Most security analysts' favorite calculations of investment value are (1) capitalized earning power, or (2) the capitalized stream of future dividends.

Fundamentalists' Beliefs

The fundamental analyst believes that stock market prices fluctuate around the underlying investment value and that the two coincide occasionally. This belief rejects the idea that, normally, stocks are priced correctly in the market, and it even implies doubt that the market behaves rationally most of the time. Because stock prices move randomly with only a weak gravitational pull toward intrinsic value, the coincidence of price and value occurs infrequently, like Halley's comet. This means that the "convergence time" is long—perhaps three to five years. The analyst using the techniques recommended in this book must have a relatively long time horizon and considerable patience. The approach is that of a "fundamentalist" or value-oriented analyst. Value-oriented analysts are not traders, but rather, they are long-term investors who look on investing as being something more like marriage than like a mere flirtation. Investment value involves forecasts of future earnings and dividends that must begin to come true before the market is likely to appreciate them. It is therefore important to understand that the value sought in this book is not the asset value, and it is surely not the market price.

Consider the following hypothetical scene: A company manager tells an analyst that the company earned $8 a share and paid out $2 in dividends. The analyst inquires why the dividend payout was only 25 percent while most other companies in that industry are paying out well over half of their earnings. The manager answers "We needed the $6 to buy more efficient machines, so that our costs and pricing would be as low as our competitors'. Our old machines were out of date." From an analyst's perspective, how much did the company earn? The retained $6 was not earnings, but made up for a short fall of depreciation, or perhaps a write-off of obsolete machinery. The "retained earnings" were not available for dividend payments, and they added nothing to the future earning power of the company. In what sense were they earnings at all? The example can be broadened into a principle: *Retained earnings that cannot result in subsequent increases in earning power are not true earnings from a security analyst's viewpoint.*

The Nature and Limitations of Accounting

Accounting grew out of a need to know, to remember, and to decide. The Industrial Revolution required the gathering of capital from many sources under a single management to gain economies of scale. The separation of ownership and management clearly required some accountability for the stewardship of capital and the profitable use thereof. Not all analysts are aware that the financial statements they receive are prepared not by auditors but by the management of companies. The philosophy of the financial reports was for many years management's statement of its stewardship of the shareholders' assets. In effect, the statements were an annual management report card in which management graded itself on the success of its activities. As a result, the annual report often focused more on operating performance and market performance than the analyst would prefer, sometimes at the expense of the clearest picture of corporate profitability. Although the stewardship notion still prevails in the minds of many management people, the direction of accounting in recent years has been more toward the needs of users.

Management Information System

The foundation or information base of accounting is the management-control and decision-making system. Such a system is designed to present what management needs to know, given the decisions it will make in dealing with individual assets and liabilities. The manager has access to these assets and liabilities, whereas ordinarily the outside investor or creditor does not. Management also needs an accounting system for tax records, regulatory reporting, SEC requirements, and other reasons. Investor needs differ from management needs in some respects because investors must make different decisions.

The Orderly Character of Accounting

Accounting is a distinctive information set in a number of respects. Its orderliness makes it subject to systematic evaluation.

Articulation.   The statements articulate both the statics and the dynamics of a company, that is, they present state and change of state.

Single Measuring Unit.   Accounting is quantified in a single measuring unit—the dollar, in the case of the United States.

Reliability.   Accounting has considerable reliability because it is audited and because it deals with transactions and events after the fact and attempts to minimize the injection of subjective estimates of the future. Unfortunately, at least some estimates have to be made, such as the useful lives of long-lived assets.

Representational Faithfulness.   Accounting is representationally faithful—it is what it purports to be. Accounting does not purport to present the actual asset, which might be a desk or a computer or a building. However, it does make representations that it will provide specific information such as unrecovered cost, fair value, or some other attribute, and this can be useful information about the desk, computer or building.

Relevance.   Much of the relevance of accounting information comes about because it is "entity specific"—emphasis is on the completed exchange transactions of the entity.

Consistency and Comparability.   Accounting provides considerable consistency through time and comparability between companies, industries, and sectors. Of course, the consistency and comparability are not perfect, because accounting cannot be applied with perfect consistency, alternatives exist, and the rules of accounting are often changed, interrupting some of the continuity.

Accrual Accounting

Today's model of accrual accounting links cause and effect by matching causal costs with resulting revenues in the same time period. The mere cataloging of cash transactions would provide far less information about the income of a period, and therefore a certain amount of matching must be provided. Accrual accounting is far more predictive of future cash flows than is the direct observation of the cash flows of a single period.[6] For example, the purchase of a major new piece of equipment in a particular period might cause a reduction in cash and the appearance of negative income, even though the equipment will be used to produce revenue for many years. Its costs should be allocated to all those periods rather than merely the one in which the equipment was purchased.

The Cash Cycle

Accrual accounting is very descriptive of the "cash-to-cash" cycles of business. Business organizations start with cash, invest in raw materials, labor, services, and parts and end up with an entirely new product or service to offer to the public. For those goods and services the company receives cash, or accounts receivables, which in turn are ultimately converted back to cash again, completing the round trip from cash outlay to cash receipt. It would be nice if all companies liquidated to an all-cash position at the end of each year and satisfied all their liabilities—there would be few quarrels about the amount of profits. Unfortunately, many cash cycles are still going on at the end of the year. Some of them are quite short cycles, and others extend over many years. Thus, accrual accounting is designed to record as well as possible the performance of the company, using various conventions that capture the part of each cash cycle that was completed during the period.

Matching, of course, can be abused. It is easy to cross the line from matching to smoothing, and the temptation is to "make it look good" rather than to "tell it like it was." The auditor must see that management's statements tell it like it was, within the confines of accounting rules and conventions. It is the analyst's job to go the rest of the way and "tell it *all* like it really *was*."

The Conservatism of Accounting

By and large, accounting has considerable conservatism built into it. Accounting tends to wait until there is reasonable assurance before recognizing revenue and profits and to reflect losses quite promptly. This is a helpful offset to the natural optimism of management.

---

[6]Financial Accounting Standards Board, *Reporting*, Nov. 1978, paras. 44–48. Concept No. 1, *Objectives of Financial Reporting*, Nov. 1978 paras. 44–48.

Conservatism is of great importance to analysts, because it contributes to their margin of safety in buying and selling securities.

Realization Principle

Accounting contains a realization principle that says revenue should not be recognized until (1) the company has performed all the activities necessary to "earn" its income and (2) the company has "realized" cash in hand or has assurance of receiving future cash. The creation of a high-quality account receivable is usually considered sufficient for the latter test.

Cash Inflows

Thus, the overall view of accounting is that it is well-structured for the analyst's further processing. Investors look to the company for cash inflows to themselves. Investor cash inflows depend totally on the company's holdings of cash and the company's ability to generate cash inflows. Recall that about all an investor gets from the company is dividend checks and financial reports. Since the market for used annual reports is modest, it is the stream of dividends to which investors look for their rewards. They have a choice of continuing to receive the stream of dividends or selling the stock in the marketplace. They do not have direct access to the assets and liabilities, as does the management of the company. The timing of the investors' cash inflows will be somewhat different from the cash picture of the company.

The Auditor's Opinion

A traditional saying of security analysts is "Read the auditor's opinion, the footnotes, and only *then* the financial statements. That way you won't forget the first two." There is much confusion about the auditor's involvement with financial statements. The auditor does not ordinarily prepare them. *Financial statements are the representations of management who actually prepare the statements.* It is the auditor's job to do certain checking and sampling, to examine the management control system, and to determine that the accounting principles followed are in accordance with generally accepted accounting principles. The auditor's qualification of an opinion is often important in determining whether a company may be looked upon as a going concern, or one likely to go into liquidation or bankruptcy. Auditors can "qualify" their opinions when they are uncertain whether the statements may be relied upon, and they can subsequently withdraw those qualifications.

Example. Coopers & Lybrand qualified the 1982 annual report of General Refractories Company with the following words: "Although certain goals of the company's 1982 business plan were achieved, the company's 1983 business plan continues to reflect the need to reduce operating losses, sell its domestic building products division, obtain additional working capital, successfully renegotiate its raw materials purchase agreement, and meet its obligations and restrictive covenants pursuant to the most recent loan agreement." By the time of the 1983 annual report, many of those uncertainties and problems had been resolved or ameliorated, and Coopers & Lybrand withdrew their qualification, stating "Accordingly, our present opinion on the 1982 and 1981 consolidated financial statements is different than that expressed in our previous report."

Limitations of Accounting

Accounting, of course, has a variety of imperfections which the analyst should know and guard against. As mentioned earlier accounting cannot measure or even observe many events and circumstances. Accounting is not a pure model in that it is not entirely based on historical cost, nor on recoverable investment, nor on current value, nor any of the other single measures that purists would love to have. For pragmatic reasons of cost and benefit and of understandability, accounting uses a mixture of attributes in measuring assets and liabilities. Yet, the end result is usable for those who understand and learn to deal with accounting's limitations.

Accounting is full of judgmental decisions and is therefore highly subjective. Someone has to determine the appropriate depreciation pattern, costs must be allocated, say, between period expenses and capitalizable inventory, and it is difficult to prove whether such decisions are right or wrong. Human frailty enters into this type of decision making, and not surprisingly self-interest, pride, inherent optimism, and other characteristics of management incline some to be biased toward reporting greater amounts of income now at the expense of lower amounts later on. For this reason, the majority of the adjustments made by analysts tend to reduce today's reported earnings and report larger earnings in the future.

Reported Earnings and "True" Earnings

Analysts' activities are somewhat schizophrenic, for they want to know two sets of earnings: reported earnings and "economic" earnings. The latter is the analysts' view of true income—income that can be (1) distributed without diminishing capital or (2) reinvested to produce greater future income. Nevertheless, the analyst would like to estimate accurately *what the company will report* as earnings for the next period. This is important because reported earnings have at least a short-term impact on the market price of a stock. A number of investing techniques have been developed using reported earnings alone, without adjustments by the analysts. *Value Line Investment Service* has been studied many times because of the consistent favorable investment results of the service's stock ranking system.[7] The two most important ingredients in the Value Line methodology are earnings momentum and price momentum. The earnings used are *reported* earnings. Many academic studies also have used reported earnings to test the speed with which information is absorbed by the market. Tests of the "price earnings" effect—a belief that low-price-earnings stocks provide higher total returns than do high-price-earnings stocks—have been published. These studies use reported earnings. Kisor studied the effects of relative earnings changes on stock prices and found that relative changes in reported earnings correlated with relative total returns over various time periods.[8]

At the same time, analysts know that dividends are paid out of the true economic earnings and not whatever was reported as earnings. Thus they have to estimate economic earnings to generate an expected stream of future dividends. Economic earnings are also essential in developing an estimate of "earning power." Earning power is more a capacity to pay dividends and increase the size of the earnings base than an accrual accounting system would report. Economic earnings that are retained always result in increased earning power if they are properly invested by management.

Some analysts lose the distinction between these two earnings, perhaps because they have misconceptions about the accuracy of earnings reports. Reported annual earnings may not be within 10 or 20 percent of the adjusted earnings that an analyst would consider to be the year's true results. Quarterly earnings reports are prepared using the so-called integral method, which makes them largely a reflection of management's estimates for the full year results. It is remarkable that the stock market reacts violently to interim earnings that are a few percentage points greater or less than expected, when the accuracy of quarterly earnings depends so heavily on subjective estimates of what

[7]Fischer Black, "Yes, Virginia, There Is Hope: Tests of the Value Line Ranking System," presented at a seminar of the Center for Research in Security Prices, Graduate School of Business, University of Chicago, May 1971.

[8]Manowm C. Kisor and Van A. Messner, "The Filter Approach to Earnings Forecasts," *The Financial Analysts Journal*, Jan-Feb 1969, 109–115.

subsequent quarters will be. This market vulnerability to earnings reports that are contrary to expectations is particularly pronounced in the case of glamorous growth stocks, where so much of the price is based on hopes and dreams and so little on assets and demonstrated earning power.

The evidence that the market reacts to reported earnings is quite powerful, but a large body of evidence indicates that the market "sees through" mere accounting differences and makes proper adjustments therefor. For example, the market will adjust the stock price of a company that uses LIFO inventory accounting so that it is in keeping with stocks of other companies that use FIFO. Similarly, the market will equalize the price of companies that use different depreciation methods.[9] We are persuaded that if the market understands the accounting differences and has the information necessary to make the adjustments, it will adjust prices properly. The effects of the market's adjustments will tend to persist over time, whereas the effects of reported earnings tend to be relatively short-lived, normally expiring in a matter of days or a few months. The importance of the adjusted earnings, which the analyst attempts to bring as close to "true" earnings as possible, is to provide a valid beginning point for forecasts of the future.

Finally, some areas of specialized accounting present very soft and subjective numbers. Outstanding examples are the percentage-of-completion method of contract accounting, and accounting for motion pictures and cable television. In each of these areas, accounting accepts the value of timeliness in exchange for a reduction in precision, rather than face the alternative of no financial information. The difficulty is not a frailty of accounting but rather the innate uncertainty in business affairs.

The Use of Adjusted Accounting Numbers

Analysts adjust the financial statements to get closer to their own notions of income and capital maintenance. These income notions may be selected partly for the decision to be made. In some cases they are devised to compare companies in an industry or a sector. All must be put on a common basis, to the degree that information is available to do so. Adjustments prepare the statements for subsequent processing and

---

[9]W. H. Beaver and R. E. Dukes, "Tax Allocation and Depreciation Methods," *The Accounting Review*, July 1973, pp. 549–555; see also R. E. Dukes, "An Investigation of the Effects of Expensing Research and Development Costs on Security Prices," in M. Schiff and G. Sorter eds., *Proceedings of the Conference on Topical Research in Accounting*, New York University, New York, 1976, pp. 147–193; G. Foster, "Valuation Parameters of Property-Liability Companies," *Journal of Finance*, June 1947, pp. 823–836; Raymond J. Ball, "Changes in Accounting Techniques and Stock Prices," University of Chicago, 1971.

analysis, which often consist of calculating ratios to determine which relationships are stable and which ones are variable. The analyst may adjust to find the true level of an item at a point in time, or what the normal level is over the business cycle. These processes require changing the accounting numbers to improve their accuracy, comparability, and consistency before measuring a trend, calculating a ratio, or taking the average of a number of years. Increasingly, analysts are using statistical techniques and mathematical models, as the profession grows more sophisticated. The most frequently used model is a financial model of the company. This is a full set of past statements, trends, ratios, equations, and relationships. These form a base for projections several years into the future. The future is where money is made—or lost.

3
Analysis of the Income Statement

All security analysis involves the analysis of financial statements. True, the weight given to the financial material may vary enormously, depending on the kind of security studied and the basic motivation of the prospective purchaser. The standing of investment-grade bonds and preferred stocks is decisively controlled by the financial record. These bonds and stocks must meet specific tests of safety, which turn upon such criteria as:

- Relation of past earnings to fixed charges (and preferred dividends)
- Dividend record
- Relation of funded debt to the property account
- Working-capital position
- Volume of business done

Although qualitative factors may be important in analyzing stocks and bonds, they cannot be used to determine risk without support from the actual figures.

Pertinence of the Past Record to the Future

In the selection of common stocks, future expectations are the primary basis of attractiveness and value. In theory these expectations may be so different from past performance that the latter could be virtually irrelevant to the analysis, but this separation of the future from the past rarely occurs. A tendency toward an underlying continuity in business affairs makes the financial record the logical point of departure for any future projection.

Most companies and industries have certain identifiable financial characteristics that remain stable or change only slowly over time, and only the trader on market movements or the heedless speculator following tips or hunches will ignore the financial results—the statistical showing—of a common stock. The investment approach to every kind of security—which is the analytical approach—requires the proper application of analysis to the financial statements.

In Chapter 2 we pointed out that the descriptive function of security analysis involves marshaling the important facts relating to an issue and presenting them in a coherent, readily intelligible manner. [1]Analysis of financial statements plays a major part in this descriptive function, and Part 2 details such analysis up to the point where the indicated results are actually to be used in the evaluation and the choice of securities.

The Typical Pattern of an Analytical Study

Every reasonably complete analysis of a corporate issue has three major divisions:

1. A description of the company's business and properties (perhaps including some historical data and some details about the management)
2. Financial material: the capitalization, the record of earnings and dividends for a considerable number of years, a funds flow analysis, and one or more recent balance sheets
3. Prospects of the enterprise in the form of projected future financial statements and the merits of the security

The Written Report

We cannot overemphasize the importance of the preparation of a written report as a discipline for the practicing analyst. This activity enhances orderliness of thought, greater attention to detail, and emphasis on facts rather than assumptions. Communication is improved and ambiguity reduced. A conclusion must be reached and a record

---

[1]See the unabridged fifth edition of Sidney Cottle, Roger F. Murray, and Frank E. Block, *Graham and Dodd's Security Analysis,* McGraw-Hill, New York, 1988.

established for future review. The good investment organization reviews its past successes and failures and learns from them. The individual analyst or advisor should do no less.

Uses of the Income Statement

The indications furnished by the income statement may be analyzed and discussed from various angles, including the average results for the period, the minimum for any year,and the trend and variability over the years. In many common stock write-ups considerable and perhaps excessive attention is paid to the current figure, which may be misleading. Well-trained analysts use past income statements primarily as a guide to formulating estimates of future earnings, or earning power, which will serve as the chief basis of their conclusions respecting the merits of a common stock. A level of earnings which has been achieved in the past is a more credible prospect than a projection of new record-high results.

Three Aspects of Income Statement Analysis

The importance attached to the income statement in security analysis makes discerning study of the published figures doubly essential. A really good job of income statement analysis may be anything but a simple matter. Many complications may have to be unraveled, many quirks or special entries guarded against, many variations between companies equalized. The broad study of corporate income statements may be classified under three headings:

1. *Accounting.* The leading question here is, "What were the true earnings for the past periods studied?".

2. *Business.* The leading question is, "What indications does the earnings record carry as to the future earning power of the company?".

3. *Security valuation.* For security valuation, the leading question is, "What elements in the earnings exhibit should the analyst take into account and what standards should be followed, in endeavoring to arrive at a reasonable valuation of the shares?"

Chapters 3 through 11 deal with the accounting aspect of statement analysis, treating the income statement, its relationship to the funds statement, and the balance sheet. Discussion of the business aspect is presented in Chapters 29 and 30.[2] Valuation is discussed in Chapters 31 through 34.[3]

Basic Procedures for Arriving at True Operating Earnings

Fraudulent and Other Misrepresentative Transactions

Analysts must start, of course, with the assumption that the figures they are studying are not fraudulent, that the various assets and liabilities in the balance sheet are honestly stated as they would appear on the books without omissions or fictitious entries. Analysts must also assume that where discretion is used in valuing assets or estimating liabilities, such estimates are based on management's informed and honest judgment.

The published annual reports of companies registered with the SEC have been audited by independent public accountants and bear their certification. This is now a requirement of law. The auditing procedures have been tightened up considerably since 1933, partly through the efforts of the accountants themselves and partly at the insistence of the SEC. Not only have the possibilities of outright fraud been greatly reduced, but—of more practical importance—analysts are now supplied with the year's results in sufficient detail and with enough explanatory comment to permit intelligent interpretation of the figures.

Prior to the SEC legislation, which began in 1933, semifraudulent distortions of corporate accounts were not unusual. The misrepresentation was almost always to make the results look better than they were, and it was generally associated with some scheme of stock market manipulation in which management was participating. Although the incidence of such practices has receded, the analyst must continue to be vigilant for cases of misleading financial statements and outright fraud.

Good Analysis Can Help to Avoid Investment in Fraudulent Companies

Security analysts are unlikely to uncover fraud, but they do have tools to reveal unusual patterns that are difficult to rationalize. A stock should never be recommended unless the analyst knows and understands the company. Companies involved in fraud or in questionable transactions are at least occasionally avoided by careful analysts who conclude that the numbers simply don't make sense.

[2] See the unabridged fifth edition of Sidney Cottle, Roger F. Murray, and Frank E. Block, *Graham and Dodd's Security Analysis,* McGraw-Hill, New York, 1988.

[3] See the unabridged fifth edition of Cottle, Murray, and Block.

The good securities analyst does not stay in touch merely with those companies that are candidates for purchase. Competitors, unions, trade associations, vendors, customers, and a host of other sources provide information and insights about trends, technical developments, share of market, trade gossip, and the like. It is through such channels that the analyst often first hears of unusual transactions or suspicious circumstances.

The analyst uses a number of sensitive ratios, particularly the activity ratios (asset turnover, inventory turnover, accounts receivable turnover, and the like) that are designed to give the earliest possible warning that something is changing in a company. Evidence of change almost always initiates inquiries to management about the causes of change. Where management explanations are inadequate, the analyst's suspicions may be aroused.

The analyst has a number of ways to predict the rate at which a company grows. Some techniques are oriented toward the company's ability to finance growth. When the reported growth exceeds that which the analyst projected the company was capable of financing, there is cause for concern.

An analyst familiar with the insurance business would know that rapid growth demands tremendous amounts of capital because of the heavy initial cost of putting business on the books. In the case of Equity Funding Corporation, an analyst might not have recognized that fraud was taking place, but the analysis of capital needs did at least turn some analysts away simply because they could find no reasonable way for the company to finance its growth goals.

Accountants' and Analysts' Results

Since the reports of nearly all companies are honestly compiled and are certified by their auditors as conforming with generally accepted accounting principles (GAAP), why should the security analyst need to meddle with the figures? A major reason is that accepted accounting principles allow considerable leeway in the statement of results. This leeway permits the company to report its earnings on a basis that may not reflect the true operating results for the year (including its interest in affiliated companies) as the analyst would present such results.

Comparability of Inventories and Depreciation.   In particular, accounting permits considerable latitude in the basis of reporting inventories and depreciation. Adjustments are necessary to permit valid comparisons. The analyst must restate and interpret the figures, not so much in accordance with permissible practices of accounting as in the form most enlightening to the investor.

Consistency Through Time. While the increased number of accounting standards has improved comparability between companies engaging in similar transactions, the accounting changes themselves have created some problems with consistency through time. Most accounting standards become effective prospectively: That is, past transactions do not have to be restated to reflect the new requirements, for several reasons, including the cost of restatement, availability of the necessary data, questions of whether the company would have engaged in the transaction had the new rule been in effect, and concern that the credibility of accounting is harmed when previously issued statements are altered. From the analyst's viewpoint the frequent changes result in trends and averages that include transactions that are accounted for using both old and new rules. Such discontinuities and inconsistencies are a small price to pay for significantly improved accounting information. If the analyst stays aware of rule changes, they can usually be dealt with.

Professional versus Practical Implications of Analysts' Adjustments. A distinction needs to be drawn between the importance of financial statement analysis as a matter of necessary procedure by the professional analyst and its importance in leading to the most successful selection of securities—particularly common stocks. If the practitioner is to use the past record as the starting point for a study, the figures must be presented adequately and accurately. Analysts who fail to make the corrections required by sound techniques do a bad professional job of analysis. From that point of view, a comprehensive training in financial statement analysis is an essential part of the practitioner's education.

Statement Analysis Less Helpful in Selecting Stocks Than Bonds. Competent marshaling of the figures can usually be depended on to lead to successful choices of bonds and preferred stocks. Here the overriding question is whether the issue meets certain minimum standards of safety based on past performance. But in the common stock field, values depend to a significant extent on expectations as to the rate of future growth of earnings. Consequently, the following four factors will largely determine the success of a common stock purchase:

Whether the analyst's expectations are more accurate than the market's

Whether such expectations are fulfilled

3. Whether current expectations about future growth rate are more or less favorable than earlier ones

4. Changes, up or down, in the market's basis of capitalizing such expectations

These determinants of market value and the success of common stock purchases are by no means closely related to the past record. In view of the present preoccupation with the tempo of the future, much of the analyst's work in an accurate presentation of the past may appear rather irrelevant and of little practical value when applied to the choice of common stocks. It would be unrealistic not to recognize that the emphasis of common stock investing is on the future.

Nonetheless, the analyst should continue to do this searching and critical analysis of the past—for several reasons. First, professional standards must be maintained in whatever the analyst does, even though the market may, at times, seem to pay little heed to such presentations. Second, it is still true that in a number of individual instances this critical analysis will lead to worthwhile conclusions as to the overvaluation of certain issues and, particularly, the undervaluation of others. Often the analysis of earnings merely confirms that the earnings figures presented by the company are reasonably accurate and the net adjustments are so small as to be insignificant. Very often this is an indication that the market is dealing with the correct earnings number and that there is little likelihood that the stock will be priced other than in line with the market. It is just as important to eliminate fairly priced stocks from consideration as potential purchases as it is to discover those that are undervalued or overvalued. Third, regardless of the valuation model used—a multiplier of earnings, dividend discount model, or whatever— the current level of earnings is the starting point of the calculations and projections. To project properly for a given company, the current earning power must be determined as accurately as possible. Earning power might be called "the capacity to earn," and this capacity is not found solely in the accounting records. Leading questions are whether the company has the physical, manufacturing, distribution, managerial, financial, and other capabilities necessary to achieve the projections. If a company does not have those capacities in place, can the company acquire them? If the company has "done it before," the projections of the future have been demonstrated to be at least reasonable. Finally, the stock markets of the future will reflect periods of optimism during which a price is willingly paid for expected future success far exceeding the past—and more pessimistic times when even proven accomplishments can be bought at miserly prices.

Overview of the Seven Steps in the Analysis of Income Statements

To arrive at the indicated earning power for the period studied, the analyst should follow a standard procedure consisting of seven steps (the first two are discussed at length in this chapter):

1. *Deal properly with nonrecurring items.* The analyst must eliminate nonrecurring items from a single-year analysis, but include them in most long-term analyses.

2. *Eliminate unjustified income recognition.* Analysts need to eliminate any reported income that is not justified by economic substance. For example, if a company awards key officers and employees compensation in the form of stock options that have economic value but are not considered to be compensation by accounting rules, the analyst should record the estimated value of the option as compensation expense, less its tax effect, and thereby reduce the company's earnings. (Proper income recognition is indirectly a subject of all chapters on financial statement analysis, i.e., Chapters 2 through 20.)

3. *Direct entries to surplus.* Earnings must be adjusted to include inappropriate direct entries to surplus (Chapter 4)

4. *Use comparable inventory and depreciation methods.* The analyst should place the inventory valuation (Chapter 5) and the depreciation and amortization expense (Chapter 6) on a common basis, suitable for comparative study. (This may not always be possible.)

5. *Consolidate affiliates.* Analysts adjust earnings for the operations of subsidiaries and affiliates (Chapter 8), e.g., joint ventures, grantor trusts, investments carried on a cost basis, to the extent they are not included but available. Determining whether a legal entity is an affiliate should be based on the economic substance of the arrangement, and not its legal form.

6. *Provide for income taxes.* The analyst must now adjust the income tax expense to place it in proper relationship to the adjusted earnings before tax (Chapter 9).

7. *Record absent assets and liabilities.* The analyst should include the effects of certain unrecorded assets and liabilities, such as operating leases, some operating loss carryforwards, and some unconsolidated subsidiaries (Chapters 10 and 11).

Nonrecurring Items

Events That Occurred in Past Years

As is evident from the name, nonrecurring gains or losses arise for reasons outside the regular course of the business. The entries are of two main types. The first type relates entirely to events that occurred in past years, such as the following:

Tax Adjustments and Tax Forgiveness.   Payments of back taxes or tax refunds, not previously provided for, and interest thereon (sometimes accompanied by adjustments in depreciation reserves), and tax forgiveness are nonrecurring items.

Example. The Tax Reform Act of 1984 included several areas of tax forgiveness. As a result, the 1984 annual report of Archer Daniels Midland Company showed a $12 million reversal of deferred taxes previously provided on unremitted Domestic International Sales Corporation (DISC) earnings; the new law had eliminated all income taxes on unreversed timing differences outstanding on December 31, 1984.

Example. Similarly, the 1984 income statement of Aetna Life and Casualty Insurance Company carried a $65 million "fresh start adjustment" as an income tax credit resulting from the 1984 Act's requirement for a recomputation of policy reserves with permanent forgiveness of the taxes that otherwise would have resulted from that recalculation.

Litigation, Claims, and Renegotiation.   Results of litigation or other claims (e.g., renegotiation, damage suits, public utility rate controversies) are nonrecurring items that relate to prior years. *Accounting Trends and Techniques* (1985)[4] showed that 339 out of 600 companies showed loss contingencies as a result of pending litigation. In the vast majority of cases, no liability number was shown, as is customary in the case of litigation. Litigation is by far the largest cause of loss contingencies.

Example. AM International, Inc., in the year ended July 31,1984, settled a lawsuit with Richard B. Black, former chairman of the board, by certain stock transactions (the value of which was not clear) and by canceling a note of $1,668,750 owed by Black to the company.

Changes in Accounting and in Accounting Estimates.   Another nonrecurring item is the cumulative effect of an accounting change or a change in an estimate (for the latter see the Bethlehem example in Chapter 6).

[4]AICPA, *Accounting Trends and Techniques*, New York, 1985, p. 52.

Example. In the year ended September 30, 1984, Ashland Oil, Inc., changed the actuarial cost method used in calculating its pension obligations to one that "more closely resembles the method of accounting for pension costs proposed by the Financial Accounting Standards Board." This change decreased the net loss by $6,262,000 ($0.23 per share) in 1984. The pension footnote also indicated that the company's 1984 estimated accumulated plan benefits were calculated based on an 8.9 percent interest rate in 1984 as compared with 10.1 percent interest rate in 1983, resulting in an actuarial loss that would be spread over future years. No figures were given for the effects of the interest rate change.

Prior Period Adjustments and Restatements

Example. Statement 52, *Foreign Currency Translation,*[5] required adjustment of the opening balances to the new requirements by applying current exchange rates to certain foreign subsidiaries. Abbott Laboratories' 1985 form 10-K includes a footnote which states "Translation adjustments for 1983 include opening balance adjustments of $49,376" (thousands).

Events That Occurred in the Current Year

The other type of special transaction originated in the current year but is nonetheless of an exceptional character which sets it off from the ordinary operations. The following are examples of this category:

Sale of Assets. Profits or losses on the sale of fixed assets—or of investments, for a noninvestment company—are such nonrecurring items.

Major Asset Sale Programs

Major asset sales programs often involve sums that dwarf the ordinary activities of the company. That is, the gain or loss on sale of a major portion of the business may be several times the company's ordinary earning power. The most frequent and important nonrecurring items arise from the sale or other disposition of productive assets—plant or equipment. Such dispositions are often related to sale or discontinuation of a division, product line, or subsidiary. Other expenses of terminating employees, loss on inventories, and the like may be provided for at the same time if the sale is part of a major restructuring.

[5]Financial Accounting Standards Board, Statement 52, *Foreign Currency Translation,* Stamford, Conn., 1981.

The standard accounting treatment, as for other similar transactions, is to show the pretax amount in the income account before (ordinary) net income. The item qualifies for treatment by the analyst as "extraordinary."

Allocating the Gain or Loss to the Proper Years

Allocating such gains to the proper years is often difficult. In most cases, attribution to a single year does not give the right answer. In some cases the loss will be event-oriented, such as an environmental protection ruling, a new law, an abrupt decline of the dollar in the foreign exchange markets, a technological breakthrough, or some other event that is specific and can clearly be identified with a single time period. More often, restructuring, plant shutdowns, product abandonments, and the like are brought about by steadily deteriorating conditions over a relatively long period. Similarly, many gains on sales of assets resulted from price appreciation that occurred over 10 or 20 years, but the gain is recognized in accounting when the sale takes place. The analyst must make a decision, once the time period has been identified: What pattern of spreading the gain or loss best describes the economics of the situation? Although straight-line spreading is the easiest to calculate, the economics may dictate some other attribution of the gain or loss to individual years. The analyst must remember that the pattern of gains or losses that was recorded—all in one period—is the least appropriate one, because it is almost certainly the wrong pattern.

The gain or loss on such dispositions may be excluded from the income account by the analyst, but any related tax effects resulting from the excluded gain or loss should also be excluded. Care must be taken to use the proper tax rate (ordinary income, foreign, state, or U. S. rates).

Example. Ideal Basic Industries, during a period of restructuring, made provisions for shutdowns, write-downs, and gains and losses on facilities sold in the amounts of a $15,000,000 loss in 1980, $15,000,000 loss in 1981, $11,768,000 loss in 1983, and a $940,000 gain in 1984. The analyst should exclude these items from the results of each individual year but would probably choose to include them in calculating a five-year average. In 1983 and 1984, the company showed extraordinary gains on early extinguishment of debt in the amounts of $4,663,000 and $4,198,000, respectively. During the years 1982 to 1984, new debt was issued well in excess of the amounts retired in the extinguishment. As a result, interest expense rose rapidly from $32 million in 1982 to $46 million in 1984. There appears to have been no economic gain on the extinguishment, and the gains should be excluded from the income of the individual years. Treatment of such gains over longer periods is arguable, but, in general, they should be excluded.

In the middle 1980s many financial institutions, in an effort to improve their capital ratios, sold off office buildings which had appreciated substantially over the years and leased them back for extended periods. Such sales are not expected to recur, and give little insight into the earning power of the company. They should be excluded from ordinary earnings. In contrast, auto rental companies, such as Hertz, Avis, and National, optimize their use of automobiles by selling them when they reach either a specified age or mileage. Those companies operate their own used car lots, and the sale of cars is clearly a part of the ordinary recurring operations of those companies.

Write-up or Write-down of Investments.   Another nonrecurring item involves adjustments of certain investments to market value, for a non-investment company, or write-down of nonmarketable investments. An example of the latter was the 1985 write-down by American Can Company of its holding of New TC Preferred Stock by $40 million because of losses of the mortgage insurance subsidiary of New TC.

Adjustment of Foreign Assets.   Write-downs or recoveries of foreign assets are also nonrecurring items. In 1979 ITT Corporation made a provision for a $305 million loss on its Quebec pulp mill, "with no tax benefit."

Losses on foreign operations have frequently arisen through both political and financial (foreign exchange) disturbances. Formerly, many companies with diversified foreign interests set up reserves, usually by charges to income, to absorb possible future losses of this kind. The income statement was thus spared if and when the loss arose. Statement No. 5, *Accounting for Contingencies*,[6] issued in March 1975, bans general reserves of this sort. A provision is made only when the loss becomes "probable," as defined, and it must go through the income statement rather than directly to surplus.

Life Insurance and Other Insurance Gains.   Proceeds of life insurance policies collected are for most companies an irregular source of cash inflows, and not a part of the ordinary activities of the company. Certain other insurance gains are nonrecurring in character. The 1985 annual

---

[6]Financial Accounting Standards Board, Statement No. 5, *Accounting for Contingencies*, Stamford, Conn., 1975.

report of Fluorocarbon Company showed as an extraordinary item $966,000 of insurance collected in excess of the carrying amount of its Birmingham, Alabama, fluid sealing plant which burned in August, 1984. Although fires are a recurring part of the business scene, gains on insurance coverage that exceed the carrying amount of plant and equipment should not be considered a part of the normal operating earnings of a company.

Discontinued Operations.   Income from discontinued operations will not recur, although some capital may remain from the discontinued activity. That capital can be reinvested in other profitable operations.

Unusual or Infrequent Items

In general, today's accounting calls for an all-inclusive income statement, with rare exceptions (e.g., certain gains and losses from foreign currency fluctuations, pensions, and marketable securities). The term *extraordinary* has long been restricted to those events that are *both* infrequent and unusual. Extraordinary items are presented below the line called "Net Income" and are presented "net of tax." At the same time events that are *either* unusual or infrequent, but not both are shown separately on the face of the income statement, above net income, and must be shown without the tax effect. Footnotes usually reveal the related tax effect. The analyst will generally conclude that items that are either unusual or infrequent should be treated as nonrecurring.

Twofold Status of Nonrecurring Items in Analysis

Most nonrecurring items play a double and contradictory role in security analysis. They should be excluded from the results for a single year, but they should be included in the overall results for a period of years. A substantial refund of overpaid taxes, for example, has nothing to do with the current year's operating profit, and it is a misuse of language to call it part of the "earnings" of the year in which it was received. Because the analyst is interested in trends, the results of events need to be placed in the years in which the events occurred. If a tax refund is received in 1987 for overpayment of taxes on income earned in 1984 and 1985, the analyst should restate the taxes for 1984 and 1985 and eliminate the refund from 1987.

In a 7- or 10-year analysis of average earnings, a tax refund pertaining to the period belongs in the picture just as much as the profits or losses against which it accrued. In a long-range analysis of past results, the best rule is to take in every real profit or loss item unless it is quite unrelated to the normal operations of the business. Voluntary markups or markdowns of capital items, such as plant or intangibles, should not be considered a real gain or loss.

Analysts frequently encounter factors that influence income favorably or unfavorably for the short term, but that will change significantly during the period for which they are projecting income. Examples might include:

- Low-cost debt that will mature in a few years
- A favorable lease that is soon to expire
- The near-term expiration of patents, royalties, and supply and other contracts

Analysts will adjust projections to reflect, say, that the old 4 percent bonds which mature in two years are likely to be refinanced with 10 percent bonds.

Rules for the Treatment of Nonrecurring Items

Clearly, where substantial nonrecurring items exist there cannot be any completely satisfactory statements of earnings by single years, for neither the inclusion nor the exclusion of such items will do full justice to the situation. It is doubtful, in any event, that really worthwhile indications of earning power and intrinsic value could be obtained from a study of the current year's results alone. Fuller consideration of this point must be reserved for the discussion of the significance of the earnings record in Chapter 29.[7]

However, the security analyst does face the problem of properly interpreting, and perhaps restating, the earnings reported for relatively short periods. A logical and consistent approach to the various kinds of nonrecurring items is needed. The analyst may be helped by the following three suggestions for the treatment of nonrecurring items in the income statement:

1. Small items should be accepted as reported. For convenience, *small* is defined as affecting net income by less than 5 percent. If a number of items are involved, the cumulative effect shall be considered in applying the 5 percent rule.
2. When an item is excluded, a corresponding adjustment must be allowed for in the income tax deduction.

---

[7] See the unabridged fifth edition of Sidney Cottle, Roger F. Murray, and Frank E. Block, *Graham and Dodd's Security Analysis,* McGraw-Hill, New York, 1988.

3. Most nonrecurring items excluded from the single year's analysis must nevertheless be included in a statement of long-term or average results.

Gains and Losses on the Company's Securities

Gains and losses on the early extinguishment of debt raise two issues. A gain may reflect a recent rise in interest rates or perhaps a decline in credit rating that occurred over many years. The economic cause of the gain must be determined to identify the year or years in which the gain should be placed—if any.

A second issue is whether the gain should be included at all. An appropriate question is whether the company is really any "better off." If the company is merely substituting a smaller face amount of high-coupon bonds for a larger face amount of low-coupon bonds, the cost of capital stays about the same for the ongoing firm. What was gained in the face amount of bonds outstanding will be lost in the higher coupons which will be paid in future years. (The present value of the new and old bonds is the same.) Yet, for a firm facing near-term liquidation, the gain is very real because it will be available for distribution to shareholders.

Whatever the source of funds for the extinguishment, a cost of capital or an opportunity cost was incurred at the same market level as that at which the debt was extinguished. For the ongoing firm, gains and losses from all capital transactions are best excluded at least from the current year's results.

A particularly troublesome transaction is a gain on extinguishment of debt when it is accomplished by a swap for the company's equity securities. The tax effects of extinguishment of debt through use of the company's stock are somewhat unusual. Any gain is considered income by the IRS, but the income can be avoided by electing to reduce the tax-cost basis of depreciable assets, if any exist. Thus, although the income will be free from immediate taxation, the reduction in depreciation in future years will increase future taxable income by exactly the same amount, so that income taxes will be paid in subsequent years. Thus, deferred income taxes should be provided on the gain.

A key question is whether the company sold stock at a favorable or unfavorable price. Gains on the extinguishment of debt often occur because interest rates have risen. When interest rates are high, it is likely that stocks are depressed. Thus, the analyst may wish to determine whether management has made a wise decision under the circumstances. The company, of course, could have sold stock without paying off the debt, which suggests that the fact that they paid off the debt is somewhat irrelevant. For purposes of determining earning power, such "internal" transactions are irrelevant. Yet the longer-term record should include the tax expense, because it probably will become payable.

Capital Gains and Losses of Financial Companies

Financial companies are those whose assets are almost exclusively in the form of cash, receivables, and securities. They include:

- Banks
- Insurance companies
- Investment companies and mutual funds
- Holding companies that do not report on a consolidated basis
- Credit or finance companies

In all but the latter group, investment in marketable securities is a major or at least a significant part of the business. Gains or losses from the investment portfolio, both realized and unrealized, will usually be significant in relation to what is called its ordinary or operating income. Should such changes in portfolio values be viewed as recurring or nonrecurring items in the analysis of income accounts of financial companies?

The question has no categorical answer. These gains and losses are certainly recurring in the sense that they occur every year in a greater or lesser amount, and they are without doubt related to the regular business operations. But they are not recurring in the sense that under normal operating conditions the business would be geared to make a certain normal profit out of security price movements. The year-to-year fluctuations in prices of equity securities are much larger than the expected annual average capital appreciation, and will not give a representative number, even if averaged over several years. Thus, their inclusion is likely to give misleading signals about the future. In contrast, the interest and dividend income from the securities owned is reasonably stable and predictable.

There seems to be a sharp distinction between realized and unrealized profits or losses. The former are necessarily entered on the books; they have income tax consequences; in the case of most investment funds, realized profits result in corresponding distributions to stockholders.[8]

---

[8] Under the tax code, regulated investment companies may reduce or avoid income tax by distributing their income and realized security profits in a prescribed manner.

However, a change in market value may be left unrecognized or is perhaps mentioned only in a footnote to the balance sheet or as a direct entry to equity, depending on the industry. Whether a security profit or loss is "real" until it is realized is a less important issue than it appears—the real distinction is between the overall long-term results, which are of major significance, and the more or less fortuitous changes in security values during a single year.

In a single-year analysis, the analyst should group together the realized and unrealized portfolio gain or loss. (This is done in the standard or conventional form of reporting the income statement of insurance companies.) The figures for the 12 months should be presented in two parts: (1) ordinary income and (2) portfolio profit or loss. Comparatively little significance will attach to the latter component because it is governed mainly by security-market conditions in the year, but the former may serve as a guide to future projections.

In a long-term analysis the portfolio results must always play a part; for investment funds, portfolio results are particularly significant in determining the relative accomplishment of the management. Former editions of this book suggested that the period taken for study be one between substantially equal levels of the stock market (the "equal level method"). For such a span the portfolio profit and loss would properly enter into the analysis on a par with the other components of earning power, providing a measure of the skill of the management in this important part of the operations of a financial company.

Because markets move to new record high levels, such comparisons are not always available—the ending level may be far above any useful starting point. An alternative is to calculate (or estimate) portfolio betas and use them to adjust the observed returns for market risk. Comparisons of risk-adjusted returns over time are as useful as results from the equal level method. In either case the time period should be at least five years, preferably longer.

Such comparisons of portfolios should seek to bring together companies with similar general policies, objectives, and portfolio compositions. It is obvious, for instance, that an all-stock fund would be expected to show better results during a rising stock market than would a balanced fund with a substantial bond component.

4

Effect of Reserves, Contingencies, and Valuation Accounts on the Income Statement

Use of Reserves Restricted

Reserves have played a prominent but not always helpful part in corporate accounting. The unhelpful type of reserves consisted of arbitrary amounts of income set aside by management to provide for general and unspecified contingencies. Such reserves were set up in good years, and the amounts brought back in poor years, thereby smoothing the earnings trend. The word *reserves* continues in use today, but FASB Statement No. 5, *Accounting for Contingencies*,[1] eliminates most questionable uses. This statement requires that a loss contingency be accrued by a charge to income if

1. It is probable that an asset has been impaired or a liability has been incurred at the date of the financial statements

2. It is probable that future events will occur confirming the fact of the loss

3. The amount can be reasonably estimated

[1]Financial Accounting Standards Board, Stanford, Conn., 1975.

If the amount cannot be determined, disclosure is required.

The recognition of gain contingencies in income is forbidden. Current accounting eliminates reserves for general or unspecified business risks and many remote contingencies such as:

- Guarantees of indebtedness of others
- Standby letters of credit
- Guarantees to repurchase receivables
- Self-insurance

The write-down of operating assets was specifically excluded from Statement 5. Special problems of write-offs resulting from restructurings are treated in separate sections of this chapter, as are postemployment benefits and foreign currency translation.

Three Classes of Reserves Generally

The word *reserves* is commonly used to describe three types of accounting items:

- Valuations accounts
- Liabilities
- Reserves against future developments

Valuation Accounts.   The standard reserves to reduce assets in valuation accounts are those against:

- Receivables, for uncollectables
- Fixed assets, for depreciation and other amortization
- Marketable securities to mark down to current price
- Other investments and net foreign assets to estimated current value or recoverable amount
- Inventories, to a figure below cost
- Loans and mortgages, for doubtful accounts

Liabilities.   Some routine liabilities arising from the past are called reserves, usually when the liability is *noncurrent and uncertain as to timing or amount.* Liabilities include reserves for taxes, for renegotiation, for pensions (especially where "book reserve" pension accounting is used), for claims in litigation, and for similar liabilities.

Other liability reserves are especially important in specific industries, for example:

Industry	Reserve
Insurance	Unearned premiums
	Policy reserves
	Loss reserves
Credit	Unearned finance charges
Transportation	Injuries and damages
Shipping	Recapture of subsidy
Public utilities	Rate adjustments and refunds

All these may be called reserves, simply because of uncertainties of timing or amount, but they are really liabilities.

Reserves against Future Developments.   Reserves to provide for probable losses include: plant impairments and similar costs for proposed plant restructuring, closure or abandonment, and discontinuation of a product line.

Balance Sheet Treatment of Reserve Items

The reserve type of transaction appears in the income statement under such titles as "Provision for Plant Shutdown," "Special Charge," or "Reserve for Rationalization." In each case, there will be a balance sheet effect:

1. An asset will be eliminated or reduced.
2. A liability will created or increased.
3. Stockholders' equity will be reduced.

Special Rules for Treatment of Certain Reserve Items

Small Items.   Reserve items that effect net income by less than 5 percent when all such items are aggregated should be accepted as they appear.

Deferred Taxes.   Deferred income taxes should be considered ordinary deductions from current income, unless they relate clearly to a nonrecurring item or have some other special characteristic.

Discussion of Frequently Used Reserves

The following paragraphs discuss a few reserve items because of their frequency or because of some peculiar characteristic. However, reserves relating to inventory accounting (Chapter 5), depreciation (Chapter 6), and deferred taxes (Chapter 9) are of such importance and complexity that we shall deal with them separately.

Reserves for Bad Debts

Reserves for bad debts are nearly always accepted as stated for nonfinancial companies. Certain financial institutions, such as banks, have special optional rules which may require adjustment by the analyst. The 10-K usually provides charge-off-information that is useful in judging the adequacy of bad debt reserves which are tax-deductible for some companies. Many bank analysts use the actual charge-offs in preference to the "provision for loan losses" (now being phased out for tax purposes for banks having assets of $500 million or more). Those analysts consider such reserves to be a device for smoothing earnings. For companies in installment selling or in the lending business, credit losses are important and may require special scrutiny.

The Treatment of Loan Loss Reserves of Banks

The loan loss reserves of banks can be used both as a device to smooth earnings and as a hidden reserve. As a result, bank analysts often eliminate changes in the reserve for loan losses from the income statement and substitute therefor the actual charge-offs and recoveries of the individual years. This results in more volatile income statements that are probably more reflective of what actually happened in a particular year. Averaging the actual charge-offs and recoveries gives a better picture of earning power than averaging the loan loss reserve as a percentage of loans. At times, bank stock analysts will make major adjustments to the loan loss reserves of these institutions. For example, in the middle 1980s, the reserves were clearly inadequate for banks operating in the "oil patch" to the extent that they were involved heavily in real estate loans and in oil drilling loans. Similarly, analysts made significant adjustments for expected losses on loans to less developed countries.

High-Risk Industries

Certain industries, from time to time or regularly, are at high risk of credit losses. Their loan loss or bad debt provisions require the analyst's special attention. For example, the credit losses of gambling casinos are highly variable from year to year. The shell home business typically makes sales with a very small down payment, and the risk is substantial that buyers will "walk away" from their loans. Those savings and loan associations that face massive withdrawal of deposits may have to sell substantial amounts of mortgages to raise the necessary funds. If the mortgages are under water or of doubtful quality, the ordinary loss provisions may be inadequate.

Allowance for Marketable Securities

These valuation accounts are not tax deductible until losses are actually realized (except for security dealers). FASB Statement No. 12, *Accounting for Certain Marketable Securities*, requires recognition in income of unrealized gains and losses in portfolios of marketable equity securities that are classified as current assets. *Realized* gains and losses are included in income of the period regardless of the current or noncurrent classifications; some, but not all, *unrealized* gains and losses of noncurrent portfolios of equity securities are shown in the equity section of the balance sheet, but they bypass the income statement. Certain industries have specialized accounting for marketable securities.

For nonfinancial companies, changes in such reserves should be regarded as nonrecurring, but they are rarely important enough to require adjustment of the income account. In the analysis of financial companies, distinguishing between unrealized depreciation (or "quotational losses") on portfolio securities and losses actually taken does not seem practicable.

Example. In 1982 Resorts International, Inc., reported a net gain of $16.7 million from marketable securities. This number included $42.2 million from the sale of U.S. Treasury bond futures contracts and certain Treasury bonds, losses of $6 million from the sale of marketable equity securities, and dividend income of $2.7 million. The gain triggered recognition of the benefit of $4.2 million of tax loss carryforwards. In addition, working capital was enhanced by $45 million by reclassification of marketable securities to current assets. Although the company's primary business is hotels and casinos, it has had an interesting history of investing in interest rate and metals futures contracts as well as fixed income and equity securities. The investing activities have been sufficiently large to justify the analyst marking the portfolio to market and calculating annual investment results.

Reserves Against Other Investments

In general, reserves for investments apply to subsidiary or affiliated companies. Valuation accounts are applied to subsidiaries and affiliates under several sets of circumstances. If management has determined to sell or liquidate a subsidiary, a loss may be recognized based on the estimated proceeds, net of expenses. Occasionally foreign subsidiaries will be nationalized with inadequate compensation, and the compensation may be in dispute, involving either negotiations or litigation. Under those circumstances, an estimate of the loss is made, and the carrying amount of the investment is reduced to reflect the expected loss.

Renegotiation and Litigation Reserves

A significant source of the reserve type of liability is the various amounts that are set aside or should be, for renegotiation of contracts in dispute and for the outcome of litigation. Some examples are:

- Disputes in defense contracts
- Disapproval by the commissioner of insurance premiums charged
- Refund order by a state utility commission
- Litigation over a force majeure cancellation of contract
- Litigation over a tax dispute
- Litigation over application of price control regulations

Example. The 1985 Exxon Corporation annual report showed a line item in the income statement titled "Hawkins provision" in the amount of $948 million, with a footnote on the face of the statement that the amount, net of related taxes, was $545 million. This case concerned a price dispute about oil produced in the East Texas Hawkins Field. Disclosure was suitable throughout the years of litigation. An analyst would normally spread a loss of this sort over the years in which the oil was produced. We know now that the earnings of those years were overstated.

Property and Casualty Insurance Reserves

In the fire and casualty insurance business, damage claims—both those litigated and those settled peaceably—are a basic part of operations. The results for any year and the equity shown for the stockholders will depend in large measure on the method followed in computing reserves for unsettled and unreported losses. The regulatory bodies require that specific formulas be followed in setting up the minimum reserves for personal injury claims in automobile insurance and for workers' compensation claims. (If the company's own estimate, on a "case basis," indicates a larger liability, that figure must be used instead.) Liability under other types of claims is a matter for management to determine, subject to a triennial or quadrennial check by insurance commission examiners. There is room for a considerable degree of either overestimation or underestimation in this field.

Unearned-Premium Liability. Analysts give credit in the income statement for certain unearned premiums. Today these are always "short-tailed" policies in which all claims are fully reported shortly after the expiration of the policy. The following formula is used by some analysts to calculate the value of these policies, representing approximately the cost of putting the business on the books.

$$\text{Adjustment} = \left(\begin{array}{c} \text{Increase in} \\ \text{unearned} \\ \text{premium} \\ \text{reserve} \end{array} \right) \times \left(1 - \text{tax rate} \right)$$

$$\times \left(\frac{\text{Overall expenses} - \text{loss expense}}{\text{Premiums written}} \right)$$

Analysts must use only the increase in unearned premiums for the particular types of policies for which they wish to give credit, using information from the Commissioners' Standard Report. Once the adjustment is calculated, the resulting number is compared with the prices acceptable to reinsurance companies for insuring the same liability. This procedure is recommended.

The previous practice of including in income 35 to 40 percent of the unearned premium on long-tailed policies, such as product liability, has proved to be a poor practice because of failure to make the proper tax adjustment and because of a tremendous underestimation of the cost of claims in an era of inflation. Very few analysts or financial services continue this previously popular procedure. It is interesting that the Tax Reform Act of 1986 embraced this repudiated form of income for the first time, subjecting 20 percent of the increase in unearned premiums to taxation.

Other Common Reserves

Reserve for Unearned Finance Charges

The accounting for finance charges "paid" by the borrower in advance—by having them added to his debt—is essentially identical with that for insurance premiums paid on issuance of the policy. A reserve is set up for that portion of the finance charges that has not been earned by the passage of time. The amount is properly deductible from the receivables themselves on the asset side along with the bad-debt reserve.

Undoubtedly the stockholders have some equity in these unearned finance charges, since they partly reflect expenses incurred in putting the business on the books, as do the unearned-premium reserves of insurance companies. It is not customary to allow for such an equity in any official calculation of earnings or net worth. Caution would suggest that such values be used as additional motivation for purchasing a stock already considered undervalued rather than putting them into the valuation calculation itself. Our conservatism is bolstered by the current abuses of somewhat similar fee income by some financial institutions.

Reserve for Unexpired Subscriptions

The liability of newspaper and magazine publishers for unexpired subscriptions is similar to that for unearned premiums. Unexpired subscriptions offer an interesting example of an unbooked asset. Subscriptions are liabilities to pay money or deliver the publication, yet the liability is more than offset by the value of the customer list. When a magazine ceases publication, other publishers are pleased to purchase the customer list for cash and, in addition, assume the liability for the subscriptions. The acquiring publisher then offers the old subscribers the choice of a new publication or return of the remaining portion of the subscription price. Since most subscribers choose the new publication, the purchase is an attractive and inexpensive way of increasing circulation. Again, we would not be anxious to include in the accounts any value for the unexpired subscriptions, but they are an incentive in the decision to buy a stock already determined to be reasonably priced. The analyst has no way to value a subscription list because that would require knowledge of subscriber demographics, such as age, location, income, wealth, and hobbies.

Reserve for Rate Adjustments

Public utility companies have frequently been subject to regulatory proceedings looking to reduce rates and charges. In some cases such reductions, if ordered, will be retroactive. Many of these rate cases result from plant abandonments due to excess capacity, to construction delays which increase the interest costs of plants, and to unexpected inflation. Consumer groups and others often vigorously resist the resulting increase in the cost of utility products and services. Rate commissions have disallowed some costs as being imprudently incurred; in some cases both return on investment and recovery of investment have been disallowed. Utility companies have been extremely reluctant to write down the assets in question, because they believe that once they do so the rate commission will be far less likely to grant them recovery. Thus, they would prefer to maintain the old carrying values until the final judicial appeal has been turned down. This, of course, can extend over several years in the case of appeals that must go through several levels of the court system. This delayed recognition of losses when they become probable is not justifiable. In such cases, analysts should attempt their own estimates of an appropriate adjustment and treat it as a nonrecurring item.

Valuation Accounts for Loan and Mortgage Portfolios

Portfolios of loans and mortgages held by thrift institutions, such as savings and loan associations and mutual savings banks, are ordinarily carried at cost, adjusted for amortization of premiums and accretion of discounts. A loan loss reserve is provided. However, that loan loss reserve is an estimate of credit losses and has nothing to do with the market value of the portfolio. Under some circumstances, the thrift institution may be forced to liquidate a significant portion of its portfolio in order to raise cash either to pay interest or cover the withdrawal of deposits. Since accounting does not require these portfolios to be carried at market value, it is incumbent upon the analyst to make an estimate of market value and of the degree of invasion of the portfolio that is likely to take place when a thrift institution gets into trouble. Such a calculation is not necessary, of course, if the institution is profitable and the maturities of its loan portfolio are reasonably well matched against the maturities of outstanding deposit instruments.

Provision for Losses on Major Restructurings

Major Write-Downs

Discontinuation of a product line, sale of a segment, reorganization of a division, or other restructuring, are nonrecurring items which usually require that a provision be set up for expected losses. These write-downs and write-offs are presented in the accounts with a variety of descriptive titles, some of which tend to soften the negative aspects and sometimes leave the impression that the whole affair is a bit of good news. Losses are recognized based on a management decision to dispose of assets and activities and the amount is a management estimate, usually based on a written plan that has been approved by the Board of Directors. The problem is that plans do change, and the program may ultimately turn out to be much larger or smaller than originally thought. In general, accounting for management intentions is a perilous activity. Analyzing such accounting is equally perilous and analysts often find themselves waiting for the other shoe to drop. The bookkeeping entries may include both a reduction in the carrying amounts of assets and setting up a liability. A major cost is the various termination benefits given to employees. These amounts include early retirement incentives, aid in finding employment, counseling, moving and traveling expenses, and special separation bonuses and are often more significant in amount than the losses on inventory and plant. The analytical issues include both the estimation of the loss and its treatment as a nonrecurring event.

Table 4.1   Armco, Inc.

(In Millions of Dollars)

			Nonrecurring items					
			Special charges					
Year	Income from continuing operation	Oil field equipment	Steel operations	Fabricated products and services	Nickel	Other	Gain on sale	Total
1986	(361.6)*	(108.0)	(235.0)	—	—	7.4	—	(335.6)
1985	(143.2)*	25.1	(110.0)	69.9	—	42.0†	167.9‡	55.9
1984	(249.3)*	(190.0)	(10.0)	(10.0)	—	(135.0)§	(172.5)¶	(172.5)
1983	(506.2)	—	(235.9)	—	—	(60.8)	—	(296.7)
1982	(359.8)	—	(300.0)	—	(71.9)	(88.4)	—	(460.3)
1981	220.9	—	—	—	—	—	—	—

*As restated in 1986.
†Includes $58 tax benefit of loss carryforward.
‡Aerospace and strategic materials and $33.2 gain on sale of tax benefits.
§Includes $120 provision for future losses of Armco Financial Services Group.
¶Coal operations.

Example. Table 4.1 shows the series of special write-offs, provisions
for losses, gains on sales, and related nonrecurring transactions resulting
from Armco, Inc.'s efforts to restructure nearly all of its operations
during the years 1982 through 1986. Several characteristics of such
restructurings are shown in the table and deserve mention. First, the
initial write-off, write-down, or loss provision is generally a round
number, indicating that it is a rough estimate rather than a realized gain
or loss. Second, it is not uncommon for a company to discover that the
first cut was not deep enough, and that additional write-downs and loss
provisions are necessary. This is seen in the company's steel operations
in which a sizable provision was made in 1982. In 1983 there was an
additional loss that probably represented realized losses, such as sale of
assets, payments to terminated employees, and the like (a nonrounded
number of $235.9 million). Then, again, further losses were provided
for in the subsequent two years (round numbers), with the final resolution
lying yet ahead. Fabricated Products and Services is somewhat similar. An
initial $10 million provision was made, a round number, followed by a
more precise $69.1 million loss. Income from continuing operations has
been restated for the years 1984 to 1986 to include the losses of Armco
Financial Services Group. Earlier Armco had announced intentions to
dispose of that group, but has concluded that another five years will be
necessary before those operations can be sold.

Allocation by the Analyst

What should analysts do in situations such as Armco's? It seems clear that the amount of special items shown in each of the years does not pertain purely to the year in which it was reported. Simply adding up all of the gains and losses of the nonrecurring nature and spreading them evenly over some arbitrary period would be an improper technique. The correct technique is to place each gain or loss in the year or years in which it is believed to have occurred. The proper procedure is to examine each loss or gain, seek its cause, and deal with it individually.

Profits in the steel industry peaked in 1979 and, overall, turned into losses for the years 1982 to 1986. An analyst might spread the steel operation losses over the years 1982 to 1986 or perhaps start a year or so earlier.

In the case of the oil field equipment loss and gain, the numbers should be combined and applied to the years when that industry turned unprofitable. Profits in the oil service industry peaked in 1981, losses began in 1983, and by 1985 losses and large charge-offs were pervasive. Given industry conditions, the analyst might spread the net oil field equipment loss over the years 1983 to 1986, admitting that a case can be made for going back as far as 1982.

The outright sale of the coal operations and the aerospace and strategic materials division resulted in gains that were realized in the years they were reported. They should be excluded from estimates of normal earnings, but included in longer term averages. The proceeds of such a sale are, of course, available to earn profits and will add to future earning power.

The loss on the nickel operation probably belongs in 1982, which is about the time that industry turned unprofitable.

Clearly, the benefits of the tax loss carryforwards, which were realized in 1985, came about through the losses accumulated from 1982 through 1985. They should be spread over that period. The tax benefit appears to be a part of normal earnings for those years, in contrast to the other nonrecurring items in the table.

One of the most interesting and unusual of the nonrecurring items in Table 4.1 is the $33.2 million gain on sale of tax benefits. In effect, 1985 net income was credited with an amount which ordinarily would have been tax deductions for subsequent years. Ideally, to place it properly in terms of a normal earnings calculation, it should be spread evenly over future years rather than taken in 1985, although normally the issue is one of spreading nonrecurring items over past years rather than future years.

Analysts also must make decisions about the pattern of allocation among years. They may choose to spread an amount evenly or in proportion to some factor (such as spreading the tax loss carryforward in proportion to the past losses), or even choose an accelerating pace, putting the larger amounts in the later years and smaller amounts in the earlier years.

Cash Flow Timing May Differ

The paragraphs above have encouraged putting the gain or loss in the proper year, but have not addressed the question of cash flows. One of the interesting characteristics of write-offs and provisions for restructuring is that the cash flow may not take place in the year the loss is recorded. Often it occurs the following year or over a period of several years. The analyst should be alert to this fact, since what appears to be a healthy net current asset position may not have received any of the impact of the provision, and an examination of the facts may indicate that liquidity will undergo some strain when the cash outflows actually take place.

Big Bath Accounting

An equally difficult aspect of these major write-offs is so-called big bath accounting. Big bath accounting does not occur when an unprofitable activity is sold or liquidated. It comes about when the activity is continued, but the inventory, plant, and equipment have been written down, resulting in lower subsequent expenses.

Including the Kitchen Sink.   Once it is decided to take a major write-down, there is little additional embarrassment in charging off every possible doubtful asset, thereby preparing the way for accounting prosperity. In subsequent years, cost of goods sold and depreciation will be reduced proportionately, so that the company may show excellent profits and a fine return on capital. The cause of the earnings recovery is still clearly visible in the first year after the write-down, because the analyst can see more than one year's financial statements in the annual report. However, a few years after that, the bath may no longer be visible and the analyst is apt to conclude that the company is highly profitable. The dangers of being misled by big bath accounting make it necessary for the analyst to review financial statements covering a history of at least 5 to 10 years before reaching a conclusion about the profitability of a company, the quality of its management, the efficiency of its operations, and similar matters.

Example.   In 1969 and 1970 Lockheed Corporation made an aggregate provision of $340 million for losses on Department of Defense contracts. Depreciation expense dropped $8.5 million from $56.3 million in 1970 to $47.8 million in 1972. The lower depreciation, and probably lower cost of goods sold, made an appreciable contribution to 1972 profits of $13.0 million.

Foreign Currency Translation Adjustments

The most frequent cause of changes in dollar-carrying amounts of the assets and liabilities of foreign subsidiaries whose functional currency is the local currency is the fluctuation of the dollar value of that currency. When the foreign currency declines relative to the dollar the beginning net worth of the subsidiary and its earnings during the period will be reduced accordingly, but the loss will bypass the income statement and be shown in an account in equity, generally entitled "Foreign Currency Translation Adjustment." *Adjustment*, in this case, is a nice but misleading term for real gains and losses. Most of them should be included in income.

Transactions and Translation Adjustments

Transactions. An important but sometimes misunderstood technical difference exists between foreign currency *transactions* and foreign currency *translation adjustments*. Transactions result in gains and losses when an entity holds monetary assets (cash, receivables and the like) or owes liabilities which are denominated in a currency that is different from the currency in which the entity measures its results and, before settlement, the relative values of the currencies change. For example, an entity which uses the peso as its *functional currency* will suffer a transaction loss if it owes French francs while the franc rises relative to the peso.

Translation Adjustments. Translation adjustments arise in the process of converting the foreign affiliate's financial statements from the local currency into the parent company's home currency. If the currency of the parent is the same as that of the affiliate, no translation adjustment arises. However, if the currencies of the parent and the affiliate are not the same, gains or losses which appeared in the affiliate's statements will usually be different when remeasured in the parent's currency. A subsidiary's gain may even turn out to be a parent company loss, or vice versa. Thus, remember that translation is the process of *remeasuring* the results so that they reflect what happened in terms of the parent's currency—that in which the parent's dividends and borrowings are paid. Remeasuring reveals real gains and losses for those who expect to be paid in dollars—not merely a mechanical "adjustment."

The Importance of a Dollar Perspective. The most fundamental decision in measuring anything is selecting the appropriate unit. When measuring a U.S. company's ability to pay dividends and debt, obviously the measuring unit must be the dollar. Investors and creditors from the United States cannot make decisions other than in terms of the number of dollars they expect to receive. An extreme example will make it obvious why translation adjustments reflect real gains and losses.

Example. Assume that a British subsidiary owns a $100 bill. At the beginning of the year 1 pound is selling at $2. From the viewpoint of the British manager, the company has an asset worth 50 pounds. At the end of the year the pound has dropped to $1. The British manager then calculates that bill is worth 100 pounds, resulting in a 50-pound foreign currency transaction profit, which must be reported in the subsidiary's income statement. This amount will be translated into dollars as a $50 transaction gain. It will appear in the parent's income statement.

The translation process, which converts the statements from the local (pound) perspective to a dollar perspective, recognizes that the $50 transaction gain does not exist in a dollar world and that the $100 bill has not changed in dollar value. Therefore the parent must enter a $50 foreign currency translation adjustment (loss) to wipe out the nonexistent gain. The problem for the analyst is that translation adjustments go directly to equity, leaving the economically nonexistent gain in income. Thus, if the translation adjustment is not recognized for what it is—a loss—income will be overstated. Obviously in this case the analyst would subtract $50 translation adjustment loss from the income statement to offset the incorrect gain that would otherwise be reported.

Are All Translation Adjustments Gains and Losses? It is less obvious what to do when the assets of that subsidiary include, say, a building. The analyst will ask the questions: "If the pound declines, will the parent really suffer a loss on this building? Is it likely that the future flows of dollars from the building will decline?"

The Answers Are Situational. If the building were a warehouse leased to someone for 20 years at a rent of 10,000 pounds per year, it does appear clear that the dollar flows to the parent company and its U.S. stockholders would go up and down with the pound.

However, if the building is a manufacturing plant that produces parts for a product that is sold in the United States for dollars, fluctuations in the pound would not appear to affect very much the expected future dollar cash flows generated by the plant. Thus in the second case the translation adjustment is probably not an economic loss and should not enter income (or the balance sheet either, for that matter). Unhappily, most situations are not nearly so clear as these two examples. The effects of exchange rate changes on plant and equipment will rarely be subject to reliable analysis.

The Difficulty for Analysts Is Lack of Information.   To a security analyst, foreign currency translation adjustments are among the most difficult of the reserve types of transactions to analyze with confidence. Often the necessary information is simply not available.

The Answers Lie in Each Asset and Liability.   The gains and losses that arise as a result of foreign currency fluctuations do so because *individual* assets are owned and liabilities owed and because particular revenues and expenses occur. Exchange rate changes have widely differing economic consequences for different types of assets and liabilities. For a given rate movement, one asset may become more valuable and another less valuable.

Individual Assets and Liabilities Are at Risk—Not the Affiliate's Net Worth.   Yet, many companies, and even accounting itself, take the view that it is the net worth of a foreign subsidiary that is at risk to currency fluctuations, and not the individual assets and liabilities that make up that net worth. As a result, many companies do not keep track of the sources of their various translation gains and losses. Instead, they simply calculate the total amount for the year using a simple short cut formula.[2] Companies that hold that particular viewpoint and use the short-cut method may not be able to answer the analyst's questions about how much of their foreign currency translation adjustment came from the plant account or how much from long-term debt. Clearly foreign currency is not only difficult to analyze, but also lacking in consistent and organized disclosure of the desired details.

---

[2]Setting aside certain adjustments for hedging transactions, the foreign currency translation adjustment equals (1) the opening net worth multiplied by the change in the rate of exchange from the beginning of the year to the end of the year plus (2) net income times the difference between the average rate and the year-end rate. Other companies simply observe the discrepancy between net income and the change in net worth on the balance sheet after both have been translated into dollars. That difference is added to or subtracted from the adjustment balance and though of as a sort of errors and omissions account.

A Compromise Adjustment Technique

Adjustments Arising from Working Capital Should Be Included in Income. The values of short-term monetary items, such as cash, receivables and payables, fluctuate with the value of the foreign currency in which they are denominated. If they are classified as current, they will soon be converted into cash, and the gains and losses will be realized. Similarly, since inventory will be sold in a relatively short time—probably before there is a major change in exchange rates—their adjustment gains and losses should also be included in income. Ideally, gains and losses from working capital items, adjusted of course for tax consequences, are the *minimum* the analyst should include in income.

The Assumptions Behind the Working Capital Recommendation. Several assumptions were made in our recommendation to recognize the translation gains and losses from current assets and liabilities. They should be examined carefully. The inventory assumption is important and it is not inconsistent with today's accounting model. Evidence of the rapid turnover of inventories is abundant. The assumption that inventories can and will be sold is required to justify existing carrying amounts. And the assumption that today's foreign exchange rate is the best estimate of tomorrow's is the basis for recognizing transaction gains and losses on those same assets and liabilities.

Funds Statement May Tell. There is a technique which will often permit the analyst to determine the gains and losses from working capital items. The information is often found in the funds statement. Many funds statements reconcile to changes in working capital. Foreign currency translation adjustments are among the contributors to changes in working capital, which is further evidence that the adjustments are likely soon to become realized gains and losses. This method will not always work because of the flexibility available to management in the presentation of the funds statement. Sometimes they give precisely the number that is wanted: the effect of foreign currency translation on working capital. In other cases, it may be possible to divine the desired number by working back and forth between the two balance sheets and the funds statement.

Current Effects Equal Total Effects Minus Noncurrent Effects. An alternative method is available for estimating the translation effects from working capital if the funds statement fails to tell the story. Since we know the total foreign currency translation adjustment (the year-to-year changes in the amounts in equity), we may be able to estimate the portion from noncurrent items and subtract that from the total to obtain the current portion. The principal noncurrent items are

1. Plant and equipment
2. Long term debt
3. Deferred taxes

The effect of currency fluctuations on plant, property, and equipment is often shown in Schedules V and VI of the 10-K report, or can be estimated from the segment disclosures and other sources. The amounts and currencies of long term debt are usually available in sufficient detail for estimating their exchange rate gains and losses. Deferred taxes are less significant abroad than in the United States because the books are usually kept on the tax basis. Unless the company is forthcoming, the analyst probably will not have enough information to estimate the effects arising from deferred taxes.

The exclusion from income of gains and losses from the noncurrent items may not be particularly harmful to the analysis of a company. First, the realization of those gains and losses, even if exchange rates remain exactly where they were at the end of the year, will take place over a long period of time as plant and equipment are used up and as interest and principal of obligations are paid. Second, the extreme difficulty of determining whether translation gains and losses on plant and equipment represent economic gains or losses raises questions whether the analyst has the ability to deal with them. As a result, in the ordinary case, it is adequate to include in income those translation adjustment gains and losses that arise from working capital only.

Inconsistent Treatment of Translation Effects in the Funds Statement

Table 4.2 presents the treatment by four companies of foreign currency translation adjustment effects in the funds statement. The four companies are similar in certain respects:

- Each had an aggregate foreign currency translation adjustment gain.

- Each reconciled to cash and equivalent.

The treatment of the foreign currency translation adjustment and the funds statement was dramatically different for the four companies.

The presentation by American Brands was ideal. The description of the number was perfectly clear and the analyst would simply add the $24.1 million, less an appropriate provision for income taxes, to net income.

Table 4.2 Foreign Currency Translation Adjustments from 1985
Funds Statements

Company	Funds statement reconciles to	Total foreign currency translation adjustment ($million)	Adjustment— Method of presentation and amount ($ million)
American Brands	Cash	75.3 gain	"Effect of foreign currency rate changes on work capital..............................24.1"
Abbott Laboratories	Cash	28.2 gain	"Cash used in operations: Translation adjustment (28.2)"
IBM	Cash	1,482.0 gain	"Sources ⋮ Uses ⋮ Translation effects..........677.00"
United Technologies	Cash	74.4 gain	Not mentioned

Abbott Laboratories listed its entire foreign currency translation adjustment from both current and noncurrent sources under the broad title "Cash Used in Operations." A subordinate line entitled "Translation Adjustment" gave as the amount a negative $28.2 million. The implication would be that, because it was a negative number, it was a *source of cash* from operations. Probably only a small amount of the adjustment gain was a source of cash and equivalent holdings, and there was no hint of what portion might have come from current or from noncurrent assets and liabilities. The information is useless and misleading.

IBM presented "Translation Effects" in the amount of $677 million as a separate line item below the items referred to as "Sources" and as "Uses." Some addition and subtraction had to be done to determine that it was a gain. Comparative analysis of the balance sheets and the funds statement showed that the amount was the gains from holdings of cash and equivalent items. Other information from the 10-K and annual report permitted an estimate of the gains on noncurrent assets and liabilities, but too many assumptions and guesses were needed to permit a reliable estimate. The analyst should adjust income *at least* for the known gain on cash items.

United Technologies Corporation did not mention the foreign currency effects in its funds statement, although they were doubtless present in some form.

Funds statements that reconcile to working capital have a much better batting average in providing information on the gains and losses from working capital items than do the funds statements reconciling to cash. However, either method can be inconsistent and confusing.

Pensions and Other Postemployment Benefits

Defined Contribution Pension Plans Present No Analysis Problems

Defined contribution plans present no particular problems for the analyst. If the company has made the contribution, it has no liability for any further payments. If a contribution has not been made, the amount is shown on the balance sheet as a current liability. In either event, the cost of pension expense will have been properly reflected in income.

Multiemployer Pension Plans and the Withdrawal Liability

Multiemployer plans become complex only if the company is likely to withdraw from the plan and thereby generate a withdrawal liability under the Employee Retirement Income Security Act of 1974 (ERISA). Once the withdrawal liability is known or becomes estimable the recommended procedure is for the analyst to see that any additional liability (less its tax effect) is recorded as a loss in the income statement, but treated as a nonrecurring item. The balance sheet, too, should be restated.

Defined Benefit Pension Plans

Uncertainty of Pension Liability.   The pension benefit obligation falls in the broad category of reserves for a noncurrent liability of an uncertain amount and timing of payment. Estimations of the size of the pension obligation and its proper present value are a staggering exercise. A 20-year-old man may be working for a company with at least some probability of receiving pension payments 60 years from now. The amount of the payments may depend upon his salary 45 years from now. The actuary must discount using estimates of interest rates over as much as 80 years.

Different choices of salary progression and interest rate assumptions can give defendable answers of which some are five times as large as others.

Opinion 8 Was Too Flexible.　The costs and liabilities of defined benefit pension plans were not comparable under Accounting Principles Board (APB) Opinion No. 8 because almost any actuarial cost method, except "pay-as-you-go" and "terminal funding," was acceptable for purposes of funding and for determining pension expense. In addition, great freedom was available in the selection of actuarial assumptions and in changing them. Comparability of pension expense between companies occurred only by happenstance. The most popular actuarial funding method was "entry age normal," largely because it provided the company with the greatest flexibility in tax planning. Entry age normal is one of the more conservative funding methods, although it can be and often is used with very unconservative methods of dealing with actuarial gains and losses. It calculates the actuarial benefits expected to be paid and then solves for that constant percentage of projected payroll that will fund the benefits by the time they come due. This procedure tends to stabilize profit margins and thereby reduce fluctuations in earnings.

Disclosures Have Been a Stopgap Answer.　Since 1980 footnote disclosure of the actuarial present value of vested and nonvested accumulated plan benefits, plan assets at market value, and the interest rate assumption have been available. The first of these items gave a rough approximation of the liability which would be owed under ERISA if the plan were terminated. No information was given on salary projections, which are a necessary component of the ultimate liability of a final pay plan for an ongoing firm.

New Pension Accounting Required by Statement 87.　In December 1985, the FASB issued Statement No. 87, Employers' Accounting for Pensions. For most of the requirements of Statement 87, the effective date is the first fiscal year beginning after December 15, 1986. That is, for calendar year companies most of the requirements will be in place for the 1987 annual report, although the requirement for recognition of certain pension liabilities is deferred for two additional years.

Ongoing Firm Rather Than Liquidation Approach.　Statement 36 had called for information on accumulated benefits, which are simply the benefits earned to date based on the present salary level. Accumulated benefits are the amount workers would be entitled to if they stopped working for the company at the date of the financial statements—a liquidation notion. Statement 87 calls for a number that is more suitable for the ongoing firm with a final pay plan—the benefits earned for the services rendered to date based on future pay rates—not today's level.

Projected Unit Credit Includes Salary Progression.   All companies will be required to use the same actuarial method—the "projected unit credit" (also called "unit credit with service pro rate") actuarial cost method, which includes the salary progression that results from inflation, promotions, and productivity gains. In addition, limitations are put on the freedom to select actuarial assumptions. The interest rate assumption must give consideration to rates of return currently available on existing plan assets and reasonable estimates of the rates at which future contributions, dividends, interest, rent, and maturities will be reinvested. There is an additional admonition that the company should consider rates at which the liability for pensions could be extinguished by purchase of annuities. Here again, the requirements force more realistic and more comparable interest rate assumptions than are commonly used. The salary progression number must be consistent with the interest rate assumption, which should eliminate some game playing in the spread between the interest rate and the salary progression. These two are the most important assumptions in pension calculations. Consistency would require that both incorporate the same inflation assumption.

Prior Service Obligations Arise from Plan Changes

Prior service obligations come about when a plan is initiated or amended and gives benefit credits for previous service. The new accounting calls for amortization of prior service costs and of actuarial gains and losses over the remaining service lives of the existing employees rather than the more typical 30 or 40 years. This forces a more consistent pattern of amortization than has existed in the past. Previous practice for amortization of prior service costs and actuarial gains and losses delayed the larger portion of such effects for unreasonably long periods of time. The amortization period for prior service cost often extended well beyond the work lives of the workers benefited.

Pension Plan Can Be Consolidated by Analysts

Components of Pension Expenses.   There will be an extensive set of disclosures, including the following components of pension expense:

1. Service cost
2. Interest cost
3. Actual return on assets
4. Net total of the other components
   a. Net asset gain or loss during the period deferred for later recognition
   b. Amortization of the net gain or loss from earlier periods
   c. Amortization of unrecognized prior service cost
   d. Amortization of any transition net asset or liability existing at the date of initial application of the statement

Income Statement Consolidation

First Method.   Given this information plus pension balance sheet information, the analyst may take at least two routes toward consolidating the pension results into the income statement. In one method, the net periodic pension cost for the period would be subtracted from compensation expense, and the service cost component and the various amortization items are added to compensation costs:

- The interest cost is added to the company's other interest expense.
- The return on plan assets is added to the company's "other income."
- Income tax expense is adjusted.

This approach views the pension plan as (1) an investment, with an investment return, (2) a borrowing from the employees, with an interest cost of that borrowing, and (3) a labor cost that includes the amortization of various gains and losses and prior service costs.

Second Method.   A second approach to consolidation subtracts the net periodic pension cost for the period from labor expenses and substitutes the service cost component. The interest cost and the investment income are treated as above, but the actual gains and losses for the year are reflected in the income statement as "pension gain or loss" or under some similar title. Taxes would be adjusted. The second method introduces into income all the gains and losses, including investment portfolio results. There are no deferrals or smoothing.

Pension Plan Balance Sheet.   All the information needed to construct a pension fund balance sheet will be shown in footnotes including the fair value of plan assets, the pension liability, and details of the unrecognized prior service cost, gains and losses, and the like.

Balance Sheet Consolidation. Simply knowing the pension assets and liability permits setting up a pension fund balance sheet, since the difference between the assets and liability is the net worth or net deficit. If desired, the analyst can consolidate the pension fund's balance sheet into that of the plan sponsor. First, any pension liability or asset shown on the sponsor's balance sheet should be removed and equity adjusted for its removal. Then, the plan assets are added to the assets of the sponsor, the pension liability is added to the sponsor's liabilities, and the difference between the two (the net worth or net deficit of the pension fund) is added to or subtracted from the net worth of the sponsor, less the tax effect. The tax liability would be adjusted for the consolidation.

Such consolidation is encouraged for some purposes, such as analysis of fixed-income securities or the potential to withdraw excess pension assets. However, consolidation can be misleading because of limitations on the prompt access to pension assets, inaccuracy in the estimated pension liability, and the inherent volatility of marketable securities. The analyst is cautioned against consolidation of the pension fund in studies that attempt to determine normal earning power. Fluctuations in the market value of plan assets or a change in a single actuarial assumption might wipe out or double a company's earnings for a particular year. The effects of such fluctuations may distract analysts from more significant matters, such as the company's basic operating activities.

How to Treat Prior Service Cost

A broad question for the analyst is whether payments for the account of past services under a pension plan should be considered a discharge of a past obligation, a nonrecurring charge against earnings, or an ordinary operating expense. What is the practical significance of each choice?

The Creation of Prior Service Liability. A liability for prior service cost occurs when a plan is initiated or amended and gives credit for services that were rendered in previous years. (This book uses the terms *prior service cost* and *past service cost* interchangeably, as does Statement 87.) In effect, the company has an immediate liability, and the worker could walk away the next day, render no more services, and be entitled to the increased benefits under the plan formula. Under ERISA, prior service obligations resulting from plan amendments are phased in over a five-year period for purposes of calculating the ERISA termination liability.

Spreading Prior Service Cost. However, whether or not there is an immediate legal liability, accounting has generally viewed prior service cost as an expense that should be spread over subsequent years.

Recognizing the entire prior service liability as a charge to income at once could result in a noncharacteristic level of earnings.

Past Service as an Ordinary Charge Against Income. Both practical and logical reasoning suggest that the annual pension contributions resulting from past service be included as an ordinary charge against income. Such payments are allowed as annual deductions for tax purposes and are not subject to capitalization in inventories, as are other pension expenses. Past service costs are the result less of events in the distant past than of a voluntary or union-enforced decision to pay out sums in the future. They will represent actual and regular cash disbursements over a period of years, not offset by additional assets for the company. Thus they come much closer to being an ordinary and current expense than the discharge of a past debt, such as the paying off of a serial bond issue.

Nonrecurring Treatment Is Contradictory. The effect of treating the annual payments as a nonrecurring charge is contradictory: They are ignored in the true earnings for a single year but are deducted from the long-term results. Obviously, any *regular* charge that figures in the long-term analysis should also be deducted in a single year's analysis. Otherwise the result is simply to create an unnecessary difference between the successive short-term and the long-term results. (It is only the *irregular* nature of large nonrecurring items that makes it preferable to exclude them from a single-year analysis.)

Actuarial Gains and Losses

Nature of the Gains and Losses. The amortization of actuarial gains and losses is another difficult analytical problem. Actuarial gains and losses are really not quite like ordinary gains and losses. They are not measured from zero but rather from the actuarial assumption. If the assumption is that the portfolio will earn 6 percent and the year's return is 4 percent, an *actuarial loss* equal to 2 percent is multiplied by the opening balance of the plan assets. Obviously, the pension fund did not actually lose money—it made 4 percent. It may turn out that the average rate of return for the next 100 years will be precisely 4 percent, which really means that the actuary and the company should have agreed on 4 percent as their assumption of return on plan assets. In such a case the problem is not that the performance of the plan assets fell short but that the actuarial estimate was too high. Similar arguments can be made for the various other actuarial estimates, whether they be salary progression, turnover, mortality, or whatever.

Changes in Assumptions Are Called Gains and Losses. A change in an actuarial assumption changes the liability, and this is also called an "actuarial gain or loss." It is the peculiar nature of the actuarial gains and losses that appears to justify spreading them over some reasonable period, such as the working lives of the employees, rather than recognizing them at once. In addition, immediate recognition of actuarial gains and losses would tend to inject into the income statement the full effect of the fluctuations of the stock and bond markets. Although those fluctuations are important, they should be studied separately from operating earnings.

Settlements, Curtailments, and Termination Benefits

In recent years it has not been unusual for a company to terminate its pension plan, purchase annuities covering all the company's pension obligation, and take down some of or all the excess assets from the plan. Previous accounting would permit recognition of a gain on the "asset reversion" only if the company did not start up a new defined benefit pension plan. Statement No. 88, *Employers Accounting for Settlements and Curtailments of Defined Benefit Plans and for Termination Benefits*, requires recognition of a gain to the extent that assets are taken down by the plan sponsor. Plan sponsors can leave assets in the pension fund and recognize only part of the gain if they choose. For example, in 1984 AMAX Corporation had about $150 million of excess plan assets but chose to take down only about $100 million in its asset reversion. This left a voluntary $50 million reserve—in effect, prepaid pension expense that is not shown on the balance sheet. The analyst can recognize a gain on *all* the excess assets resulting from a plan termination, treating it as a nonrecurring item, or recognize no gain at present, but instead project lower pension expense in future years as a result of the excess assets left in the plan. Your authors are not of one mind on this matter.

Other Postemployment Benefits

Disclosure of the annual costs of other *post*employment benefits (OPEB) is required. These benefits consist primarily of health and life insurance that are continued after the employee has reached retirement age. Often the spouse is covered. The amounts are potentially very large. In 1985 the average cost of medical care for persons over age 65 was about $4800 per annum. Medicare paid for approximately 60 percent of that number, leaving the rest to be paid by the elderly people and/or their previous employers. The amount and nature of coverage, the deductibles, caps and other characteristics of the plan will vary from company to company, but there is little doubt that many companies are obligated for very substantial amounts of health benefits for many years into the future. Accrual accounting would seem to call for recording the liability and the expense for those benefits over the working lives of the employees rather than on a pay-as-you-go basis (the current practice). The recommended procedure for accruing an OPEB balance sheet liability is to multiply the annual expense number by a factor between 10 and 15, with the factor rising with the age of the work force. Annual changes in the liability should be added to the reported expense number, with an appropriate tax adjustment.

Example. The following data are based on information provided by a company which has a large number of divisions, nearly all of which offer postretirement health care and life insurance benefits. The benefits are generally similar, but not identical for all divisions. Table 4.3 shows the benefits in 1985 in a typical division.

Table 4.3. Other Postemployment Benefits

Postemployment Medical Benefits	
Eligibility	Retirees and dependents
Hospitalization	100% of reasonable and customary charges
Surgical	$500 schedule
Deductible	$100–$150 per individual (based on pay)
	80–100% after $1000 employee
	out-of-pocket expense
Maximum	$25,000 per 3 years
Integration with Medicare	Carve-out
Part B Reimbursement	$12.26
Employee contributions	None
Dental benefits	None in 1985

Postemployment Death Benefits (Nonpension)		
	Company-paid	Contributory
Benefit at retirement	$1,000–5,000	None
Ultimate benefit	Same	None
Employee contributions	—	None

In 1985 the company's pay-as-you-go expense amounted to $5,740,000. If the company were to reflect the expense of benefits earned to date (the equivalent of the unit credit method) and amortize the accumulated benefits over 10 years, the expense would rise to $23,104,000, assuming 9 percent inflation in medical costs and a 9 percent investment return. A projected unit credit approach would raise the expense item to $36,364,000. The balance sheet liability for all accumulated liabilities would be $110,000,000, and the projected benefit obligation would be $195,000,000. Use of the projected unit credit method would have reduced profits and net worth by about 5 percent. The average age of the work force was in the low thirties.

5

Inventory Valuation and Cost of Goods Sold

From the standpoint of security analysis, the problems of inventory accounting and of depreciation accounting have a generic relationship. Both can have an important bearing on reported earnings, and in both cases the amounts are determined in accordance with principles and theories rather than as the simple result of cash or credit transactions during the year under review. Chapter 5 discusses inventory and depreciation accounting briefly before concentrating on inventory valuation.

Methods of Valuing Inventories and Calculating Depreciation

The standard method of valuing merchandise inventory is to carry it "at cost or market, whichever is lower." The standard method of calculating depreciation (and other amortization) is to write down each depreciable item from cost to salvage value by regular charges against income extending over its expected life. Until recently the chief job of the security analyst in these fields has been to make sure that the standard accounting practices were followed in the corporate reports examined.

In general, the departures were in the direction of overstatement of income, e.g., by failure to mark down inventory to market or by omitting or skimping the depreciation charge. Less frequently, the income and assets were understated by an overconservative policy in valuing inventory or figuring depreciation and amortization.

Since the end of World War II, the questions of inventory valuation and depreciation policy have taken on a somewhat different complexion. Many corporate managers have thought that the standard accounting practice was not well-suited to a protracted period of rising prices. On the one hand, profits were increased by a nonrecurring and probably illusory gain arising from the marking up of inventory values to their ever-higher replacement levels. On the other hand, the tax-allowed depreciation, based on cost, was becoming grossly inadequate to provide for the replacement of worn-out facilities at these same higher price levels. When the tax laws were changed to permit faster depreciation, many companies changed their accounting practices to minimize the impact of inflationary forces upon the income statement. The issues involved here have implications beyond the area of accurate reporting to the stockholders. They have led to a vigorous demand for the right to charge higher depreciation against earnings for tax purposes during inflationary times, and they have also figured prominently in labor disputes where the "real" profits of business and its consequent "ability to pay" have been in controversy.

Inventory Profits and Inflation

The Recent History

The post–World War II years could be divided (somewhat arbitrarily) into five phases of inflation. The 1947–1957 period reflected pent-up inflationary forces, held down by wage and price controls during World War II, and the effects of the Korean War. The 1958–1965 years signaled peace and moderate growth, accompanied by relatively moderate inflation and virtually no inventory profits. Deficits from the Viet Nam War and large social spending and turmoil in the international monetary markets led to an acceleration of inflation and inventory profits in the years from 1966 to 1972. The fourth period ends abruptly in 1983 because the awesome inflationary effects of the OPEC oil cartel and the collapse of the Bretton Woods Agreement (fixed exchange rates) seem to have run their course and then abated. The 1984–1986 period benefited from declines in oil and other commodity prices and a stronger dollar. Table 5.1 demonstrates the expected pattern—high inventory profits tend to accompany high inflation rates, and the opposite holds true for lower inflation.

Table 5.1. Inflation and Inventory Profits, 1947–1986

Period	Average annual inflation rate (%)*	Corporate profits before tax ($ billion)	Inventory mark-up ($ billion)	Mark-up as percent of corporate profits
1947–1957	2.6	40.3	1.7	4.2
1958–1965	1.4	56.5	0.2	0.3
1966–1972	4.2	85.5	4.4	5.1
1973–1983	7.8	187.4	23.3	12.4
1984–1986	3.0	196.1†	−1.1†	0.0†

*Compound annual rates of change in the Consumer Price Index for all clerical and factory workers, prepared by the Department of Labor.

†Fourth quarter of 1986 reflects preliminary figures.

Sources: Corporate Domestic Product of the National Income and Products Accounts is prepared by the Department of Commerce. Data taken from Department of Commerce, *Business Statistics*, 1984, p. 201; *Business Conditions Digest*, April 1984, pp. 95, 99; *Survey of Current Business*, February 1987, pp. 5–6.

It is clear from Table 5.1 that inventory profits tend to follow the pattern of acceleration and deceleration of price changes in the economy. The nineteenth-century economic history of the United States shows that prices sometimes follow a downward course for extended periods. The effects on profits would be just the opposite under such circumstances, since they would result in inventory mark-downs rather than mark-ups.

Security Analyst's Approach to Inventories and Depreciation

Adjust to Normalize Expense. The security analyst is interested in these matters from two practical standpoints. First, analysts must decide what treatment of inventory and depreciation will help in calculating the normal earning power and—less important—the actual asset values.

Seek Comparability. Second, to the extent possible, the analyst must develop a means of placing all companies in a given industrial group on the same accounting basis, as regards inventories and depreciation, to permit a proper comparative analysis.

Inflation Accounting

From 1976 to 1986 most large companies were required, first by the SEC and then by the FASB, to report the effects of inflation on their inventories and plant accounts. In 1987 the information became voluntary, but some companies may continue to provide it. The FASB requirements included presentations in a constant-dollar mode, using dollars of constant purchasing power, which made the information more complex.[1] Analysts could prepare constant-dollar numbers from the annual report without the help of the companies, but none thought it worthwhile. The current cost and replacement cost numbers are potentially useful. They permit analysts to place FIFO companies on a LIFO inventory basis, which we consider to be a better measure of earning power.[2] The current cost and replacement cost information on the plant account and on depreciation may be helpful in estimating the costs of new plant and equipment, but these figures are not very accurate.

Analysts' Resounding Apathy
Is Not Justified

Although the inflation accounting information has enjoyed little interest among users of financial statements,[3] we encourage the analyst at least to consider the implications provided by the information for

- Converting FIFO income statements to LIFO
- Estimating future capital expenditure levels
- Working capital requirements
- Liquidating values
- Potential as takeover candidates

---

[1] For many years accountants have worried about the unstable nature of the dollar, or any other currency, as a measuring unit when its purchasing power changes. Many feel that accounting has an obligation to measure in inflation-free units. If analysts were to use such dollars of constant purchasing power in their projections, the mathematics of the process would require that they forecast future earnings and dividends in constant dollars. This would require a correct forecast of future inflation. Even worse, the dividends would have to be discounted to present value using the *real* interest rate, which has been hypothesized but never observed. Analysts bypass this problem by dealing in nominal dollars and nominal interest rates, which already have an inflation premium built into them.

[2] LIFO and FIFO methods are discussed extensively in the next section of this chapter.

[3] William C. Norby, "Application of Inflation-Adjusted Accounting Data," *The Financial Analysts Journal*, March–April 1983, pp. 33–39; Robert H. Berliner, "Do Analysts Use Inflation-Adjusted Information? Results of a Survey," *The Financial Analysts Journal*, March–April 1983, pp. 65–72.

Inventory Calculation

FIFO and LIFO

The two most important ways of calculating inventory costs are known as *first-in, first-out* (FIFO) and *last-in, first-out* (LIFO). Both are subject to the "lower of cost or market" requirement. FIFO is based on the usually correct *flow assumption* that a company will deliver the oldest inventory first, before "moth and dust doth corrupt." LIFO inventories must also be carried at cost, but cost is calculated using the assumption that the newest inventory is sold.

The basic difference between FIFO and LIFO is generally illustrated by a company's coal pile. If the coal bought is piled on top and the coal used is taken from the bottom, we have a typical case of first-in, first-out. The old coal is used up first, and the stock remaining would naturally be valued on the basis of the most recent purchases. But if the coal used is taken off the top, the physical flow would be the typical last-in, first-out situation. The coal on hand at the inventory date would include some old or original purchases which would be valued at an unchanging price from year to year.

During a period of sharply rising prices, FIFO calculations mark up inventories to about current replacement cost. Hence computed earnings are increased by a special profit (called "holding gains" by accountants) arising from the sale of older and cheaper materials at advancing quotations. Under the same circumstances, the LIFO method will hold down the carrying value of a given quantity of inventory to its original low level and thus exclude year-to-year inventory profits from the reported earnings.

Increased Use of LIFO

Annually, the publication *Accounting Trends and Techniques* compares many of the accounting practices of 600 companies. The number of companies using LIFO accounting for a significant part of their inventories rose from 194 (32 percent) in 1960 to 400 (67 percent) in 1984.[4] The first-in, first-out method was widely used before the recent inflation, because it seemed to correspond to the actualities of business.

Use of Multiple Methods

LIFO accounting is not acceptable for tax or reporting purposes in most foreign countries, and for that reason most multinational companies

---

[4] American Institute of Certified Public Accountants, *Accounting Trends and Techniques*, 1961 and 1985.

carry foreign inventories on a FIFO basis. Diversified companies often use specialized inventory accounting techniques ordinarily employed by the industries in which they operate. Thus, a conglomerate that owns a retailing operation is likely to include the retail method among its inventory accounting methods. Subsidiaries engaged in the production of agricultural commodities or precious metals will usually mark such inventories to market prices instead of carrying them on a cost basis. Still other companies use several different inventory accounting methods because they have made acquisitions and either have not had time to change the subsidiary's inventory method or have not found it worth the trouble. In the footnote on accounting policies, companies list the principal inventory cost methods used, but they do not always give much information on how large or small a part of the total inventory is carried on a particular method.

The Economic Logic of LIFO

In continuous production or merchandising, older goods are normally sold first if possible so that those remaining on hand may be fresh and up to date. The newer LIFO idea is thus in reality a somewhat artificial concept, which recommends itself, however, because of its stabilizing effect on corporate results. Beyond this, it has the support of economic theory. For instance, calculations of national income by the Department of Commerce exclude gains or losses from inventory valuation, as unrelated to the actual production and distribution of goods. (Similarly the Department includes a capital consumption adjustment from corporate profits to reflect inadequate depreciation charges, similar to the effects of using replacement cost depreciation.) Finally, the LIFO method is a permitted method of accounting, subject to certain limitations, under the Internal Revenue Code.

Example. The difference between the FIFO (formerly the standard) and the LIFO methods of computing cost of goods sold and inventory on hand can be illustrated by the following simplified and hypothetical example (see Table 5.2): A company starts with 10 million pounds of copper, buys 10 million pounds each year for three years, and sells the same amount each year at a 2-cent advance above current cost price. The initial cost is 10 cents; the average and closing cost price is 15 cents the first year, 20 cents the second year, and 10 cents the third year. We assume that the company has no operating expenses.

Obviously the company ends up where it started in inventory and has made a continuous profit of 2 cents per pound. Common sense would insist the company has made $200,000 each year. But the standard or

Table 5.2.   FIFO and LIFO

	First year		Second year		Third year	
			FIFO			
Proceeds of goods sold......................		$1,700,000		$2,200,000		$1,200,000
Cost of goods sold:						
Opening inventory.........	$1,000,000		$1,500,000		$2,000,000	
Purchases............	1,500,000		2,000,000		1,000,000	
Totals...........	$2,500,000		$3,500,000		$3,000,000	
Less closing inventory (lower of cost or market) ...	1,500,000	1,000,000	2,000,000	1,500,000	1,000,000	2,000,000
Gross profit...........		$ 700,000		$ 700,000		$ (800,000)
			LIFO			
Proceeds of goods sold......................		$1,700,000		$2,200,000		$1,200,000
Cost of goods sold (same as purchases during year)...................		1,500,000		2,000,000		1,000,000
Gross profit...........		$ 200,000		$ 200,000		$ 200,000
Closing inventory...		1,000,000		1,000,000		1,000,000

FIFO method of accounting would show a profit of $700,000 in the first year, the same in the second year, and a loss of $800,000 in the third year. In general, operating losses can be carried back 3 years or forward 15 years for tax purposes. Thus, the $800,000 operating loss would be carried back against the profits of the previous two years, resulting in a tax refund.

However, by the last-in, first-out method, the profit would work out as $200,000 each year—the sensible figure, and income tax would be payable on this amount in the proper years.

LIFO Problems and Issues

The example we have given places the LIFO method in a particularly (and misleadingly) favorable light, because it excludes two complicating factors: (1) the triggering of profits by layer invasion, and (2) use of questionable versions of LIFO.

The Liquidation of LIFO Cost Layers

Most companies either grow or simply go out of business. Those that grow do an increasing volume of business, which requires a larger volume in inventory. Thus, a company may have 100 units of inventory at the end of year 1 and 175 units at the end of year 2. If prices are rising, the 100 units bought in year 1 will have a lower cost than those bought in year 2. These yearly increments are referred to as "layers." Over a period of time, a company will accumulate many layers in a given pool of products, each at a different price. If a year comes along when the physical volume of inventory declines, the first layer invaded is the most recent one, and if the volume decline is large, additional layers will be invaded, which means that older and older costs are leaving the balance sheet and entering into the costs of goods sold. Since in inflationary times these older costs are presumably lower costs, they increase the profit margin.

IRS Conformity Rules

One of the original requirements for use of LIFO accounting for tax purposes was that the company report its costs of goods sold to shareholders precisely the same way as to the Internal Revenue Service (IRS). This was called the "LIFO Conformity Rule." In addition, the IRS has been rather strict about the size of the LIFO pools (groups of related products) it would accept for tax purposes. Naturally, the companies wanted tax pools that were as all-encompassing as possible, and the IRS was anxious to keep the pools as small as possible to ensure accidental invasion of lower-cost layers, which would result in the larger amounts of tax revenue.

Pools and Puddles

Internal Revenue Service LIFO conformity rules have been relaxed so that companies now can report large "pools" for tax purposes and small puddles to stockholders. Layer invasion occurs less frequently when the inventory pools are large; small pools give management an opportunity to report larger profits almost at will by deliberately reducing the physical volume of certain pools at year end or, say, by setting up pools by model year. The footnote reconciling income taxes with the statutory rate will reveal if a company is using significantly different LIFO pools for tax and stockholder reporting purposes. The footnote on inventories will reveal the amount of LIFO reserves and the amount by which income was increased as a result of invasion of layers. Layer invasion does not always result in an increase in profits. Some older layers have *higher* costs rather than lower costs.

Often, layer invasion occurs by accident, or because a company is discontinuing certain product lines or reducing its size in a restructuring.

Example. Firestone Tire & Rubber Company reported reductions in inventory quantities during 1983 resulting from a partial liquidation of LIFO costs. The effect of this partial liquidation was to decrease cost of sales by $55 million in 1983. Net income for 1983 was $111 million.

Example. The Deere & Company 1985 annual report reported: "During the last three years, the company inventories have declined due mainly to lower levels of production and increased emphasis on inventory reduction. As a result, lower costs which prevailed in prior years were matched against current year revenues, the effect of which was to increase net income...." Of the $158.7 million total income for the three-year period, $151.2 million came about through inventory layer invasion. Yet, at the end of fiscal 1985 the company still had $971 million of LIFO reserves.

Variations of LIFO Calculation

LIFO calculation is not a single method, but rather a family of methods that can give a wide variety of results. Some methods are so misleading that they are not permitted by the SEC. The analyst should realize that management has great flexibility in determining just what expenses shall be capitalized as inventories or written off as period expenses. Accounting requires that at least some factory overhead be included in inventories. The rule may be "If it's here in town it's SG&A (selling, general, and administrative expense), and if it's out at the plant, it's inventory." Thus if the personnel department were located in town, its activities would be expensed; if it were located at the plant, at least part of its expenses would be capitalized as inventory. Conservative managements lean toward capitalizing direct expenses and as few additional costs as possible. More liberal managers capitalize anything related to production, a view encouraged by the 1986 Tax Reform Act. If the procedure is not patently misleading, there is really no way to prove that one inventory judgment is right and another wrong.

Do not automatically assume that a company using LIFO has more conservative accounting than one using FIFO. In certain industries in which costs are dropping dramatically, such as semiconductors and computers, placing the latest costs in inventory decreases costs rather than the opposite. It is interesting that in 1984 only 38 percent of the industry groups that include computers and semiconductors were using LIFO, although the average for all industries was 67 percent. For companies with declining costs, FIFO calculation produces lower profits as well as lower taxes, thereby yielding the traditional advantage of LIFO accounting.

LIFO Reserves

For practical reasons most companies keep their internal inventory records on a FIFO basis and calculate the LIFO numbers only when the financial statements are prepared. Most use pools of dollar value and make the adjustments by applying internal price indexes to the dollar amounts rather than to physical units.

The dollar difference between the LIFO and FIFO inventory amounts is often called the "LIFO reserve," "the excess of current cost over the carrying amount of inventories," and similar terms. A few companies show the reserve on the balance sheet, but most companies using LIFO figures reveal either the reserve or the FIFO amount in footnotes.

Example. Norton Company reported in its inventory footnote for 1984, "If the average or standard cost (first in, first out) method of inventory evaluation (which approximates replacement costs) had been used for all inventories by the company, inventories would have been $62,115,000 higher than reported at December 1, 1984 ($61,327,000 at December 31, 1983)." Note that the LIFO reserve increased only $788,000 as a result of using LIFO during 1984, whereas net income for the year was $60,425,000. The difference in inventory method would have changed earnings by only 1 percent, yet the LIFO reserve was about 10 percent of total shareholders' equity.

Inclusion of LIFO Reserves in Calculating Certain Ratios

The Norton example does call attention to an issue involved in calculating such ratios as return on equity and return on invested capital (discussed in Chapter 12). LIFO inventories are sometimes stated at absurdly low numbers on the balance sheet, and the sorts of ratios just mentioned attempt to relate the amount of return earned to the amount of capital employed to earn it. That capital should include the LIFO reserve less an appropriate tax provision. The increment should simply be added to stated capital in the denominator, whether the income in the numerator is LIFO- or FIFO-based. This procedure will make the return on equity of companies using FIFO and LIFO accounting much more comparable, because the denominator will be the same and the numerators are normally not very different.

Other Inventory Methods

The Base Stock or Normal Stock Method

The base stock method of inventory valuation is a variation of LIFO accounting; it is applied to some minimum level of raw materials, usually metals or agricultural commodities, and the rest of inventories are accounted for on some other basis. Because past practice was to write the base stock down to nominal amounts, some companies had significant hidden assets. The method is based on the theory that the company must regularly carry a certain physical stock of materials and that there is no more reason to vary the value of this normal stock from year to year—because of market changes—than there would be to vary the value of the manufacturing plant as its price or level of operations rises or falls.

When part of a normal stock inventory is sold, bringing the amount on hand below the basic requirement, earnings have to be charged with a reserve for the replacement of the deficiency. In effect this cancels out the large profit made on the sale. Thus, base-stock figuring differs from the LIFO method in the matter of layer invasion profits.

On the whole, the base stock method probably produces more conservatively stated and more stable earnings over an extended period than does the LIFO method.

The Average and Standard Methods

The average cost method is used by about 39 percent of companies for at least part of their inventories. Since the average includes both older and newer inventory, the expense tends to fall somewhere between LIFO and FIFO figures, but it is closer than either to the actual cost of specific items.

Standard cost is usually applied to work in process and finished goods based on past patterns of cost and productivity. Unusual costs are thus excluded from the carrying amount and are, therefore, expensed. Except for the expensing of unusual costs, the standard cost method's results are close to average cost results.

The Retail Method

An accepted method of valuing retailers' inventories, including those of department stores and chain stores, starts with the current retail selling price of each item and deducts an appropriate "mark-on." The resulting value gives a calculated replacement cost which corresponds to the expected realization less normal expense and profit. This figure is regarded as more closely reflecting the true value of each inventory item to the store than either the actual recorded cost of each item or its current quotation in the wholesale market.

LIFO For Retailers

Retail stores that follow the LIFO method use a special technique based on an official index of retail prices. The inventory in each department is first valued according to the retail method, and then the cost is reduced in inverse proportion to the advance in the official index number. The IRS makes an exception here to its normal rule of requiring the LIFO indexes to be internally derived.

The Security Analyst and Inventory Valuation Methods

LIFO or FIFO?

If, in a period of inflation, there are two generally similar companies and one reports on the LIFO and the other on the FIFO basis, the second will probably show somewhat larger earnings than the former. Should the analyst accept both earnings statements as correct? If not, what adjustments should be made?

Comparability

Two companies cannot be fairly compared unless a substantially similar method of inventory valuation is applied to each. For this purpose either the LIFO or the FIFO method could properly be used, if the data are available. Since most companies are now at least partly on a LIFO basis, adjusting the inventories and earnings of those using FIFO methods to conform with the majority might seem wise. However, this will be possible only if the FIFO companies report current cost of inventory and costs of goods sold under Statement 33 or are willing to release the needed information to the analyst. Too often that information will not be available, and the analyst will have to adjust the LIFO-based companies to FIFO figures. Disclosure of the LIFO reserve and/or the FIFO inventory amount is required by the SEC for the 10-K and these figures are almost invariably in the annual report. Even per-share figures are often given. Thus, comparable figures are almost always available on a FIFO basis.

Adjusting Formulas.   The adjustment to either method from the other is straightforward using these formulas:

Formula 1. Beginning inventory plus purchases minus ending inventory equals cost of goods sold

Formula 2. LIFO inventory plus LIFO reserve equals FIFO inventory

Note that no special adjustment to these formulas is needed when there is LIFO layer invasion.

Table 5.3.   Selected Data from the 1985 Annual Report of the Maytag Company
(In Millions of Dollars)

	1985	1984
1. LIFO reserve	37.3	39.1
2. Inventories (LIFO)	78.5	77.7
3. Total = FIFO inventories	115.8*	116.8*
4. Cost of sales	432.9	421.5
5. Stockholders' equity (LIFO)	256.6	228.9
6. Stockholders' equity (FIFO)	276.7†	250.0†
7. Net income (LIFO)	71.8	63.1
8. FIFO net income	70.8‡	

* From Formula 2.
† FIFO stockholders' equity = [(1 − tax rate) × (LIFO reserve)] + LIFO stockholders' equity. The tax rate was 46% at the time of this example.
‡ FIFO net income = [(1985 LIFO reserve − 1984 LIFO reserve) × (1 − tax rate)] + 1985 LIFO net income.
NOTE: Years ended December 31.

Example.   The 1985 annual report of Maytag Company, highlighted in Table 5.3, provides a useful example. The table includes certain FIFO numbers which are footnoted to show how they were calculated from the other information in the table. Since we have the beginning and ending inventory numbers and the cost of goods sold, we can easily calculate, using Formula 1, that the purchases during the year were $433.7 million ($432.9 + $78.5 − $77.7 =$433.7). The amount of purchases is independent of the inventory method.

The third line of the table is simply the result of applying Formula 2. Having the beginning and ending FIFO inventories and the purchases for input in Formula 1 permits calculation of the FIFO cost of goods sold of $434.7 million ($116.8 + $433.7 − $115.8 = $434.7). This is $1.8 million more than the LIFO cost of goods sold and is the same as the decline in the LIFO reserve. FIFO after-tax income is $1.8 million × (1 − tax rate), or $1 million less than the LIFO after-tax income. Note that the tax rate was 46 percent at the time of this example—not 34 percent.

The U.S. income tax rate should be used for these LIFO-related adjustments, because LIFO inventories are usually domestic. For some purposes analysts should consider the effects on available tax loss carryforwards, the percentage limitation on the investment tax credit, and other aspects of the ever-changing Tax Code and regulations.

Which Basis Should the Analyst Prefer?

Use FIFO on the Balance Sheet. In balance sheet studies the current cost or the replacement cost of inventories are often the most informative figures for the analyst to use. Using FIFO inventories or including the LIFO reserve and an appropriate tax adjustment for LIFO-based companies gives a better picture of the net current assets and the capital at work by putting all companies in the same industry in a comparable position and avoiding price levels related to dates arbitrarily selected in the past. If the analyst believes the current price level is vulnerable, allowances can be made for any expected degree of decline.

Use LIFO in the Income Statement. However, the use of LIFO cost of goods sold in the income statement analysis has its own advantages. The most recent costs give information that is useful in predicting the next year's costs. LIFO accounting does not suffer the problems of a full current cost accounting system. The dynamics of the going firm are expressed in the completed cash-to-cash cycles. Conservatism is well served by maintaining the realization principle and avoiding inventory profits. Requiring that the earnings process be complete before earnings are reported reduces opportunities to overstate operating results.

Problems of Using Both Methods at Once

There are problems in the simultaneous use of LIFO in the income statement and FIFO on the balance sheet. First, the income statement and the balance sheet no longer articulate. That is, changes in equity are no longer explained by the income statement. Second, inventories are marked up by the LIFO reserve, less appropriate taxes, but sooner or later, layer invasion will cause the unrealized gains to become realized and flow through the income statement to equity. Since those gains have already been reflected in equity, care must be takento see that they do not get counted twice. This problem has been referred to by accountants as the "recycling" or the "reclassification of equity" problem. If the analyst calculates a growth rate of book value per share using FIFO inventories on the balance sheet, the trend will include FIFO profits—

not LIFO ones. The exercise is further complicated by the need to provide deferred taxes for the inventory write-up.

Limit the Use of Mixed Measurements

Clearly, there are advantages to treating inventories differently in the income statement and the balance sheet. At the same time, the inconsistent measurement system strongly suggests that the analyst should not treat the statements as if they were integral. It is recommended that the FIFO inventory adjustment should be limited to use (1) in balance sheet ratio calculations, and (2) in balance sheet analyses that are oriented toward liquidating values or asset values, rather than "going concern" or earning power values. The distinction between the analysts' investment value approach and accounting's asset value approach must be kept in mind. The use of LIFO cost of goods sold in the income statement offers considerable useful information for estimating earning power, the cornerstone of investment value.

6

Effect of Depreciation and Amortization on Taxes and Income

Expenses That Must Be Allocated Over Time

Depreciation, depletion, and amortization have a common characteristic: They involve costs or expenses that must be allocated to a number of periods rather than be absorbed in a single period.

A critical analysis of an income statement must pay particular attention to the amounts deducted for depreciation and other noncash charges. These items differ from ordinary operating expenses in the following ways:

- They do not usually signify a current and corresponding outlay of cash.
- They represent the estimated shrinkage in the value of the fixed or capital assets, due to wearing out, to technological or economic obsolescence, to using up, or to their approaching extinction for whatever cause.
- They ensure that the capital invested in the asset is returned in cash from the revenue stream.

- They create timing differences between amounts that are tax deductible and amounts that are reported to shareholders as expense, resulting in deferred taxes.

Depreciation and Amortization

Leading Questions Regarding Depreciation and Amortization

The accounting theory that governs depreciation charges appears simple enough. If a capital asset has limited life, provision must be made to write off the (unsalvaged) cost of that asset by charges against earnings distributed over the asset's useful life. But behind this simple theory lie five complications:

Accounting rules themselves permit a value other than cost as the basis of the amortization charge.

Companies have wide latitude as to the choice of allocation method and the length of an asset's life.

Certain companies may not follow accepted accounting practice in stating their amortization deduction in the income statement.

In most cases a company will use one permitted basis of amortization in its tax returns and another in its published statements.

Sometimes an allowance that is justified from an accounting standpoint is not justified from an investment standpoint.

Apart from these technical issues, some tend to regard the depreciation deduction as in some sense an "unreal" expense and to concentrate attention on earnings before depreciation and amortization, or so-called cash flow.

The Analyst's Basic Approach to Depreciation and Other Amortizations

In this rather complex area we suggest that the analyst be guided by the following basic principles:

The analyst should make certain that the amortization provision is adequate by conservative standards.

The analyst should seek, as far as possible, to apply uniform measures of depreciation, making the necessary adjustments in comparative studies.

3. The analyst must maintain a sense of proportion—avoiding those items that might have no appreciable influence on the conclusions reached.

Amortization Charges in Corporate Accounts

The attention that the analyst will give to depreciation will vary with its significance. If a poor choice of depreciation method or the length of useful lives has only a small effect on net income, the depreciation question needs little attention. Where the customary relationship requires, say, a dollar of investment in plant to generate a dollar of annual sales, the analyst will study the depreciation question with great care. If a company has a relatively small amount of fixed assets, its amortization charge will have only a minor influence on its profits. This situation will be found generally in the major divisions of financial, trade, and service enterprises. In the manufacturing field the plant investment and associated depreciation is less important for light operations of the assembly type than for the heavy and integrated operations of basic industries. In mining, chemicals, oil and gas production, and the public utility and railroad industries, the fixed assets bulk very large, and amortization is correspondingly important.

Industry Depreciation Characteristics

The relationship between the depreciation tax deduction and other major financial elements for various industry groups is summarized in Table 6.1. The data are taken from 1983 Corporation Income Tax forms, the latest released by the Internal Revenue Service (IRS). Observe that for manufacturing companies generally the amortization charge was more than 9.5 percent of depreciable assets, about 3.9 percent of sales and 47 percent of taxable income before such deduction. The right column illustrates the wide divergence between industries as to the importance of depreciation in its impact on profits. Clearly, where the ratio is high, a very small error in estimating the useful lives of plant and equipment assets could result in a very large error in the income number. (Note that the taxable income shown in Table 6.1 is before foreign, state, local, and U.S. possession income taxes, totalling about $25 billion for all corporations in 1983.) Profits before amortization were divided fairly evenly among depreciation, all income taxes, and final net income.

Table 6.1 Corporate Tax Depreciation Rates, 1983[*]

	Total receipts (millions)	U.S.income taxes after credits (millions)	Taxable income[†] (millions)	Depreciable assets (millions)	Depreciation deduction (millions)	Ratio of depreciation to assets	Ratio of depreciation to taxable income
All corporations	$7,135,494	$51,862	$218,686	$2,730,372	$241,492	8.8%	110%
Sectors							
Mining	132,420	722	4,623	85,787	7,786	9.1	168
Construction	290,799	1,393	5,505	57,711	6,281	10.7	101
Manufacturing	2,552,831	24,961	113,610	1,051,144	99,416	9.5	88
Transportation and utilities	657,421	5,430	25,612	901,874	56,162	6.2	219
Wholesale and retail trade	2,119,445	10,653	33,503	246,665	27,667	11.2	83
Finance, ins., real estate	902,822	5,697	22,470	193,098	19,654	9.9	88
Services	416,462	2,674	11,840	162,395	21,194	13.1	179
Selected industries							
Metal mining	50,701	25	47	6,118	370	6.0	787
Coal	15,669	115	256	10,995	1,014	9.2	396
Oil and gas production	103,637	489	4,049	60,221	5,806	9.6	143
Food and kindred products	305,288	2,581	9,434	78,572	8,502	10.8	90
Paper and allied products	69,614	707	1,159	43,441	3,290	7.6	284
Printing and publishing	93,783	1,980	5,509	33,374	4,120	12.3	75
Chemical and allied	236,327	2,631	14,013	122,298	10,463	8.6	75
Petroleum refining	511,125	3,722	30,092	220,043	18,223	8.3	61
Machinery (except electrical)	179,634	2,210	11,271	82,237	9,266	11.3	82
Electrical and electronic	202,754	2,077	8,036	78,676	9,284	11.8	116
Motor vehicle	171,176	1,178	5,678	65,054	7,911	12.2	139
Transportation	235,696	1,535	5,954	176,993	14,749	8.3	248
Telephone	120,585	525	5,732	235,491	20,097	8.5	351
Electric and gas utilities	281,028	2,911	12,565	478,062	19,736	4.1	157

[*]Department of Treasury, Internal Revenue Service, *Statistics of Income—1983, Corporate Income Tax Returns*, pp. 16–21.
[†]Income before U.S. Possessions', Foreign, State, and Federal Taxes.

The figures in our table demonstrate that for most industries the depreciation and amortization allowance is of major importance in relation to net income. Consequently analysts must determine what is normal or adequate depreciation for companies generally and for industrial groups, and they must detect and evaluate individual or group departures from these norms.

Standard Methods of Computing Depreciation

The Diversity of Depreciation Practices— An Analyst's Challenge

Four theoretical approaches to the writing off of property during its useful life are found in current account practice. In addition, the useful lives used by different companies for stockholder reporting purposes cover an extremely wide range, and these differences can produce dramatic results. For example, a chemical company had been using conservative useful lives for its chemical plants but changed its accounting to use the same useful lives as prevailed among its principal competitors. The effect of this change in estimate was a doubling of the company's earnings in comparison to the amount it would have reported under the old depreciation schedule.

Straight-line

For many decades the usual approach to depreciation has been the *straight-line method,* which charges off the same dollar amount each year. That amount is the difference between book cost and estimated salvage, divided by the estimated years of useful life.

Accelerated Methods

A more conservative approach assumes that an asset loses a larger portion of its economic value in the earlier years of use than in the later years, and with this method the depreciation charge diminishes over the asset's life. These accelerated methods include *double declining balance, 150 percent declining balance,* and *sum-of-the-years' digits.* At present companies may depreciate, for tax purposes, assets placed in service between 1980 and 1986 using the modified *accelerated cost recovery system* (ACRS) schedules. Assets placed in service after 1986 may be depreciated for tax purposes using straight-line, 150 percent, or 200 percent declining balance methods depending on the asset class life and other factors. The present class life asset depreciation range (CLADR) system provides ranges of useful lines that are shorter than the economic lives but not as conservative as either ACRS lives or the ADR lives that apply to assets put in service between 1970 and 1981. ACRS was designed to offset the effects of inflation by permitting the use of special depreciation schedules with very short useful lives. Use of even the less liberal modified ACRS of the Tax Reform Act of 1986 for financial reporting purposes would still overstate depreciation expense by a good margin in the early years and have no depreciation charge at all in the later years. Even the present CLADR system tends to have that effect, but to a lesser degree.

Calculating the Sum of the Years' Digits. Mechanically, most accelerated depreciation methods are fairly straightforward. In the case of the sum of the years' digits, a piece of four-year equipment would have a sum of the digits of $1 + 2 + 3 + 4 = 10$. Thus, in the first year, the depreciation would be $\frac{4}{10}$ of cost-minus-salvage value, the next year $\frac{3}{10}$, and so on.

Declining Balance Calculations. The double declining balance method first calculates straight-line depreciation as a percentage of cost-minus-salvage and then doubles that percentage as the first year's depreciation. The second year's depreciation will be that same doubled percentage multiplied by the remaining balance to be depreciated. At some point, the formula's depreciation reaches an amount less than straight-line depreciation and for the asset's remaining life the straight-line method is used. Other declining balance methods are calculated similarly.

Unit of Production

The third commonly used method is based on the principle that wear and tear is a function not only of the passage of time but also of the use made of the facilities. Companies using this approach will vary the depreciation rate in some proportion to the rate of operations during the period. This calculation, usually called the *unit-of-production* method, tends to smooth earnings.

Example. In 1983, Bethlehem Steel Corporation changed its depreciation policies. The new depreciation method is a base of straight-line depreciation with adjustments not to exceed 25 percent in either direction for the level of operation of the plants. Bethlehem also adopted the policy of capitalizing the cost of relining blast furnaces and depreciating the capitalized cost on a unit-of-production basis. A footnote explained that the management believed the changes would provide a better matching of revenues and expenses and bring Bethlehem's accounting practices in line with those predominant in the steel industry. The depreciable lives were also lengthened. The changes were mainly applicable to facilities producing steel and raw materials.

Mortgage or Sinking Fund Methods

A fourth approach to depreciation permits *smaller* deductions in the earlier years than in the later ones. This amortization charge is set aside —sometimes just for purposes of computation—and will earn compound interest until the property is retired. This method has been considered appropriate for public utility companies by a few utility commissions in the western United States. Proposals of similar so-called sinking fund or mortgage methods for other industries have been resisted by accountants.

Depreciation on the Phase-in of New Utility Plants

The FASB is currently considering the appropriateness of phase-in depreciation for newly completed nuclear electricity plants. These phase-in plans are meant to reduce the shock of the large rate increases needed to pay for the plants. Some of these plans in effect book *negative* depreciation in the early years through writing up the plant by an amount greater than the reported depreciation. Such procedures may be suitable for rate-making purposes, but they are totally unjustified for accounting use by any reasonable notion of wear and tear, obsolescence, or return of capital. (Oddly, a staff paper of the California Public Service Commission calls such a calculation "economic depreciation"!)

The Portfolio Problem

Portfolio problems arise when companies have a choice of levels of aggregation at which to measure depreciation. At one extreme, an entire factory and its machinery can be considered a single asset and depreciated using one of the accepted methods. This large portfolio of individual assets could have been broken down into smaller portfolios such as, say, individual production lines. These in turn could have been broken down into individual machines and pieces of equipment. Or all machines of a similar type could be aggregated into a portfolio of, say, machine lathes. The large aggregation, such as the entire plant, allows accountants to expense some expenditures immediately as "maintenance" rather than capitalizing and then amortizing them over a period of years. Large aggregations can also obscure obsolescent equipment that rightfully should have been written down to salvage value. Thus, in comparing depreciation expense, analysts should consider not only the method and the assets' useful lives but also how the method is applied. In general, information on the latter is not provided in the financial reports and must be obtained by discussions with management. Maintenance expense is often given in 10-K and certain regulatory reports, and can sometimes give useful clues about internal operations, depreciation, and the like.

Depreciation and Current Values

When plant and equipment are written up or down, depreciation expenses usually rise or fall proportionately. In the first third of this century, write-ups were a widely used method of stock manipulation, and a source of the expression *watered stock*. In the early thirties, write-downs were common as companies sought to relieve their income statements of the depreciation burden.[1]

Capitalization of Interest and AFUDC

The capitalization of interest as a cost of acquiring plant and equipment presents a difficult analytical problem. Once accounting formally endorsed interest capitalization, it quickly became a requirement for income tax purposes. For tax purposes the capitalized interest is an asset amortizable over a period up to 10 years rather than an investor's return when the asset was earned and paid for.

Interest Cost Is a Return on Investment— AFUDC Is Not

The analyst should consider the cost of capital in terms of the distinction between return *on* capital and return *of* capital. Interest is a return on capital, since it is the reward earned for use of capital. Surely no bondholder would imagine that an interest check received is a return of the original investment. Yet, capitalized interest never appears as such

---

[1] Many political historians believe that the testimony of Professor Soloman Fabricant on the practices of writing assets up or down to current value, and the unfortunate results for investors who were misled by such accounting, was the persuasive evidence of stock manipulation that led Congress to pass the 1933 Act creating the SEC.

on the income statement. The absence of the interest expense results in immediately higher reported income and higher taxable income. That higher reported income, of course, will be offset over the years by higher depreciation expense of the overstated asset that was acquired.

Capitalized interest is shown in a footnote each year. In subsequent years the reader of income statements sees only *depreciation*, which is, by definition, a return *of* capital. Thus, the capitalized interest never appears in the financial statements as a return *on* capital. Unless the interest is adjusted by the analyst, the company's return on invested capital over the years will be permanently understated. The return on equity will be front-ended, although total earnings over the years will be exactly the same for the common stock.

The allowance for equity funds used during construction (AFUDC) has even less justification than capitalized interest. It is merely direction from a utility commission to a public utility to make bookkeeping entries—to record a profit and an imaginary asset—*without any trans-action!* In effect, the commission is saying "It's bad politics to raise utility rates right now, but you must *seem* profitable to survive, so report a profit, and maybe we can raise rates later on." If nonutilities reported profits on such fantasies, some would accuse them of fraud.

It is a matter of some difficulty to unwind the accounting. To do so perfectly would require information on the useful life and depreciation method applied to the specific assets acquired and the amount of interest and AFUDC included in their carrying amounts. Depreciation could then be adjusted to exclude those amortizations, and the capitalized interest could then be shown properly as return on capital in the year paid. Lacking such detailed information, the analyst should use the company's normal depreciation rate expressed as a percentage of gross plant and equipment, or some other reasonable approximation, to eliminate the amortization of the capitalized interest and AFUDC.

Adjustment for Capitalized Interest

The following hypothetical example may help explain the effects of interest capitalization and why the analyst must adjust for it. Assume that a company takes two years to construct a machine. The out-of-pocket costs of building the machine are $100, the average investment in the acquired equipment during the acquisition period is $50, and the applicable interest rate is 10 percent; 10 percent interest for two years on $50 amounts to $10. Thus, interest will be capitalized to the extent of $10, and the initial carrying amount of the machine will be $110. During the two-year acquisition period, interest will be capitalized rather than run through the income statement as an expense. Thus, over the two years, the apparent earnings for the common shareholders will be increased by $10 before taxes or $6.60 after a 34 percent income tax rate.

If the machine has a five-year useful life and zero salvage value, the annual depreciation will be one-fifth of $110, or $22. Without interest capitalization, the depreciation would have been $20 a year. This $2 of additional depreciation a year brings the total pretax earnings for the common stock down by $10, or $6.60 after taxes during the depreciation years. Thus, the increase in earnings during the acquisition period is exactly offset by a decrease in earnings during the depreciation period.

The potentially misleading effect arises because the interest cost never appears on the income statement. Thus, an ordinary calculation of return on investment will never show that $10 of return unless the analyst makes an adjustment for it. The appropriate adjustments would be to return the $10 of interest expense to the income statements in the years in which it was paid out and to reduce taxes paid or payable by $3.40 over the two years. In the subsequent five years the analyst would reduce depreciation by $2 per year and increase tax expense and the deferred tax liability by $0.68 each year (34 percent of $2).

On the surface, reconstruction of such transactions seems hardly worth the effort, until one considers that in capital-intensive industries, especially those whose plants require many years to construct, the interest numbers can become enormous. The interest component on a nuclear power plant can easily approach half of the total cost. If a company's construction program is large, its entire interest expense for the year may disappear from the income statement, with 66 percent of that amount flowing to net income. This can easily increase net income by 25, 50, or 100 percent in the years of interest capitalization.

The old accounting adage "You make money selling things—not by buying them!" seems most appropriate to this situation. Accepting badly distorted earnings and a permanent error in a company's historical rate of return on investment are too high a price for the analyst to pay for avoiding work. The analyst must restate the record to eliminate the capitalized interest, its amortization, and the related tax effects (see "Depreciation" in Chapter 9).

Deferred Taxes and Accelerated Depreciation

The Statement of Depreciation Policy

The depreciation policies of the more important companies are summarized in the detailed descriptions appearing in the financial manuals.

They must be set forth in a registration statement and prospectus covering the sale of securities, in proxy statements relating to mergers and similar transactions, and in annual reports. In recent years the depreciation footnote in many annual reports has diminished to a statement that a particular method is used "over the estimated useful lives." Many companies used to give more useful ranges of lives for the major classes of assets.

Example. The International Paper Company's 1984 annual report was more helpful than most. It provided the following information about useful-life estimations for company assets:

Buildings	2.5 percent
Machinery and equipment	5 to 33 percent
Woods equipment	10 to 16 percent
Start-up costs	5 years
Timberlands	As timber is cut
Roads and land improvements	Over economic lives

Investment Tax Credit

To encourage the construction of new plant and equipment, the Congress from time to time during the post–World War II period has allowed tax credits equal to a specified percentage, usually 10 percent, of the cost of certain plant and equipment. Two methods are acceptable for accounting for the investment tax credit. The most widely used is *flow through*, which reflects the full value of the credit in net income in the year taken. The *deferral* method, used primarily by public utilities, defers the credit and amortizes it over the life of the asset. Those in favor of the flow through method argue that the credit is *earned* by acquiring the asset. Those who favor deferral and amortization believe that the tax credit is a subsidy that merely *reduces the cost* of the asset and should be deferred and amortized in the same fashion as the asset itself. The Tax Reform Act of 1986 eliminated the investment tax credit.

Post-SEC Practices

Between, say, 1935 and 1954 the vast majority of companies used the straight-line method of depreciation applied to the cost (less salvage) of their assets, as required on tax returns. The year 1954 marked the beginning of the trend toward more liberal tax depreciation. For a time companies tended to change their financial reporting depreciation toward these faster tax methods. That trend has been reversed because the earnings penalty was too painful. In 1984, 567 of 600 companies used straight-line for some of or all their depreciable assets; 60 used unit-of-production calculations; 54, declining balance; 15, sum-of-the-years' digits; and 76, unspecified accelerated methods.[2] Companies that used more than one depreciation method did so because they had recent acquisitions, because they were fulfilling foreign accounting requirements for certain subsidiaries, or because they wanted to keep certain divisions in accord with the practices of the industry in which they operated.

Deferred Tax Effects

Book-Tax Timing Differences. The use of accelerated depreciation and of ACRS for tax purposes are the largest causes of the difference between the taxable income recorded on the tax form and the profits shown in the published financial reports. A survey of sources of book–tax depreciation timing differences of 600 companies in 1984 showed that 488 had timing differences due to depreciation.[3] No other type of timing difference was nearly as widespread nor as large in magnitude.

Contribution to Cash Flow. Since in recent years the deferred tax effect has been one-third to one-half of the difference between book depreciation and tax depreciation, deferred income taxes have become a very important contributor to a company's cash flow. Even at a 34 percent tax rate and using the new asset depreciation range lives, the impact is large.

Normalization of Reported Earnings

Taxes are deferred when a company reports faster depreciation on the tax form than in the financial statements. The simple example in Table 6.2 may help explain why the recording of a deferred income tax liability improves the reporting of after-tax income to investors and also has favorable cash flow consequences.

Assume that the company has only one asset, a machine with an expected useful life of six years. The machine cost $300. The company has annual revenues of $100, and no expenses other than depreciation and taxes. Assume also that the tax laws permit such a machine to be depreciated straight line over a period of three years.

---

[2] American Institute of Certified Public Accountants, *Accounting Trends and Techniques*, 1985, New York, p. 268.

[3] American Institute of Certified Public Accountants, *Accounting Trends and Techniques*, 1985, New York, p. 275.

Table 6.2.   Comparison of Shareholder and Tax Reporting

		As Reported to Shareholders				
Year	Revenue	Depre-ciation	Pretax income	Tax expense at 34% rate	After-tax income	Cash flow
1	$100	$50	$50	$17[*]	$33	$100
2	100	50	50	17[*]	33	100
3	100	50	50	17[*]	33	100
4	100	50	50	17[†]	33	66
5	100	50	50	17[†]	33	66
6	100	50	50	17[†]	33	66

		As Reported on the Tax Form		
Year	Revenue	Depre-ciation	Pretax income	Taxes paid at 34% rate
1	$100	$100	$ 0	$ 0
2	100	100	0	0
3	100	100	0	0
4	100	0	100	34
5	100	0	100	34
6	100	0	100	34

[*]Additions to the deferred tax liability.
[†]The deferred tax account is reduced by this amount.

The report to shareholders reflects accurately the economics in the after-tax income column. The six years of revenue are charged with a reasonable allocation of the cost of the $300 machine. The tax expense shown in the report to shareholders represents annual increases of $17in the company's deferred tax liability for the first three years. At the end of the third year the company would have a $51 tax liability related to the machine. During each of the final three years $17 of deferred tax liability would "mature," and $17 of new tax expense would come about from operations, so the company would have to make tax payments in the amount of $34 in each of those three years. (Accountants refer to this maturing phenomenon as a "reversal of book-tax timing differences.")

The cash flows of this company in each year equal the sum of net income plus depreciation plus the increase (or minus the decrease) in the deferred tax liability.

A Comparison of Depreciation Rates and Methods

The Renaissance of Straight-Line.   Table 6.3 shows depreciation rates and methods for 29 major industrial companies in 1984 and selected earlier years. The average depreciation rate as a percentage of gross plant advanced from 5.0 percent in 1949 to 5.6 percent in 1959 and to 6.6 percent in 1984. The effect is a reduction in reported earnings of about 10 percent over the 25 years, and the question is whether the newer depreciation rates are appropriate.

By themselves, the depreciation methods give little evidence about the adequacy of the depreciation amount or the effect of the related deferred income taxes. The letters SD, DB, and AM all represent accelerated methods that give more rapid depreciation than straight-line in the early years and less in the later years, and are thus considered to be conservative. A switch from any of those three methods to straight line would appear to be a move away from from conservatism. Nine of the companies switched from one of those three accelerated methods to the straight-line method between 1959 and 1984. In five of the cases, depreciation as a percentage of gross plant declined, but, in the other four, the ratio *increased*. Presumably in those cases the movement to a less conservative method was offset by more conservative useful lives, although this cannot be said with certainty because the mix of assets held might have changed. Overall, the 1984 rate of 6.6 percent appears to have risen more through use of significantly shorter lives than through change of method. This probably occurred because most companies prefer to use the same lives for both tax and reporting purposes.

Units-of-Production Growing in Popularity
An interesting trend between 1959 and 1984 was the shift toward depreciation methods that reflected levels of activity—the units-of-production method—that occurred in raw materials industries such as steel, oil, and paper.

Proper Useful Lives, Properly Applied

Depreciation Rate Is the Reciprocal of the Useful Life. If the rate of depreciation to gross plant is 5 percent, it is implicit that the average fixed asset, excluding land, has an expected life of 1 divided by 5 percent, or 20 years. A decline in the depreciation rate suggests that longer useful lives are being estimated. This is not necessarily nonconservative because the mix of depreciable assets can shift considerably over time. In contrast, obsolescence, whether competitively or technologically caused, can shorten the lives of assets considerably. A decline in foreign competition due to a weak dollar can lengthen the life of a piece of equipment otherwise near retirement.

Table 6.3. Comparative Depreciation Allowances for Twenty-Nine Companies

	1984		1959		1948	
	Ratio to gross plant	Method	Ratio to gross plant	Method	Ratio to gross plant	Method
Allied Signal	7.1%	SL	5.4%	SD	3.7%	SL
Alcoa	5.3	SL	4.8	SD	2.3	SL
American Brands	7.8	SL	4.2	SL	4.0	SL
American Can	6.7	SL	4.4	SL	3.6	SL
American Tel. & Tel.	7.2	SL	4.7	SL	3.4	SL
Bethlehem Steel	3.8	UP	4.3	DB	2.7	SL
Chevron Corp.	6.1	UP	4.5	SL	5.5	SL
Chrysler*	9.9	SL†	6.3	SL	9.3	SL
Du Pont	6.3	SD	7.5	SL	8.3	SL
Eastman Kodak	7.0	AM	6.0	SD	5.1	SL
Exxon	6.3	UP	5.3	SL	4.9	SL
General Electric	7.5	SD	7.5	SL	7.7	SL
General Foods	6.1	SL	6.3	SD	4.3	SL
General Motors*	11.9	AM	6.7	AM	6.3	SL
Goodyear	5.3	SL	6.3	SD	5.9	SL
INCO Ltd.	3.8	SL	2.5	SL	2.8	SL
International Paper	4.6	UP	6.3	DB	4.7	SL
Manville	5.2	SL	5.5	SD	4.4	SL
Navistar Int'l	7.0	SL	6.0	SL	4.7	SL
Owens Illinois	5.9	SL	5.0	SD	4.8	SL
Procter & Gamble	4.9	SL	3.8	SL	3.3	SL
Sears Roebuck	4.9‡	SL	5.5	SD	7.5	SL
Swift Independent	7.7	SL	4.5	SD	4.4	SL
Texaco	7.7	UP	6.7	SL	6.7	SL
Union Carbide	4.6	SL	6.2	SL	4.0	SL
U.S. Steel	5.5	UP	3.2	UP	3.9	UP
United Technologies	7.7	AM	9.9	SD	7.4	SL
Westinghouse Electric	7.8	SL	6.2	SL	4.3	SL
Woolworth	12.1	SL	6.1	SL	5.8	SL
Average	6.6		5.6		5.0	

NOTE: These companies were in the Dow-Jones industrials average in 1959. Anaconda has been omitted due to its acquisition by another company. SL = straight line, SD = sum of the years' digits, DB = declining balance, AM = accelerated method, UP = units of production or activity related.

*Includes amortization of special tools.
†An accelerated method is used for assets acquired before 1980.
‡Merchandising division only.

Useful Lives Are Affected by Shifts in the Economy.   The U.S. economy has been characterized in the postwar years by a shift away from the old basic industries and toward new technological products and the service industries. Both areas include higher technology content, which suggests that the new sectors might see an increasing influence of technological obsolescence in the lives of assets.

Decline of Basic Industries: Are Write-Downs a Suitable Substitute for Adequate Depreciation?   Part of the problem in the old basic and raw materials industries has been the growth of those industries in the stronger third-world countries. Those countries have low wages and, in some cases, more modern equipment than their U.S. counterparts. The average depreciation rate in the basic industries probably should have been more rapid in the past to reflect the economic obsolescence. Yet the record shows very low depreciation rates. It is in those industries that we observe today the largest number of plant write-downs, plant closings, abandonments, restructuring of product lines, and the like. The average depreciation rate in 1984 for the loss-ridden steel industries was 4 percent, which implies a 25-year useful life. A leading question therefore is: Are large write-downs of obsolete plants a suitable substitute for adequate depreciation?

Intra-Industry Depreciation Ranges Should Be Narrowed by the Analyst.   In contrast to the integrated steel companies, the average depreciation rate of a dozen electronics companies in 1984 was 10 percent, implying a 10-year average life for plant and equipment. Given the short life cycle of new products in the electronics industry, this rapid depreciation may well be justified. Regardless, the analyst should be uncomfortable with the *range* of depreciation rates in the electronics industry (from 7 to 16.1 percent) and in the steel industry (from 2.6 to 5.5 percent).

Are Depreciation Charges Adequate?

At least two sources of useful information provide background on the reasonableness of depreciation lives for the entire corporate sector: current cost data and the National Income and Product Accounts.

Current Cost Information.   Statement 33 required, through 1986, that some 1200 companies present current cost depreciation in their annual reports. The difference between the current cost and historical cost amounts represents the additional amounts needed to replace at current prices the operating capability used up during the year. Current cost depreciation exceeded historical cost depreciation by 37 percent in 1980 and averaged 31 percent from 1980 to 1983.[4] These figures suggest a serious short fall in the provision for replacement.

National Income and Product Accounts. The National Income and Product Accounts include Table 1.12, Gross Domestic Product of Corporations. This is a partial income statement of the domestic business of U.S. corporations, and the table includes a capital consumption adjustment (CCA), which is the amount necessary to bring depreciation to a current cost number. In 1985 the capital consumption allowance was $197.4 billion before adding the capital consumption adjustment of $71.8 billion. This suggests that historical cost depreciation should have been increased by 36 percent to cover the current costs of consuming fixed assets in 1985.

Although both the current cost data and the National Income and Product Accounts information paint a gloomy picture, there are some offsetting factors. Many companies use the IRS class life asset depreciation ranges (CLADR) for their ordinary depreciation, which place the useful lives on a significantly conservative basis. Second, although technological change has undoubtedly increased obsolescence, at the same time it has brought significant increases in efficiency and improvement in product quality which are not reflected in the replacement cost prices. The industries in which depreciation has seemed the most inadequate are the ones which have taken large write-downs and write-offs over the last few years and which have shown the poorest profit histories. Their share of the economy is declining, making their depreciation practices less significant on an overall basis. History will tell us the truth of it, but on balance today's depreciation rates are probably adequate if inflation stays under, say, 5 percent.

Adjust for Comparability
An Example of the Recommended Procedure

The recommended way of dealing with disparate depreciation methods and lives is to put all companies that are to be compared on a comparable basis. A method recommended for its simplicity places all companies in an industry on a straight-line basis, using the industry-average depreciation rate which is calculated as the ratio of depreciation expense to gross plant. Straight-line calculation is the easiest method because the

[4]Price Waterhouse & Co., *Inflation Accounting*, New York, 1981.

assets' ages are not needed; the amount of depreciation is simply gross plant divided by a conservative useful life.

Airline Depreciation Rates

Table 6.4 shows the depreciation rates for seven large airlines in 1984 (the year to June 30, 1985, in the case of Delta Airlines). To make the depreciation figures for these airlines more comparable, the analyst might calculate the average ratio of depreciation to gross plant, which in this case turns out to be 6.82 percent. That average percentage would be multiplied by the gross plant of each airline to determine whether

Table 6.4.   Major Airline Depreciation Rates, 1984

	AMR Corp.	Delta	Eastern	NWA Corp.	PanAm Corp.	Trans- Air	UAL Inc.
Gross plant ($ million)	4759	4423	4505	2643	2762	3428	6714
Depreciation ($ million)	307.7	346.5	287.7	167.2	207.7	224.1	445.6
Net income ($ million)	233.9	175.6	37.9(d)	56.0	206.8(d)	29.9	282.4
Depreciation to gross plant (percent)	6.47	7.83	6.39	6.33	7.52	6.54	6.54
Depreciation adjustment to 6.82% after 46% tax ($ million)	+9.0	+24.1	−10.5	−7.0	+10.5	−5.2	−6.5
Adjusted net income ($ million)	224.9	199.7	48.4(d)	49.0	196.3(d)	24.7	275.9

SOURCES: *Moody's Transportation Manual*, New York, 1985: *Standard & Poor's Corporation Records*, New York, 1985.

reported depreciation was above or below average. If, as in the case of Delta Airlines, the company appeared to be overdepreciating, a depreciation adjustment would be calculated:

$$(7.83\% - 6.82\%) \times \$4423 \times (1 - 46\%) = \$24.1$$

The excess depreciation, expressed as a rate, is multiplied by gross plant and equipment and the result is tax-adjusted at the 1984 tax rate of 46 percent to obtain the proper adjustment to net income. Similar adjustments for the other airlines result in some increases and decreases which change earnings by a significant percentage.

The precision of such adjustments would be greatly improved by a more detailed analysis of each company. Some of these companies operate hotels, reservation systems, automobile rental subsidiaries, and the like. The conscientious analyst would seek separate financial statements for these divisions and affiliates to calculate more precise weighted average depreciation adjustments.

Amortization Charges of Mining and Oil Companies

These important sectors of the industrial field are subject to special factors bearing on amortization. In addition to ordinary depreciation on buildings and equipment, they must allow for depletion of their ore, oil, and similar nonrenewable reserves. Mining companies also incur exploration and development expense; the corresponding charges for oil and gas producers would come under the headings of unproductive leases, dry holes, and drilling costs in which "intangible drilling costs" have a special accounting and tax status. These items are significant in their bearing on the true profits, and they are often troublesome to the analyst because different enterprises use varying methods to deal with these figures in their accounts.

Depletion Charges—A Recovery of Costs

Depletion represents the using up of exhaustible capital assets, mainly underground, by turning them into products for sale. It applies to companies producing oil and gas, metals and many other minerals, sulphur and other chemicals from deposits, clay, limestone, and other similar materials. Timber companies also face depletion costs, although their wasting asset is above ground and may be renewed by reforestation. As the holdings, or reserves, of these products are exhausted, their cost must be gradually written off through charges against earnings so that the original capital will be returned. In a company's own accounts such charges are made by deducting that percentage of the cost of the property which the mineral extracted bears to the total mineral content. This units-of-production method can be applied also to depreciation of oil and gas wells and other equipment, the service life of which is governed by the same factors. For tax purposes, however, an important departure from the standard method of computing depletion has been permitted—percentage depletion.

Percentage Depletion Is a Tax Rule— Not a Recovery of Costs

The concept of percentage depletion arose because searching for minerals and hydrocarbons underground is highly risky, and most exploration efforts fail to discover economically useful deposits. To make the reward commensurate with the risk, Congress allowed a special tax deduction, which was calculated as a specified percentage of the sales value. The percentage differed according to the mineral in question. The overall effect of this incentive was that successful explorers would receive profits and cost recovery on their own investments, plus an additional bounty equal to recovery of the unsuccessful explorers' costs and their expected returns. Exploring for minerals would then, in the aggregate, be economically attractive—a positive sum game. Regardless of the merits of the concept behind percentage depletion, it has sparked much political controversy. As a result, Congress has reduced the tax benefits in recent decades. Table 6.5 shows the percentage of sales value allowed under the tax codes in 1954 and in 1987 for a few minerals.

Table 6.5.   Percentage Depletion Deductions

	Percentage depletion allowed	
	1954	1987
Oil and gas	27.5	0 *
Sulphur and uranium	23	22
Gold, silver	15	15
Metal mines	15	14
Coal	10	10
Clay, shale	5	5–22†
Gravel, peat	5	5

*For producers who are also refiners or marketers and for production over 1000 barrels per day of oil or 6000 mcf of gas per day.
†Depending on grade and location.
Source: *Internal Revenue Code of 1986*, vol. 1, Commerce Clearing House, Chicago, 1986, pp. 5310–5311.

The percentage depletion allowance is limited to not more than 50 percent of net income before depletion for each producing property. Thus, the overall allowance can exceed 50 percent of a company's *total* net income if other operations of the company are losing money. For tax purposes, the company must take the larger of percentage depletion or the ordinary cost-based depletion. In the past, percentage depletion was almost always larger than cost-based depletion and over time accumulated amounts in excess of the cost of finding and developing deposits. Typically, reports to stockholders include only cost-based depletion, and the amortization of intangible drilling costs is also significantly lower than the amounts expensed on the tax return.

Note that any excess of percentage depletion over book depletion is a *permanent* tax-timing difference that will not reverse. That is, that difference will never appear in the statements issued to stockholders, nor will a time come when reported depletion expense will be less because of that difference. The effect of the excess percentage depletion is the same as the permanent difference that exists on interest from tax-exempt bonds: Permanantly tax-exempt income is created, and the analyst need make no provision for deferred taxes.

Oil Accounting Practices

Two basic accounting methods are used in the oil and gas industry:

- *Successful efforts.* Capitalize only the wells which discover oil and gas.
- *Full cost.* Capitalize all the costs of a field or area if at least some wells are successful enough to ensure recovery of the costs.

Some full-cost companies define the field or area very narrowly, and their results are close to successful efforts in accounting. In other cases, the area of interest may be an entire country or a large area such as "off-shore United States." Nearly all small exploration companies use full-cost calculations, although many large companies remain on successful efforts accounting. It is very difficult for the analyst to put companies using these two accounting methods on a comparable basis.

Reserve Information—More Important Than the Accounting Method. Although the lack of comparability is frustrating, the analyst should not lose sight of a much more important fact; usually, the oil-producing company's largest asset, oil and gas underground, is not on the books at all. The books show only the costs of wells that lead to the oil, plus other equipment. Information about the reserves, including the quantities, quality, and locations, and the "standardized measure" of discounted future net cash inflows are important information. The latter discounts expected future net cash inflows from proved reserves, based on year-end prices and costs, using a 10 percent discount rate. The oil analyst is probably better served pursuing information about existing reserves and their future cash inflows than by spending the same amount of time trying to untangle the accounting differences.

Accounting for Intangible Drilling Costs. Intangible drilling costs represent the labor and overhead costs incurred in drilling oil and gas wells, as distinguished from the cost of pipe and other tangible materials. The income tax law gives the option of capitalizing and amortizing the costs or immediately writing them off. Companies normally take the immediate write-off for the tax benefits. The active and expanding producers have always kept ahead of the tax collector in their increasing intangible drilling accounts, a cause of frequent debate in Congress.

Oil Royalties. Taxes paid to foreign governments result in credits that reduce U.S. taxes. Payments to foreign governments as oil production occurs can be described with many captions—for example, royalties, severance taxes, or income taxes. From the company's viewpoint, payments as foreign income taxes are desirable to get the foreign tax credit rather than a mere deduction. The more payments are structured to look like income taxes, the greater the concern of the foreign government about the transfer price at which the oil or gas is sold to the company's refinery or pipeline in another country. Thus, political developments both at home and abroad can overwhelm the statistical record, as can the more obvious risk of nationalization of foreign reserves. In underdeveloped countries, nationalization usually occurs when the government ceases to need the company's capital and skills.

Depletion of Mining Companies

Depletion is no longer an important item in the published accounts of mining companies. Some have written off their exploration costs when incurred or over too short a period and have no costs left to amortize. Others show a deduction based on the cost of their mining properties, but this figure is almost always comparatively small. In former years some concerns deducted the percentage depletion allowed by the tax law, and the analyst had to restore such amounts to net income and deduct instead a cost depletion amount to recover the actual investment.

At one time financial services used to state the per share earnings of mining companies "before depletion." That unfortunate practice is no longer common. Failure to recover the investment in reserves is failure to maintain the capital of the company. Income is not properly stated without such a charge.

Income Effects of Operating Leases and Capital Leases

Operating Leases

A major development of the past quarter century has been the growth of assets accounted for as operating leases. The reported expense is the rental cost, a level expense that tends to smooth earnings. (See Chapter 10.)

Capital Leases

Under a capital lease, a liability is shown on the balance sheet and the asset is presented separately from other plant and equipment. The asset is depreciated, usually straight-line. The interest component of the borrowing is reflected using the mortgage or interest methods. The effect is to reduce the early years' net income and to increase income in the later years of the lease.

Amortization of Intangible Assets

Intangible assets fall into various classes, depending on how they may be amortized in the tax returns and on the varying treatment accorded them in corporate accounts. These items usually have a small effect on reported earnings, but there are exceptions, particularly when goodwill is large. (Intangible drilling costs are not really intangible and are invariably carried in the balance sheet as part of the tangible property account.) Four classes of intangibles are discussed below, based on their tax or accounting treatment.

Items to Expense or Amortize

Exploration Costs and Mine-Development Expense.   Exploration costs and mine development expenses are almost always written off for taxes, but their treatment on the books varies. Productive exploration and development expense is regularly capitalized and amortized over the life of the property.

Research and Development Costs.   Research and development costs must be charged to current expense. Most research and development is unsuccessful, and there is no consistent relationship between (1) the value of the discovery, process, or product, and (2) the amount of money spent. Clearly, when successful, research and development are a real economic asset. However, analysts rarely have the information to determine the cost of that asset or to estimate the useful life over which it should be amortized. Setting up such an asset would require company guidance regarding the allocation of research and development costs between expense and the cost of successful products.

Much of what is called research and development is ordinary engineering related to cost reduction, styling, and production—the ordinary engineering application of known processes and materials to some existing function or part. These ordinary and recurring expenses should be charged to expense as incurred. It is in the exploratory research of the sort found in drugs, electronics, and biotechnology that analysts have attempted to reflect in some way the results of successful research efforts. For example, analysts following the drug industry have devised such adjustments as adding back half the cost of research to reported earnings for purposes of comparing companies. Another method is to adjust earnings upward or downward by a figure that represents the amount the company's research expenditures (expressed as a percentage of sales) deviate from the industry average.

Items to Amortize on Tax Returns

Intangibles which are amortized on the tax return include:

- Patents
- Licenses
- Royalties
- Motion pictures and television programs
- Sound recordings
- Costs of leases

(Leasehold improvements—often buildings erected on leased land—should be considered the equivalent of tangible assets with lives coterminous with the leases involved.) In the past most companies "conservatively" wrote off the cost of patents against *surplus* and thus relieved future earnings of the usually small amortization charge. Today the cost of patents and licenses is regularly amortized against income. Regardless of the treatment of such items on the tax return, the analyst should follow the general rule of eliminating intangibles and their amortization unless they are known to be marketable or to have a direct stream of revenue attributable to them. In many cases, it will be obvious to the analyst that the intangible asset has great value. For example, RCA pioneered in radio and television and continues to receive substantial royalty income for use of its patents. The film libraries of the movie companies generate substantial income from leases to television stations and reissue of old classics—note, for instance, the $1.5 billion paid by Turner Broadcasting System for MGM Entertainment Company. However, usually the intangibles have little or no value, but that information is seldom revealed to the security analyst unless management is asked specifically about it.

Development Items to Expense on Tax Returns

Development items include advertising, start-up costs, early deficits, and the like. In some rather varied cases these have been capitalized in the accounts, increasing the reported earnings. If such items appear on the balance sheet, analysts should eliminate them and their amortization. The magnitude of these items is sometimes proportionate to the ineptitude with which the expenditures were incurred.

Purchased Goodwill and Other Doubtful Debits

The fourth group of intangibles includes those which may be neither expensed nor amortized on the tax returns. Chief of these is goodwill, especially the important element of "purchased goodwill," which arises when a business is acquired at a cost exceeding the fair value of its net assets in a business combination accounted for as a purchase rather than a pooling of interests.

Warren Buffett, a student and associate of Ben Graham, has commented, "An analyst can live a rich and fulfilling life without ever knowing about goodwill or its amortization." By this, he meant that goodwill and its amortization are void of information and should be eliminated by the analyst. Thus goodwill should be written off, and its amortization should be removed from the income statement. If no asset existed economically, no economic cost was incurred in using it. The analyst should not allow its amortization to affect current or future earnings. No tax adjustment is required because amortization of goodwill is not tax deductible.

Goodwill is a premium paid in excess of fair value of net assets. It represents the acquiring company's estimate of the excess of *investment value* over *asset value*. However, this estimate is soon out of date, reflecting projections of earnings under the new ownership. If the company has financial difficulties, the goodwill evaporates quickly. Thus goodwill is not a reliable asset.

Accounting requires that purchased goodwill be amortized over no more than 40 years. Its immediate write-off is forbidden. At times, even amortization over 40 years can result in significant amounts in the income statement. For example, Manufacturers Hanover Bank acquired goodwill of $626 million in 1984 in its acquisition of CIT Financial Corporation. Amortization will be over 34 years, or $18.4 million per year.

7

Analysis of the Funds Flow Statement

In Chapter 6 we discussed a number of aspects of depreciation, depletion, and other amortization, as these items appear, either actually or ideally, in the company's accounts. We are now ready to extend the discussion into the concept of cash flow, which is currently an important part of Wall Street's thinking. Two approaches are offered in preference to the conventional funds statement, and the uses and interpretation of cash flow statements are discussed.

Some Funds Statement Definitions

Reconciliation to Cash or Working Capital

A funds statement, officially called the "statement of changes in financial position," attempts to explain many changes in the balance sheet from one period to the next, from various causes in addition to net income. For simplicity we will use more familiar terms such as *funds statement* or *cash flow statement*. The bottom line is either *net changes in cash and equivalent*, or *net changes in working capital*, but many other balance sheet changes, including investing and financing activities, are included. (*Cash equivalents* typically include U.S. Treasury bills, commercial paper, certificates of deposit, and other short-term high-quality temporary investments of cash.)

Operating, Financing, and Investing Activities

Since little official guidance is given for funds statements, they vary widely. Some practices are quite common, such as presenting the statement in three categories: operating, financing, and investment activities. Since there are currently no official definitions of these categories, similar items are classified differently, based on judgments or preferences of different managements.

Direct and Indirect Methods

Discussions of the funds statement are hampered by loose usage of terminology—particularly the phrases *direct method* and *indirect method*. In this book an indirect method is any method that does not look to actual cash flows as a starting point. For example, as defined here, the typical funds statement uses the indirect method when it considers the sum of the following as sources of "cash from operations":

- Net income
- Depreciation
- Other noncash charges
- The increase (or minus the decrease) in deferred taxes

It is possible to have all those items and still have no cash inflows. Those four items are merely an approximation of net cash inflows, because they are income or expenses that are assumed not to require any current cash outflow. Implicit assumptions here are that cash revenues exist, and that the above list of items would not make any demands upon those cash inflows.

The direct method looks to direct sources of cash. Direct cash inflows include:

- Sales for cash
- Collection of receivables, rent, interest, and dividends
- Receipt of tax refunds
- Sales of securities
- Other transactions

Similarly, the direct method looks to actual cash outflows, using currency, checks, wire transfer, and the like to make payments to others, rather than to accrual bookkeeping entries.

Indirect Method Is Normally Used

Unfortunately, even though companies have the information to prepare direct cash flow statements, the custom is to use an indirect method in the funds statement. Often what is actually presented in the funds statement is a combination of *some*

- Year-to-year changes in balance sheet items (such as depreciation of equipment)
- True flows of cash (for example, cash purchase of supplies)
- Accrual entries (such as setting up a warranty reserve for products sold)

Some items are gross amounts and others are net of tax or expense.

Using a funds flow statement based on accrual accounting as a check on the accrual income statement is a sort of self-fulfilling prophecy. Misleading information about cash flows in one is liable to show up undetected in the other.

The Importance of Cash Flows

Investors and creditors can receive cash only if the company has holdings of cash or net inflows of cash. As a result, investors examine the relationship between the accrual income reported in the income statement and the related cash flow from revenues and for expenditures. Over the life of a company, use of accrual accounting or cash accounting does not matter, since income turns out to be the same. In any one year cash inflows and outflows may deviate from accruals by a wide margin. Over a period of several years a cash-based income statement should begin to approach the numbers presented in the regular accrual income statement. Some analysts use a rule of thumb that if the earnings estimated from the funds statement are within 15 or 20 percent of the reported earnings of the income statement over a five-year period, the latter number is "validated."

Bank credit officers in particular are aware that loans must be repaid with cash. They, too, would like to know whether a company generates cash from its operations in amounts sufficient to service debt, pay rental obligations, and maintain operating capability without strain. The user of financial statements can do most of the job of preparing an ordinary funds flow statement from the existing income statement, balance sheet, footnotes, and knowledge or estimates of the amount of capital expenditures. The desirability of cash flow information is clear when one considers that bankers are known to have prepared cash flow statements as early as 1863.

Dividends and Cash Flow

The security analyst is interested in cash inflows for a variety of reasons. One, of course, is the stream of dividends which constitutes a major portion of return. While the reason may not be immediately obvious, there is a much higher correlation between dividends and cash flow than there is between dividends and earnings. This occurs partly because earnings are highly volatile—much more so than cash flow—and companies attempt to pay a relatively stable pattern of dividends. Usually dividends are not cut because of what are considered to be temporary declines in earnings; often, all or most of the dividend will be continued even during a period of two or three years of deficits. The dividend will not be continued, however, if the decline in cash flow is great enough to encroach on debt service and necessary capital expenditures. Thus, the prediction of future dividends is heavily influenced by the analyst's projection of future cash flows from operations and mandatory cash outflows.

Dividend Policy

Companies budget future dividend payments the same way that they budget any other cash outflow such as debt service requirements, capital expenditures, or any forecastable demand for cash. As a result, when a board of directors sets a general dividend policy, it is often in terms of and always in consideration of projected cash flows—not earnings. Thus, the internal policy might well be described as 20 to 25 percent of average cash flow, even for companies that express their dividend policy publicly in terms of payout ratios, that is, as a percentage of earnings.

Cash Flow Approximation

Another reason for the analyst's interest in cash inflows is to determine the ability of the company to fund its growth internally—that is, from the cash it is able to generate from operations. A company cannot grow forever through increasing its leverage. The quality ratings of its debt will be downgraded, and the company will be forced to sell stock, diluting the growth in earnings per share. Thus, although some growth can be financed by debt, that debt can grow no faster in the long run than the growth of equity. Equity must grow largely from retained earnings if dilutive sales of stock are to be avoided. Since the growth rate of earnings has a major influence on the earnings multiplier, analysts must validate their projection of earnings growth with a cash flow analysis confirming the company's ability to finance the growth.

Revenues as a First Approximation of Cash Inflows

The cash flow concept can be better understood if considered in terms of the cash-to-cash cycle of the typical business enterprise. The operating cycle consists of buying raw materials, labor, and the like for cash and of subsequently receiving cash as a result of sale of output. Companies have very few nonmonetary transactions. Thus, cash, sooner or later, represents one side of most two-party transactions. Where do operating cash flows come from? Usually cash is received for outright sales or from exchange of goods and services for credit—accounts receivable, which are subsequently collected. Revenues can be used as a first approximation of the actual cash received from operations, since the cash payments on receivables from earlier periods may be about equal the absence of cash inflows from the uncollected receivables held at the end of the period.

Gross Cash Inflows

Dividends and growth are financed by the *net* cash inflows, of course. Cash revenues are not available for such uses except when they exceed cash expenses. However, analysts need the *gross* inflows from revenues and the outflows for expenses and losses for the same reasons that they need an income statement that shows both revenues and expenses. The primary use of the funds statement by stock analysts is to confirm or deny, over time, the amounts shown in the income statement. Having revenues and expenditures on a cash basis for comparison with accrual revenues and expenses permits the analyst to identify more specifically the *sources* of differences. Information about only the *net* cash inflows is deficient in that respect.

Example of a Gross Cash Inflow Comparison. Consider, for example, a company that reports growing accrual revenues but flat gross cash revenues. The difference may appear in the form of rising accounts receivable, since they can be sold. The revenue difference would initiate a series of questions in the analyst's mind:

- Has the company adopted a lenient credit policy?
- Is it selling to customers who are unable to pay?
- Has the company been "borrowing" sales from future periods?
- Is the company "parking" inventory in a financing transaction?
- Are cash sales down?

Some explanation is demanded to reconcile differences between cash revenues and accrual revenues, which in the long run must be the same. Information on only the *net* cash inflows might not raise those questions.

For similar reasons, analysts need to examine differences between accrual expenses and gross cash expenditures for operations. Those differences both raise questions and offer insights into the operating dynamics of a company. That such information has neither been available nor been demanded by users of financial statements is no reason to dismiss its potential usefulness. To the contrary, given the differences between analysts' and accountants' views of capital mainte-nance and income, the gross cash flows seem the most promising candidates to deal with the differences created by:

- Amortization of goodwill
- Treatment of other doubtful intangible assets
- Accretion or discounting of interest
- Physical capital maintenance difficulties
- Capitalization of interest

Method One: Unadjusted Indirect Calculations

Calculating Cash Flow the Indirect Way

The earlier method of calculating cash flow was to sum net income and depreciation. Depreciation was the only large noncash expense for most companies. The result was called "cash flow," and it began to take on a meaning of its own. Some still calculate it that way, for example, the *Value Line Investment Survey*.[1] Analysts and companies now calculate cash flow using a more complete version of the indirect method—adding net income, depreciation, increases in deferred tax liabilities, and other noncash charges from the income statement.[2] These other non-cash charges include:

- Amortization of goodwill, patents, licenses, and the like
- Warranty expenses
- Amortization of bond discounts

[1] *How to Use the Value-Line Investment Survey—A Subscriber's Guide*, Value Line, Inc., New York, p. 30.

[2] Allen H. Seed, III, *The Funds Statement*, Financial Executives Research Foundation, Morristown, N.J., 1984, pp. 33–34. Seed found only two companies using the direct method in 1983: SafeCard Services, Inc., and Northrop Corp.

- Amortization of leasehold improvements

(Ideally, the credits, such as amortization of bond premiums, should be subtracted from the total.)

But Depreciation Isn't Cash Flow

Of course, if there were no sales for cash or receivables collected, there would be no cash inflow from operations. Analysts must keep in mind that depreciation and the like are not a source of cash, although if there is revenue, depreciation and noncash charges are expenses that generally do not require a concurrent cash outflow. That part of the cash inflow is a *net* inflow.

Flows and Capital Maintenance—Return of or Return on Investment?

All cash flows from operations represent either return *of* capital or return *on* capital. The amounts that are properly measured expenses are return of investment. Properly calculated depreciation represents the return of the investment in a building or a piece of equipment over its useful life. After all the proper expenses of a period have been recovered, any additional positive cash flows from operations are income, or return *on* investment. A major objective of security analysis is to measure this net income as accurately as possible through making appropriate adjustments to accounting net income. The adjustments include reallocation of some of the amounts that are stated on the books as "return of capital" to "return on capital," or the reverse. (Of course, the financial statements do not actually use the terms *return of capital* and *return on capital*.)

To the analyst, the return of capital is the amount of expense for the period necessary to maintain capital—to remain "as well off." The amount of return on capital, or income, is the residual after revenues and expenses have been brought to the analysts' estimate of *correct* levels. Many of the adjustments that the analyst makes to the income statement or to the balance sheet will also turn out to be appropriate adjustments for the funds flow statement.

Cash Flows—Independent of Accounting

A point worth repeating is that cash flow is the same in any accounting system. This is seen in the deferred tax example shown in Table 6.2 in Chapter 6. Notice that the calculated cash flow will be precisely the same *regardless of whether one uses the tax statements or the stockholder report* to measure the cash inflows. Cash flows are equal, in that example, to net income plus depreciation plus the increase (or minus the decrease) in the deferred tax liability.

Criticism of Method One
Dissatisfaction with the Funds Statement

Criticisms of Format and Implementation.   The existing indirect method funds flow statement, which we shall call method one, has been criticized on a variety of grounds. Some have indicated that the format of current funds flow statements is so different from the income statement that it is difficult to relate the two. Others have pointed out that a variety of refinements should be made to the simple indirect formula so that a more accurate funds flow number is presented—regardless of whether the bottom line is changes in working capital or changes in cash and equivalent.

Working Capital as a Bottom Line.   Another criticism is the vagueness of the concept of working capital flows. It is not easy to grasp exactly what that notion is. It is clearly not part of the cash-to-cash cycle previously described, and it can be argued that most changes in amounts of various working capital items are too loosely related to income and capital notions to be helpful as a check on the income statement.

The Bottom Line Is Not Important.   It is quite easy to take a funds statement that reconciles to cash and reconstruct it to reconcile to working capital. Usually the information is shown in the funds statement itself and merely needs rearranging. If not, a bit of adding and subtracting of balance sheet items will permit that rearrangement. Thus, in terms of information, the argument for or against one or the other bottom line seems an arid debate.

Method Two: Adjusted Indirect Flows—An Easy Improvement

Custom and inertia are likely to perpetuate the prevailing indirect method for some time. However, its implied cash flows can be brought closer to actual cash flows by a series of adjustments that will bring it from a rough approximation to a reasonably close estimate.

The conventional indirect method assumes that there are no lags and leads between the times that accrual revenues and expenses are recorded and when cash is actually received or paid out. Clearly, that is not true. Accrual accounting deliberately moves revenues and expenses out of the periods in which the cash flows occurred. Some of the lags and leads are identifiable and can be used to the first approximation to make it a bit more accurate. For example, accounts receivable outstanding at the beginning of the year are usually uncollected revenues of the previous year or years. If the receivables are classified as "current" it is reasonable to assume that they fall due and are collected during the following year. The estimate of cash flows can be improved by adding to the revenues the accounts receivable outstanding at the beginning of the year.

Accounts receivable outstanding at the end of the year are amounts that were probably reported as revenue during the year but have not yet been collected. Thus, the revenues had a cash shortfall equal to the accounts receivable outstanding at year end. Making adjustments of this sort converts method one, the indirect method, into method two, an adjusted indirect method.

A wide variety of such adjustments can be made. Some are discussed below in connection with the third method. The point is that even the crude indirect method can be adjusted to improve the cash flow estimate. The analyst would still be dealing with *net* cash inflows, rather than the gross numbers. In that respect, the result is less than optimum, but the increased accuracy is worth the effort involved.

Method Three Is Preferred

A Direct Method of Estimating a Cash-Based Income Statement

Although the above-mentioned adjustments can be made to improve the net cash flow number provided by the indirect method, they can also be used to approximate the direct method. This cash flow statement focuses more closely on actual cash inflows and outflows and displays them in a format similar to an ordinary income statement.

A worksheet for this method is illustrated in Figure 7.1. The figure is a form that might be suitable for a manufacturing company that has revenues, a little interest income, and perhaps a foreign currency translation adjustment gain or loss arising from cash or equivalents.

Its expense categories include:

- Selling, general, and administrative costs (SG&A)
- Cost of goods sold (COGS)
- Depreciation and amortization

Cash Inflows from Ordinary Operations:
1. Revenues .... _____
2. Less Increase in Accounts Receivable .... _____
3. Plus Decrease in Accounts Receivable.............. _____
4. Plus Interest Income .... _____
5. Less Noncash Interest Income .... _____
6. Plus Amortization of Bond Premium .... _____
7. Plus Dividends from Equity Method Investees... _____
8. Plus Cash and Equivalent Portion of Foreign
   Currency Translation Adjustment Gain .... _____
9.   Total Cash Inflows From Operations .... ==========

Cash Outflows from Ordinary Operations:
10. Selling, General and Administrative Expense .... _____
11. Cost of Goods Sold .... _____
12. Plus Increase in Inventories........................... _____
13. Less Decrease in Inventories........................... _____
14. Less Increase in Accounts Payable .... _____
15. Plus Decrease in Accounts Payable.................. _____
16. Plus Increase in Prepaid Expenses.................. _____
17. Less Decrease in Prepaid Expenses .... _____
18. Less Increase in Accrued Liabilities.................. _____
19. Plus Decrease in Accrued Liabilities................. _____
20. Plus Increase in Other Noncash, Nontax
    Current Assets .... _____
21. Less Decrease in Other Noncash, Nontax
    Current Assets .... _____
22. Plus Cash and Equivalent Portion of Foreign
    Currency Translation Loss........................... _____
23.   Total Cash Outflows for Expenses before
      Interest and Income Taxes .... ==========

24. Net Cash Flow from Operations before Interest
    and Income Taxes (line 9 − line 23) .... ==========

Cash Outflows for Interest Costs:
25. Interest Expense .... _____
26. Less Accretion of Interest Discount................. _____
27. Plus Interest Capitalized............................... _____
28.   Total Cash Outflows for Interest Costs .... ==========

Figure 7.1.   Approximation of a cash basis income statement.

Cash Outflows for Income Tax Expense:
29. Income Tax Expense................................. _____
30. Less Increase in Deferred Tax Liability............ _____
31. Plus Decrease in Deferred Tax Liability........... _____
32. Less Increase in Income Taxes Payable .... _____
33. Plus Decrease in Income Taxes Payable........... _____
34.   Total Cash Outflow for Income Taxes .... ═════════════

35.   Cash Flows from Operations Available for
      Dividends, Capital Expenditures, and Debt
      Repayment (lines 24 − 28 − 34)................ ═════════════

Investments:
36. Purchases of Plant and Equipment .... _____
37. Less Interest Capitalized .... _____
38. Less Net Disposition of Plant and Equipment.... _____
39   Total Investments...................................... ═════════════

Cash Raised Through Financing:
40. Sale of Bonds... _____
41. Less Note Maturity....................................... _____
42. Exercise of Stock Options.............................. _____
43. Less Decrease in Bank Loans........................ _____
44. Sale of Commercial Paper .... _____
45.   Total Cash Raised by Financing................... ═════════════

46.   Dividends Paid.. ═════════════

47.   Net Increase in Cash and Equivalent (lines
      35 −39 − 45 − 46) .... ═════════════

Figure 7.1   (Continued)

Because the company borrows money, it has interest expense, some of which has been capitalized. The company has income tax expense, but part of that is deferred because of tax timing differences. The company makes investments in plant and equipment, sells off some used equipment, and even pays a few dividends to its stockholders.

The example starts with the accrual numbers from the income statement, and attempts to adjust each item from an accrual to a *cash* basis. If an income statement line item does not involve current cash flows, it is ignored. The intended result is a cash basis income statement. The model is like government accounting in that expenditures replace expenses.

A Parallel to the Income Statement

Figure 7.1 shows some similarity of format to the ordinary income statement, although differences exist. Information from the balance sheet, the present funds statement, the footnotes, and the 10-Ks is used. The outline of this particular format is:

Revenues and gains

    Less expenses and losses, excluding interest and taxes

Equals cash from operations before interest and taxes

    Less interest

    Less income taxes

Equals internally generated free cash

    Less cash spent for investments

Plus cash raised through financing

    Less dividends paid

Equals net increase in cash and equivalent

In the forthcoming paragraphs we will examine Figure 7.1. line by line, explaining the adjustments made, and reasons for them. Figure 7.1 is not a standardized form that would apply to every company. It is, instead, simply an example that sets forth certain assumptions, methods, and principles for adjusting line items to bring them closer to the actual cash flows. Yet, many industrial companies can be fitted into the form with little or no adjustment.

Cash Inflows from Ordinary Operations

Revenues and Gains and Their Adjustments. Figure 7.1 begins with the revenues as presented on the income statement. If all sales were made for cash, the revenue number would be exactly equal to the revenue cash flow. Most companies do not sell only for cash, but have a certain amount of accounts receivable from credit sales.

Accounts Receivable.   The accrual revenues should also be adjusted for the accounts receivable outstanding at the beginning and the end of the year. Note that we have made assumptions about the accounts receivable, some of which will prove to be incorrect. For example, we assumed that the receivables outstanding at the beginning of the year would be collected during the year. In some cases, such as long-term contracting, such an assumption would be inappropriate and would be rejected by an analyst. The assumptions underlying the adjustments suggested for methods two and three are not heroic, and the reader will find them to be sufferable. They do not appear in practice to create significant errors.

The Accounts Receivable Shortcut.   Since our procedure calls for us to add the accounts receivable held at the beginning of the year and subtract those held at the end of the year, our form uses a shortcut— only the changes in accounts receivable from the beginning to the end of the year are dealt with. If the change is an increase (line 2), it should be subtracted from accrual revenue to get the cash revenue number. Similarly, a decrease in accounts receivable (line 3) over the year results in an addition. The analyst may wish to review the allowance for doubtful accounts in Schedule VIII of the 10-K.

Interest Income.   Line 4 shows that the company has interest income. Some interest income may not involve any cash during the period involved. If the company has bought bonds at a discount, the accrual interest income would include accretion of interest which is not a cash flow and would not be collected until maturity. Thus we should subtract any noncash interest income (line 5). Similarly, accrual accounting would amortize a premium paid for a bond, reducing the reported interest income to a level below the actual cash received. Thus, one should add back the amortization of bond premium (line 6).

Dividends.   This company has some nonconsolidated subsidiaries accounted for using the equity method. The retained earnings are of no interest to us, since they do not represent a cash flow to the company. Thus, line 7 lists as cash income only the dividends actually received during the year—not the equity income from the income statement.

Gains.   Line 8 calls for the addition of any increase in *cash and equivalent* that came about by foreign currency translation adjustment gains. (This statement treats such gains as revenues and such losses as expenses.) If a company operates abroad and holds variously denominated cash and equivalent, translation gains and losses are an ordinary and recurring result of its business.

   Foreign currency translation gains and losses are as properly recorded in operating results as are transaction gains and losses, which also result from currency fluctuations. In addition, it does not seem fruitful to divide *translation* results among operating, financing and investing categories for the following reasons:

1. Similar *transaction* results are not divided among those categories.
2. The accrual income statement (with which this cash statement will be compared) makes no such adjustment.
3. The necessary information to make the separation is mostly unavailable.

It may very difficult for the analyst to estimate, but ideally the estimate is required because it represents a cash inflow.

   Many other types of gains and losses may occur, some involving cash and others not. For example, provision for restructuring is often a loss that occurs prior to any cash outflows; a gain or loss on litigation is often accompanied by an immediate cash flow.

Cash Revenue.   Summing these various revenue and gain items gives the total cash inflows from operations (line 9).

Cash Outflows from Ordinary Operations

Ordinary Cash Expenses.   We now examine the income statement for those line items that include substantial cash outflows. Line 10 is Selling, General, and Administrative expense. Line 11 is Cost of Goods Sold.

Exclude Depreciation and Noncash Charges.   Remember that depreciation, usually a noncash expense, may be shown as a single line item on the income statement, or it may be divided among SG&A, Cost of Goods Sold, and capitalized items. The analyst is advised to compare the depreciation number shown in the income statement with that in the funds statement, the footnotes, and in Schedule VI of the 10-K. Often this comparison provides clues as to the amount of depreciation that is in inventories or that is included under some other title in the income statement. If found, depreciation should be deducted from the appropriate line items of cash expense. The treatment of depreciation and interest under capital leases should be examined to determine that the cash outflows for rent are included in and apportioned properly between cash operating expense and cash interest expense.

Changes in Inventories.   An increase in inventories represents an implied cash outflow in excess of the cost of goods sold. Thus, over the year, increases in inventories increase cash outflows (line 12), and decreases reduce cash outflows (line 13). (However, depreciation that is capitalized in inventory does not require a current cash outflow, as mentioned in the previous paragraph.)

Changes in Accounts Payable.   If accounts payable have increased during the course of the year, expenses or losses have probably been recorded in the income statement but have not yet been paid for in cash; that is, they are not yet cash expenses. Thus, an increase in accounts payable (line 14) is assumed to reduce cash outflows, and a decrease (line 15) to increase cash outflows.

The analyst will recognize that all accounts payable do not arise from operations. Accounts payable could occur because of the purchase on credit of a new machine, which is part of investment activities rather than operations. Fortunately, that is the exception, and our assumption will be valid from a practical viewpoint.

Prepaid Expenses.   If expenses are prepaid, cash has been paid out, but the expense has not yet been recorded in the income statement. Thus, a year-to-year increase in prepaid expenses is a net cash outflow (line 16), whereas a decrease (line 17) is a net cash inflow. In the latter case, an expense recorded during the period had been paid for in an earlier period.

Accrued Current Liabilities.   If a liability has been accrued, an expense has been incurred but not yet paid for. Thus, an increase in accrued liabilities during the year (line 18) reduces cash outflows, whereas a decrease (line 19) increases them. Some authorities have recommended that prepaid expenses and accrued liabilities be associated with selling, general, and administrative expenses and that the inventory and accounts payable adjustments should be associated with cost of goods sold.[3] Although these relationships may often be correct the distinction doesn't seem worthwhile.

Other Liabilities.   If other current liabilities increase, say, salaries payable, excluding taxes and borrowings, which are treated below, the assumption is that the increased liability was an avoidance of cash outflow for an expense. It should be subtracted from cash outflows (line 20).

---

[3]Robert Morris Associates, *RMA Uniform Credit Analysis*, I.M.D. Learning Systems, Inc., Oakland, Calif., 1982, pp. 26–30.

Similarly, decreases in other current nonfinancing liability accounts (line 21) are presumed to have incurred cash outflows that have not yet become an expense.

Many noncurrent liabilities other than long-term debt and deferred tax liabilities are financial rather than operating in nature. Often they are identified as such—for example, lease obligations—and therefore should not be considered reductions in cash expense. Further information may have to be sought from the company when the amounts are significant and the details sparse.

Foreign Currency Translation Adjustment Losses. Having treated foreign currency translation adjustment gains from cash and equivalent holdings as cash revenues, losses from such holdings should be considered a part of cash expense (line 22).

Operating Cash Flows. These expenses and their adjustments are totaled on line 23. When line 23 (cash expenses) is subtracted from line 9 (cash revenues), the result is cash flow from operations before interest and income taxes (line 24). This is a key number to compare with its counterpart—operating income—in the income statement, especially the total amounts over long periods.

Cash Outflows for Interest Costs

Interest cost is examined separately, as we consider it to be outside of operating expenses. We record first the interest expense shown in the income statement (line 25). However, if bonds were issued at a discount, a part of interest expense will be the bookkeeping accretion of the discount, which is not a cash outflow. Thus, on line 26 the accretion of interest discount is subtracted. (The amount would be added if it were amortization of a premium over par.)

Capitalized Interest. A company which acquires plant and equipment that requires time for construction or acquisition is required to capitalize interest incurred during the acquisition period. This capitalized interest is normally a cash outflow (line 27) and, if so, should be added to interest expense to obtain (line 28) the total cash outflows for interest. (Note that the capitalized interest will later be eliminated from capital expenditures.)

Cash Outflows for Income Tax Expense

Income Tax Expense. This number is taken directly from the income statement. However, this is not necessarily the amount paid to the government. If there were an increase in the deferred tax liability, that increase was not paid during the year, and should be subtracted from income tax expense. If deferred taxes (line 31) decreased, that amount would represent a cash outflow and should be added to taxes paid.

An increase in income taxes currently payable represents taxes owed but not yet paid, which is a reduction in cash outflow for income taxes (line 32). A decrease (line 33) should be added to tax cash outflows because it represents payments greater than the tax expense. Line 34 is the sum of all tax items resulting in cash outflows.

Line 35 is the cash inflows from operations after taxes and interest. It represents the cash flows available for dividends, capital expenditures, and debt repayment. This is another key line for comparison with the income statement.

Investments

Capital Expenditures. Acquisitions of plant and equipment are presumed to be cash outflows and are shown on line 36. These figures include capitalized interest that has already been recorded in the interest cash outflows, and therefore capitalized interest should be deducted here (line 37). In adddition, if the company has disposed of any of its plant and equipment, the net cash received is treated as a reduction in cash outflows for investment (line 38). We consider disinvestment to offset investment. Note that the gains or losses on dispositions are not cash flows and do not change the cash revenue or expense numbers. Line 39 sums the various investment cash flows.

Financing Activities

Financing transactions are almost by definition immediate sources or uses of cash. Thus, lines 40 through 45 are self-explanatory. Selling securities brings in cash. Retiring them requires a cash outflow. Care should be taken to include bond premiums as proceeds of sales, and discounts as reductions thereof.

Operating lease transactions should be treated as financings if the leased asset is treated as an investment. They do not ordinarily involve immediate cash flows (other than rent), and a case can be made for excluding both. Treat the leased asset and the lease obligation consistently. That is, they should be treated as one of the following:

1. A cash equivalent transaction, in which the asset is an investment and the lease obligation a borrowing

2. A noncash exchange (both items are left out of the table)

Although the arguments for either treatment seem fairly evenly balanced, we incline toward including both items because the rent expense will surely be included among cash expenses.

Dividends

Line 46 shows the dividends paid to preferred and common stockholders.

The Bottom Line

Line 47 sums up the cash flow results for the period. Ideally, this number will turn out to be precisely equal to the change in cash and equivalent shown on the balance sheet, but that seldom happens. If the difference is relatively small, it is easiest to put in a plug item increasing or decreasing the operating expense cash outflows. Errors and omissions are less likely in the revenues, financing and investing activities, or dividends paid.

The Customized Approach

Figure 7.1 presents an exercise in converting accrual numbers into cash numbers. It is a simple example with a deliberately brief explanation of the recommended approach that we could have complicated by adding other transactions. For example, if the company in the example used LIFO calculation and had had a liquidation of lower-cost inventories, the cost of goods sold would have been less, but cash outflow would not have been reduced. The analyst would reduce the calculated cash outflow for cost of goods sold by the amount of the layer invasion. Similarly, if there were a large increase in the reserve for doubtful accounts, the analyst would adjust the amount of increase or decrease in accounts receivable to indicate that the change had nothing to do with cash flows from revenues but was a matter of bookkeeping entries.

Our point is that no book could cover all the adjustments that might be needed. Preparing a table along the lines of Figure 7.1 is an exercise in financial analysis, not a set of inflexible rules. The general model is simply to:

1. Begin with those accrual items that imply cash flows

2. Make all logical adjustments to bring them closer to actual cash flows

Each company analysis is customized to reflect its particular mix of transactions.

The application of the general model begins with the assumption that ordinary revenues and expenses are cash flows. The familiar noncash expenses—depreciation, amortization, deferred taxes, and the like— are assumed *not* to be cash flows and do not enter into the model unless a cash flow is indicated. Here are a few reminders of a general nature:

1. The acquisition of any asset except cash is assumed to require a cash outflow.

2. The incurrence of a liability is a net cash inflow, because it is a borrowing, or it can be presumed to be an avoidance of a cash outflow.

3. Increases and decreases in asset carrying amounts are handled on a situational basis, because some of those changes result from changes in prices rather than cash flows (for example, certain marketable securities and noncash assets and liabilities of foreign subsidiaries using functional currencies other than the dollar).

4. The carrying amounts of other assets and liabilities may change as a result of changes in valuation accounts, such as the depreciation account. Such changes do not represent cash inflows or outflows and should be handled like foreign exchange rate changes.

5. Only the effect of foreign exchange rate changes on cash and equivalents should be treated as a cash inflow or outflow—not the entire translation adjustment.

Analysis of Funds Statements Prepared by Method Three

Compare Longer Periods of Time

The cash flow statements for perhaps a 10-year period should be added together, which eliminates by cancellation many of the leads and lags caused by the timing differences between accrual and cash accounting. When these numbers are compared with the numbers in a 10-year summation of the income statement, many of the major line items will be of the same general magnitude, giving the analyst some comfort about the income statement. Certainly, revenues, cost of goods sold plus selling, general, and administrative expense (excluding depreciation), financing, and dividends should compare well. Note that in a 10-year study, only the balance sheet changes from the beginning of the first year to the end of the last year are necessary. The intervening year-to-year changes cancel out.

The Comparison of Depreciation and Capital Expenditures

A comparison of depreciation (from the income statement) with cash capital expenditures has interesting implications. Perhaps the analyst's biggest challenge will be to determine what part of the capital expenditures over the 10-year period are to be considered replacement of departed capital—a counterpart of depreciation and amortization—and what part represents an increase in the capital base. Capital expenditures that increase efficiency or capacity are viewed differently than replacement of old capacity. The increases in the capital base are a part of income.

The leading question is "Did the capital expenditures improve earning power, hold it at the original level, or were they so inadequate as to permit earning power to decline?" Analysts who find an answer to that question can probably estimate an amount of the capital expenditures made that merely serve to replace the exhausted and obsolete plant. Those expenditures, like depreciation, assure maintenance of capital. Any additional expenditures for plant and equipment, unless they were somehow wasted, represent something akin to income—to being "better off."

Estimating Conventional Income from a Method Three Statement

Similarly, increases in working capital usually contribute to an improvement in the welfare of the company. In estimating conventional income from the cash-based statement, working capital increases should be included. The income estimated from the cash flow statement would be the sum of the following less net financing:

- Increase in cash items
- Dividends paid
- Capital expenditures (in excess of those needed for capital maintenance) and other investments
- Other increases in working capital

Estimating Distributable Income

However, if the analyst is seeking distributable income, that part of any increase in working capital that is needed to do a constant volume of business should not be included in income. (A variation of the distributable income idea would adjust for increases in the company's ability to borrow to finance the increased working capital needs.) The distributable income approaches have gained more attention from United Kingdom investors than those in the United States, perhaps due to greater exposure to the ideas.

At this point a comparison of the 10-year cash flow statement with the income statement can begin to focus on income from both perspectives. If the two statements tell widely disparate stories, the accrual income number cannot be considered to be confirmed.

Comparison of the Three Methods

Three approaches to a funds statement have been discussed in this chapter:

1. The conventional funds statement, using the indirect method
2. The indirect method adjusted to reflect the implied cash flows that are suggested by analysis of the two balance sheets and other data
3. The direct method that begins with the revenues and expenses in a quasi-income statement format and makes the same adjustments suggested for the second method

Method One Is Familiar and Relatively Labor-free

The conventional funds statement has the advantage of familiarity. It requires little or no labor, other than perhaps rearranging the numbers to fit the analyst's preferred format. Its disadvantage is that it cannot be put in a format that parallels that of the income statement and is therefore more difficult to compare with the income statement. The first method does not even attempt to deal with cash flows. Instead, it handles the accrual accounting numbers. The accrual system deliberately moves revenues and expenses away from the periods in which the cash flows took place, to the degree that such changes are needed to "match" revenues and expenses. To call the resulting funds flow a "cash flow" requires an assumption that exactly the same amounts of revenues and expenses were transferred in or out of the period under study. This could only occur by happenstance.

Methods Two and Three Seek the Actual Cash Flows

In contrast, the second and third methods are attempts to capture the actual cash flows that occurred during the period. To the degree that they succeed, the analysis will provide more reliable numbers, more understandable numbers.

Differences between the Second and Third Methods

In one respect, the second and third methods are the same: All adjustments that are appropriate for one are also appropriate for the other. The difference is just that the second method begins with the first approximation of funds flow by the indirect method and is an estimate of the net cash inflow: It adds net income to the expense items that are not cash outflows. It assumes that the net income and noncash expenses will equal the portion of cash revenues that are net cash inflows.

Method three, however, will reach the same net cash flow number but begins with the gross cash flows—the approximation of revenues and expenses on a cash basis. Taking that additional step has the advantages of

1. Ensuring that the revenues are actual cash flows so that the second method's assumption is fulfilled

2. Presenting the information in a format that is much more comparable to the traditional income statement format

The latter point is important because one of the major uses of the funds flow statement is to confirm, over time, the income statement. An additional advantage of method three is the ability to determine income on several different bases. For example, a cash income number can be derived based on:

- Conventional income notions from an analyst's viewpoint of the increase in net assets

- Distributable income notions

- Income on a liquidating basis

Method Three's Distributable Income Is Controversial

The distributable income notion associated with the direct method of calculating has been criticized because it excludes some of or all the increase in working capital. In a liquidation situation, an increase in working capital is an increase in net assets and in the expected liquidating value. For that analysis, of course, working capital changes are income items.

However, from the viewpoint of a going concern, changes in working capital are a part of management's deliberate operating decisions or a result of the operating environment in which the company does business. Thus, either the changes in working capital were necessary to achieve the operating results, or they were the casualties and windfalls of the operating environment. It appears logical to consider those working capital demands as part of operations when studying the cash flow dynamics of a company. At the same time, using a more conventional view of the ongoing firm, it seems appropriate to recognize in the analysis of income the benefits of those changes to overall profits.

Technical Difficulties of Methods Two and Three

Some have critized methods two and three because certain technical difficulties exist in their application. The most significant of these technical difficulties occurs when there is a change in the reporting entity, that is, when mergers, acquisitions, spinoffs, divestitures, and the like take place between the beginning and the end of the year. Those events do cause analytical problems, not only for the funds statement but for all other analysis of the surviving company. In most cases, there is enough information in the annual report and the 10-Ks for the analyst to cope with those problems.[4] The analyst may have to go to the company for additional information to complete the analysis, but regular company contact is a routine part of an analyst's activities.

Comparisons of inventory and cost of goods sold, particularly in LIFO layer invasion situations, are technically difficult, but, again, the same problems must be faced in the regular income statements.

---

[4]Ralph E. Drtina and James A. Largay, III, "Pitfalls in Calculating Cashflow from Operations," *The Accounting Review*, vol. 60, no. 2, April 1985, pp. 314–326.

Method Three Is Preferred

The analyst should use the direct method, if possible. No more work is involved in the third method than in the second, but the benefits of grossing up expenses and revenues for analysis gives the third method an informational advantage. Clearly, using the first method will avoid a considerable amount of effort on the part of the analyst. The analyst overburdened with responsibility for too large a number of companies may not have time to apply the third method, and the first method does provide useful information. However, in every case of analysis of underwritings, leveraged buyouts, speculative fixed-income financing, takeover and acquisition candidates, other similar analyses, and meeting due diligence requirements, the third method should be used.

Confusion between Income and Cash Flows

Cash Flow as a Substitute for Income

The heavy emphasis on cash flows (as opposed to earnings and income notions) by a few writers, analysts, and managements, especially in the real estate industry, has led some to believe that certain industries should not use depreciation in calculating earnings. That capital maintenance notion is unacceptable because it does not maintain the capital invested in the item to be depreciated. At the same time, one can understand the frustration of many in the real estate business because accounting does not fully reveal the values of their properties. Many companies in the real estate field present supplementary current value balance sheets and income statements, and we consider these to be helpful.

The Real Estate Industry Encourages a Cash Flow Focus

The problem in the real estate business is that the whole is often worth more than the sum of the parts. When a real estate development company builds a shopping center, initially it is worth just about what it costs for construction and land acquisition. However, when one combines that project with favorable long-term financing, a 95 percent occupancy rate with stable high-grade tenants and heavy retail traffic flow, the property suddenly becomes worth a good deal more than its mere acquisition cost. This additional worth, of course, is reflected in improving rentals and a high return on original cost. Many in the real estate industry, however, feel that some of or all the enhanced value should be reflected as income, preferably by excluding depreciation and certain other expenses from the income statement. Some would include the increased rents and also the unrealized gain on the value of the property that resulted from the increased rents. This is a sort of double counting.

Example. A booklet issued by Koger Partnership, Ltd., states:

> Cash flow is the accepted, professional measurement of the performance and value of income-producing real estate, used by lending institutions, tax assessors, appraisers and others engaged in the real estate field. Cash flow represents earnings before non-cash charges for depreciation, amortization of deferred property costs, provision for deferred income taxes, etc.
>
> Cash flow is a major consideration in the purchase, ownership and sale of commercial real estate.
>
> Cash flow is used for the payment of mortgage amortization, future expansion and other corporate purposes, and to make distributions to investors.
>
> Net earnings are not considered by real estate professionals as the important measure of results for income-producing properties. Ideally, real estate net earnings should approach zero, as the earnings are reduced by non-cash accounting entries and protected from taxes.

Example. The 1985 Annual Report of McCormick & Company, Inc., entitles a chart "Profitability" (p. 15). The vertical bars are described as "net income before financial charges, depreciation and amortization" with a footnote that they are also exclusive of loss from Mexican peso devaluations (1982). Its subsidiary, McCormick Properties, Inc., lists operational cash flow of $10.89 million for 1985, with a footnote as follows: "Operational cash flow is defined as net income plus depreciation, other non-cash charges and deferred taxes (excluding tax benefits from leveraged automobile leases) minus after-tax profit from improved property sales and scheduled mortgaged payments."

Is Depreciation a Necessary Cost?

To test the implication that depreciation is not a proper cost, see the data shown in Table 7.1 for the *Value Line Industrial Composite* from 1977 through 1986. The composite's comparative showing on a cash income basis (up 87.5 percent) is somewhat better than on the customary net income basis (up 47.5 percent). The issue is not the relative movement of the two but whether a cash income basis has a sound capital maintenance notion behind it. Cumulative capital expenditures during the 10-year period were $40.90 per share, or 89 percent of the total cash income. It is hard to imagine that a significant portion of those capital expenditures

Table 7.1. Per-Share Cash Income and Net Income from *Value Line Industrial Composite*

	1977 to 1986*	1977	1986*
Cash income	$45.82	$ 3.04	$ 5.70
Depreciation and amortization	21.06	1.21	3.00
Net income	24.76	1.83	2.70
Net worth		13.10	23.05

* The fourth quarter of 1986 is partly estimated.
NOTE: Cash income here is taken to be net income plus depreciation and amortization.
SOURCE: *The Value Line Investment Survey, Part 2, Selection and Opinion*, February 13, 1987, p. 691.

were not replacements of plant and equipment that was worn out or technologically or economically obsolete. If only half the expenditures were for replacement, rather than expansion or greater efficiency, the necessary depreciation would have been just about the $21.06 actually charged to expense using the conventional net income approach.

No one questions the importance of cash flow—it is required to service debt and finance future growth, and it is the best predictor of the future stream of dividends. However, we reject the notion that cash flows should be thought of as being the same as earnings.

8

Results of Subsidiaries, Affiliates, and Foreign Operations

Consolidation of Results

Affiliates and Subsidiaries Defined

A subsidiary is generally defined as a company controlled by a so-called parent company which owns more than half the voting stock. (Most subsidiaries, however, are 100 percent owned by the parent.) Affiliate is a less definite term. An affiliate may be a company effectively controlled—perhaps jointly with others—though ownership may be less than 50 percent. Or the relationship may exist through control of both companies by the same owning group or parent, with resultant close commercial or operating ties. In some cases a company may be called an affiliate but really be a subsidiary.

Provision of Consolidated Reports

The great majority of companies publish consolidated reports which include in the balance sheet and income statement the results and financial position of their subsidiaries. The earnings or net equity applicable to other stockholders, if any, are shown as a deduction of minority interests. Such consolidated reports usually have no reason to distinguish results attributable to one corporate unit or another. The matter may become important, however, when a company elects to publish an unconsolidated (or "parent company only") statement or when a so-called consolidated statement excludes certain important subsidiaries or affiliates.

Foreign Activities Are Sometimes Excluded

A large area for variation in reported results—and for possible correction or adjustment by the analyst—lies in the field of foreign operations, including those of subsidiaries and branches. For a number of our larger corporations such foreign operations are of major consequence, and their proper evaluation presents a challenge both of technique and of judgment to the securities analyst. We shall first discuss the treatment of domestic subsidiaries and affiliates, and then pass over to the foreign field.

Domestic Subsidiaries and Affiliates

Deduction of Minority Interest from Net Income

Where 50 percent or more of the voting stock of a subsidiary or affiliate is owned, the standard procedure is to consolidate the subsidiary, with a one-line entry on the balance sheet for the minority interest usually placed below other liabilities but above stockholders' equity. The minority equity in net income is shown as a one-line item in the income statement as a deduction, so that the amount shown as net income is the amount applicable to shareholders of the parent only.

Use of the Equity Method for Twenty to Fifty Percent Owned Affiliates

Where the parent owns less than 50 percent but as much as 20 percent of the voting stock, the equity method of accounting is normally used. Ownership of 20 to 49 percent of the voting stock presumably gives the parent significant influence over financial and operating policies.

The equity method shows in the income statement the proportionate interest, after taxes, in the net income of the affiliate. The investment in the affiliate is carried on the balance sheet also as a one-line item that is adjusted up or down to reflect the proportionate interest in retained earnings or in losses. The investor's net income and stockholders' equity are intended to be the same under the equity method as they would have been if the affiliate had been consolidated. Intercompany profits and losses are eliminated. If an investor's share of losses exceeds the carrying amount, the investor discontinues applying the equity method and the investment is reduced to zero. Any additional losses are ignored unless the investor has made financial commitments to support the affiliate.

Example. The Universal Leaf Tobacco Company, Inc., owns (1) *subsidiaries* in which there are minority interests and (2) *affiliates* in which the holdings are 20 percent or more. Table 8.1 is an abbreviated 1985 income statement showing the treatment of minority interests and equity income.

Table 8.1. Universal Leaf Tobacco Co., Inc. Condensed Income Statement, Year to December 31, 1985 (In Millions of Dollars)

Revenues	1,078.9
Costs and Expenses	1,030.3
Income before Income Taxes and Other Items	48.5
Income Taxes	13.3
	35.2
Minority Interests	0.2
Income from Consolidated Operations	35.0
Equity in Net Income of Unconsolidated Affiliates	10.9
Income from Continuing Operations	45.9
Income from Discontinued Operations	0.5
Net Income	46.4

The Universal Leaf Tobacco presentation is fairly typical of the income statement format used by most companies for their equity method investees. The company's accounts reflect that the presumption of influence can be overcome. Footnote 1 reads, in part, "However, due to the inaccessability of certain financial information and exchange controls which restrict the remittance of dividends, our affiliate in Zimbabwe is accounted for under the cost method. A Mexican affiliate is also accounted for under the cost method since the company does not exercise significant influence over its financial and operating policies." Universal's consolidation policies, however, are somewhat unusual. Although the parent company is primarily engaged in the tobacco business, it fully consolidates its Lawyer's Title Insurance Corporation subsidiary. The resulting balance sheet is somewhat difficult to analyze. The balance sheet is classified, showing current assets of $188.8 million and current liabilities of $148.8 million. The current ratio (current assets divided by current liabilities) is rather low for a company in the tobacco industry, but the details of the current assets and liabilities reveal the heavy influence of the current portion of policy and contract claims and of insurance customer advances and deposits. The apparent weakness in the net current asset position is more than offset by the presence of a $100.7 million investment portfolio which is shown as a noncurrent asset on the balance sheet, separate from the $47.4 million equity in net assets of and advances to consolidated affiliates.

Example. Schlumberger Ltd. includes the pro rata share of revenues and expenses of Dowell Schlumberger, a 50 percent owned oil field services business, in the individual captions in the consolidated statement of income. This presentation is uncommon. The balance sheet treatment of the subsidiary is on the equity method.

Cost Methods

Investments in less than 20 percent of the voting stock are assumed to be purely investments and are usually carried at the lower of cost or market value, or on the cost method, which does not recognize losses unless they are deemed permanent.

The cost and the lower of cost or market methods recognize only dividend income. Note that the retained earnings of an investment carried on one of the cost methods are not reflected in the investor's income, but it would be difficult to say that the investors are not better off for the existence of retained earnings than they would be without them. Some analysts add the retained earnings, if they are known, to the income of the investor, effectively converting those investments to the equity method for income purposes. In their view, control is not the central issue, nor is economic integration, and the earnings simply reflect fully the "better-offness." Other analysts—probably the vast majority—make no explicit adjustment but merely consider the retained earnings of an investment carried on a cost method to be a plus factor in deciding on the attractiveness of the company.

Economic Integration and Use of the Equity Method.   When the business relationship between investor and the investee is a strong one, such as a supply arrangement, the analyst should place the income statement on the equity method. For example, oil companies often form joint ventures to build oil and gas pipelines or gathering systems. While the percentage holding might be small, the equity method seems more appropriate than the cost method in reporting the results of such integrated activities.

The Potential to Control.   The analyst should look for the presence of potential control as well as existing control. When the parent does not wish to carry an investment on the equity or consolidated method, it is quite simple to have some other party own the nominal equity while the parent holds warrants, options, convertibles, or contractual agreements that ensure control whenever the company chooses to obtain it. Some abuses of accounting have occurred in recent years in such areas of nonconsolidation as start-up subsidiaries, grantor trusts, and research and development partnerships. Particular care should be given to the footnotes on related party transactions, which will usually reveal such matters as

- Interlocking directorates
- Business relationships
- Other evidence of economic interests and unity

In addition to the footnotes to the financial statements, information on related party transactions and business relationships is provided in prospectuses, the proxy statements, and in the 10-K and other SEC filings.

Exclusion of Domestic Subsidiaries' Results

In general, consolidated financial statements are considered more useful than a mere parent company statement. Many companies, however, do not consolidate certain subsidiaries because they are not homogeneous or because of other special circumstances. For example, it is not usual for a manufacturing company to consolidate financial subsidiaries such as

- Banks
- Finance companies
- Leasing companies
- Savings and loan associations
- Insurance companies

Inclusion or Exclusion of Finance and Leasing Subsidiaries—A Contentious Issue

Large makers and sellers of durable goods and capital goods often have subsidiary finance and leasing companies to handle installment sales and leases of such products. It is customary to include the full results of such operations as a single line item in the income statement but not to consolidate the individual asset and liability classes in the balance sheet.

On or Off the Balance Sheet? The issue of consolidation or noncon solidation of finance subsidiaries is controversial. In general, the earnings of a wholly owned finance or leasing subsidiary are included in the net income of the parent company, barring extremely unusual circumstances. The disagreement lies in the proper handling of the balance sheet. If the subsidiaries are carried on the cost or on the equity method,ratios such as return on invested capital and return on total assets may appear to be higher than if there were full consolidation of the assets and liabilities on the balance sheet. At the same time, it is argued that finance companies have relatively huge liabilities to banks and others and that their inclusion in the financial statement of the parent would distort the normal credit ratios for manufacturing and distributing concerns.

Parent Guarantees of Subsidiary Debt—Is It Really Parent Debt? Several points should be considered by the analyst. First, in most cases the parent gives substantial assurances to creditors of the finance subsidiary so that the debt of the subsidiary is effectively guaranteed by the parent. Most banks would not lend to highly leveraged finance companies without such guarantees. Thus, one of the issues is "off-balance-sheet financing," where the parent is obligated to see that payments are made but shows no debt on its balance sheet..

The parent's assurances to the lender may be expressed in terms that do not make the commitment an obvious liability. A guaranty that the parent will not allow the subsidiary's cash balance or its working capital to fall below a prescribed level is effectively a guaranty to pay the subsidiary's debt if the subsidiary fails to do so. The parent may also be obligated by circumstances, for example when it depends on the subsidiary's good financial health for distribution of products or to obtain critical parts or raw materials.

Comparability. A second aspect is that comparisons between companies that do and do not consolidate are not possible on a truly comparable basis. However, companies with or without a finance subsidiary may (1) borrow from banks or the commercial paper market to finance their receivables or (2) simply sell their receivables, with or without recourse, to banks and other investors. The problem of comparability persists, regardless of the consolidation issue.

Captive Finance Companies. The picture is further blurred by the differences in the activities of finance and leasing subsidiaries. General

Motors' Acceptance Corporation (GMAC) is a subsidiary of General Motors Corporation. GMAC is essentially a "captive" finance company, set up for the purpose of financing the inventories of the company's dealer network and the installment sales of its automobiles. It is integral to the automotive operations. At times General Motors has made interest-free loans to GMAC so that it can offer bargain interest rates to buyers of General Motors cars. This is a form of price cutting for purposes of increasing auto sales. Where the operations of the two organizations are so closely integrated, separation of the financial statements of the parent and the subsidiary can be considerably distorting and difficult to comprehend. Consolidation is needed.

Stand-Alone Finance Subsidiaries. In other cases, such as General Electric Credit Corporation (GECC), the primary purpose of the finance subsidiary is not to finance the products of the parent, but rather to act as an independent financing and leasing company for purposes of generating profits and tax benefits . The case for consolidation of GECC is less clear than for GMAC, because GECC finances mostly products of other manufacturers.

A third example would be Sears, Roebuck Acceptance which finances a substantial part of Sears, Roebuck's durable goods retail sales but also finances the sales of other manufacturers and engage in other financial activities. In the case of Sears, the consolidation of retailing with such diverse financial activities as Dean Witter (a brokerage house), Sears, Roebuck Acceptance, Allstate Insurance, Coldwell Banker (real estate), and other financial services results in a balance sheet that is terribly confusing. Although the annual reports of Sears, Roebuck are outstanding in their efforts to reduce the confusion, the analyst faces a consolidated balance sheet for which determining the proper ratio of debt-to-equity, current ratio, interest coverage, or whether the cash position is adequate is impossible. About the only useful ratio that could be generated using Sears's balance sheet is return on equity, but that figure could be calculated if the financially oriented subsidiaries were carried on the equity method. There is something comforting in knowing that one has an "all-inclusive" balance sheet. The bothersome question in Sears, Roebuck's case is how to find any possible use for it.

Leasing Subsidiaries—The Same Consolidation Quandary. For a variety of reasons, the activity of leasing buildings and equipment has grown dramatically in the postwar years in response to increasing capital needs caused by inflation, a desire to keep liabilities off the balance sheet, and the ability to transfer tax credits and tax deductions from one company or person to another. In addition, a manufacturer of durable goods that owns a leasing subsidiary may be able to place products more readily through leasing to some customers than through direct sales. Thus, many companies now have leasing subsidiaries, and in most cases they are accounted for by using the equity method rather than by being consolidated. The arguments for and against consolidating finance subsidiaries apply equally to leasing subsidiaries.

Recommended Procedure.   The analyst should consolidate most *captive* finance and leasing companies, if the needed information is available. Where the subsidiary is not a captive, integral to the parent's other operations, the analyst should make the decision on a case-by-case basis. This matter is discussed further in Chapter 23 on the analysis of fixed-income securities.[1]

Treatment of Foreign Operations

Conditions for Deconsolidation

Over the past quarter century the diversity in practice concerning the consolidation of foreign operations has diminished considerably. Immediately after World War II, the foreign exchange markets were in turmoil. Many countries placed severe restrictions, if not absolute bans, on the transfer of foreign currencies across their borders. Those foreign currency difficulties have ameliorated considerably so that in recent years only occasional and short-lived restrictions occur, generally in the less developed countries. Today, a foreign subsidiary is rarely excluded from the consolidated statements except when:

- A similar domestic subsidiary would be excluded
- Genuine problems restrict the movement of currencies so that dividends and other payments cannot be remitted to the parent
- Serious political problems such as revolution, war, and nationalization are occurring

Example.   In 1982 Carnation Company wrote off its Mexican subsidiary and, in 1983, deconsolidated the Mexican operations, although it continued to operate an evaporated milk facility. The reasons for the write-off were currency restrictions, price controls, and uncertainties about the supply of certain key raw materials. A footnote to the 1983 financial statements stated that any earnings would be reflected in the consolidated financial statements if and when dividends were received.

Bear in mind that remittances received from abroad are in general subject to a U.S. income tax equal to the difference between our 34

---

[1] See the unabridged fifth edition of Sidney Cottle, Roger F. Murray, and Frank E. Block, *Graham and Dodd's Security Analysis*, McGraw-Hill, New York, 1988.

percent rate and that imposed on the earnings by the foreign government, in accordance with tax treaties. Percentage differences will vary widely between different countries.

Deferred Taxes on Unremitted Foreign Earnings

Today the larger question for analysts relates to the company's provision, or lack of provision, for deferred income taxes on undistributed foreign earnings.

- Some companies do not provide for deferred taxes on the unremitted earnings of foreign subsidiaries, arguing that no tax will ever be paid because the company intends never to remit the profits. If that is the case, one could question whether the earnings should be consolidated, since apparently the earnings will never benefit the domestic stockholders.

- Some other companies maintain that there are legal ways to return the earnings without incurring any taxes and that no provisions for taxes should be made for that reason. That type of remittance sounds very much like the sort of tax loophole that Congress often becomes concerned about.

- Finally, some companies provide fully for the payment of taxes on the unremitted profits, regardless of whether they have any near-term plans for remitting them.

Example. In 1984 American Express Company sold a Canadian subsidiary and other assets at a gain of $42 million. The company also reported a related $42 million tax expense on undistributed earnings not previously provided for. Since the transaction was voluntary, it is a reminder that the tax cannot always be avoided by structuring the transaction in a particular way. Also, decisions of the past not to distribute foreign earnings can be reversed at any time.

Unremitted Foreign Profits and Related Taxes

The diversity in treatment of this item by corporations presents a problem for security analysts. Clearly, unremitted foreign profits should not be left out of reported net income. But should they be counted at full value, regardless of possible tax liability and transfer difficulties? We think not. Such profits should be taken in, after deducting the estimated taxes that their remittance will incur, only when reasonably assured that remittances can take place in an orderly fashion under the expected exchange control conditions. Such adjustments should be made, of course, only when appreciable amounts are involved.

In general, the analyst should adopt a consistent method of treating such unremitted profits that would not depend on the company's reporting procedure. In addition, the analyst should capitalize foreign earnings at rates which reflect political and exchange risks.

Subsidiaries' Losses

The Sum of the Parts

The matter of subsidiaries' losses raises a special question that can illustrate some of the finer logical points involved in security analysis. We have asserted that both the profits and losses of subsidiaries should be fully accounted for in the parent company's earnings. But is the loss of a subsidiary necessarily a direct offset against the parent company's earnings? Why should a company be worth *less* because it owns something—in this case, an unprofitable interest? Could it not at any time put an end to the loss by selling, liquidating, or even abandoning the subsidiary?

Treat Subsidiaries' Losses as Nonrecurring If the Subsidiary Is Separable.   If good management is assumed, must we not also assume that the subsidiary losses are at most temporary and therefore to be regarded as nonrecurring items rather than as deductions from normal earnings? Some investors specialize in searching for "turnaround" situations. It is hard to imagine a more attractive turnaround situation than a company that could double its earnings by simply giving one of its subsidiaries to charity. Such a situation is even more attractive if the subsidiary can be sold, or can be gradually liquidated while generating positive cash flows.

Is Separability Really Feasible?   There is no one simple answer to the questions of (1) including or excluding a subsidiary's losses in the parent's income and (2) valuing the unprofitable subsidiary as a going concern or a liquidation candidate. Actually, if the subsidiary could be wound up *without an adverse effect on the rest of the business,* viewing such losses as temporary would be logical. But if there are important business relations between the parent company and the subsidiary, e.g., if the latter affords an outlet for goods, provides cheap raw materials or supplies, or absorbs an important share of the overhead, then the termination of its losses is not so simple a matter. It may turn out, upon further analysis, that all or a good part of the subsidiary's loss is a necessary factor in the parent company's profit. It is not an easy task to determine just what business relationships are involved in each instance. Like so many other elements in analysis, investigating this point usually requires going well beyond the reported figures.[2]

Examine the Individual Parts Separately If There Are Losses. The analyst should consider the issue of separability of the unprofitable subsidiary in connection with the notion of normal earning power. If the parts appear separable, the total value of the parts may be greater than the value of the whole. Thus, some parts of a company might be valued on a basis of normal earning power while others were valued at zero or on a basis of whatever they would bring in liquidation.

Divisional Losses versus Subsidiary Losses

This subject could lead us into the much wider field of unprofitable divisions, departments, or products. The distinction between a subsidiary, with a separate corporate name and accounts, and a not-so-separate division is likely to be one of convenience and form rather than of substance. When the subsidiary is not 100 percent owned, the presence of the minority interest usually requires the publication of its separate results. Hence the analyst is made directly aware of the existence of losses from such a source. Much more frequent, however, are losses from a wholly owned subsidiary or from a company division; the extent of such losses is usually only hinted at by the management, if revealed at all in the segment reporting. However, a competent analyst, by inquiry and probing, can in most such cases obtain a fairly accurate idea of the drain on the company's profits. The possibility of terminating the drain should not be forgotten in the analysis. Action of this kind is clearly called for, is usually taken sooner or later—though a management shake-up may first be necessary, and, when taken, may transform the earnings picture and the value picture of the company's stock.

Example. In 1985, Acme-Cleveland Corporation sold the business, related fixed assets, and selected inventory of its Shalco Systems Division, its subsidiary LaSalle Machine Tool, Inc., and certain related activities for $12.8 million plus contingent payments and an $0.8 million pension plan asset reversion. These operations had operating losses after taxes of $4.2 million in 1985 and much larger losses in 1984 and

---

[2] For a discussion of two older examples illustrating this point, Purity Bakeries and Barnsdall Oil in the 1930s, see the 1951 edition of this book, pp. 159—160.

1983. The company's net income in 1985 was a loss of $1.90 per share, including the losses of the discontinued operations, but a profit of $0.70 per share from the continuing operations.

Recommended Treatment of Subsidiary's Losses.   To avoid leaving this point in confusion, we shall summarize our treatment by making the following suggestions:

1. In longer-term studies, deduct subsidiary or divisional losses.
2. If the amount involved is significant, investigate whether or not the losses may be subject to early termination.
3. If the result of this examination is favorable, consider all or part of such losses as the equivalent of a nonrecurring item and exclude the losses from the calculation of earning power.
4. Forecasts of future earnings should account for the availability of the proceeds of sale or liquidation of the unprofitable activity.

9

Effects of Income Taxes

Analysts Must Stay Abreast of Income Taxes

Tax Calculations Required for Analysts' Calculations

Chapters 2 through 8 have pointed out many occasions when a security analyst should change financial statements. When a nonrecurring item needs to be removed from the income statement, the tax results of that item also need to be removed. Most restatements of the financial accounts are pro forma, that is, presented as if something that happened had not happened, or vice versa. Clearly, if the accounts are to be presented as if a certain event had not occurred, the tax results of that event must be eliminated, or income will be distorted by an improper tax rate and the balance sheet also will be inconsistently presented. These tax adjustments require that the analyst be familiar with the tax rates and tax laws of at least the past 10 years as well as the current ones.

Judgment of Management's Tax Skills Necessary

An analyst must also know how well or poorly the company's management handles tax planning and implementation. Analysts do not have to be tax experts but should be familiar with the general characteristics of the U.S. tax laws and the specialized tax treatment of the industries in which the analysts have an ongoing interest.

Characteristics and Features of the Tax Laws

Taxes — A Moving Target

All security analysts should know a number of broad structural characteristics of the tax laws. The U.S. tax laws and regulations are changed nearly every year in some way. The practicing security analyst must stay abreast of new tax legislation when it is proposed and when it has passed, paying particular attention to the unique tax situation of the industries and companies followed. Some tax situations are very complex because various tax elements interact. In those cases, straightforward analysis and simple rules of thumb become quite unworkable.

The Effective Rate Often Is Not the Statutory Rate

We shall first consider why a given amount of *taxable income* on a corporation Form 1120 may not be taxed at the ordinary income tax rate of 34 percent. (The effective date of the 34 percent rate was July 1, 1987. Previously the rate had been 46 percent going back to January 1, 1980, and it was 48 percent for a number of years prior to that.)

Important Features of the U. S. Tax Code

Progressive Corporate Tax Rates.   Like the personal income tax, the U.S. corporate income tax is progressive. The following rates apply:

- Taxable income up to $50,000 is taxed at 15 percent.
- The next $25,000 is taxed at 25 percent.
- Above $75,000 is taxed at 34 percent.

For a corporation that earns $100,000 or more, the progressivity feature is gradually eliminated by a surtax of 5 percent of the excess income over $100,000. Thus when a corporation's taxable income has reached $310,000, it has become subject to a flat rate of 34 percent on its *entire* income. Nearly all corporations investigated by security analysts would have at least that income in normal years, so for all practical purposes the analyst may act as if ordinary income were taxed at a flat rate of 34 percent.

Alternative Minimum Tax.   The 1986 tax law introduced a minimum tax with real teeth in it. It is expected to raise $22 billion over the 1987–1991 period. A number of new tax preferences were added to those of the previous law. An interesting feature of the new alternative minimum tax (AMT) is that book income, that is, what is reported to investors and creditors, will enter into the determination of tax preference. Thus, 50 percent of the excess of book income over AMT taxable income is a tax preference item. The alternative tax is imposed at a 20 percent rate on the AMT income above $40,000 if that amount is greater than the normal tax calculation. In effect, all companies must calculate the AMT to determine whether they owe it. In selecting the tax preferences, Congress rounded up the usual suspects: accelerated depreciation, mining exploration and development costs, completed contract accounting, the last vestiges of installment method accounting, intangible drilling costs, tax-exempt interest on private activity bonds issued after August 7, 1986, and unrealized gain on charitable contributions of appreciated property.

All this will take place merely as a transition through 1989. After that, an undefined earnings and profits concept will come into play. Apparently, "earnings and profits" will be an adjusted book pretax income. Since most of the adjustments are to be determined by Congress in future years, that is not a very useful piece of information.

Because the 34 percent rate applies only to the second half of 1987, and the 46 percent to the first half of the year, the full year may be treated as if there were a flat rate that averages the two—that is, a 40 percent rate. In adjusting years prior to 1987, the 46 percent rate should be used from 1980 to 1985, and the 48 percent before 1980.

Tax-Exempt Interest.   Interest received on nearly all state, municipal, and other local government bonds is tax exempt and is thus excluded from taxable income. Under the 1986 tax act, tax-exempt bonds issued for private purposes such as industrial development bonds, bonds for sports stadiums, pollution control, and other private purposes became fully taxable for federal income tax purposes. Tax-exempt interest was the most important reason that many banks paid little or no federal income taxes and has been an important factor in the effective tax rate of insurance companies. A formula applicable to life insurance companies that would make tax-exempt interest partially taxable, was eliminated by the 1984 Tax Act.

Eighty Percent Dividend Exclusion.   Only 20 percent of dividends received by domestic corporations from other domestic corporations are taxable. Thus the effective rate is 34 percent of 20 percent, or 6.8 percent. In 1986 and prior years, the dividend exclusion was 85 percent, but at a 46 percent tax rate, the effective rate was 6.9 percent. Because of the low effective tax rate, preferred stocks have long been a favorite investment for insurance companies. Because of the tax advantage to corporate investors, preferred stocks provide yields that are below those of similar quality corporate bonds but above those of similar quality tax-exempt bonds.

Capital Gains.   Prior to 1987, capital gains realized on the sale of capital assets held more than six months (in excess of corresponding long-term capital losses) were subject to a tax rate of 28 percent. Capital gains now are treated as ordinary income.

Tax Credits.   Tax credits come and go with the whims of Washington, often promoting socially desirable but economically unjustified actions by business organizations. The appeal to Washington is that use of tax credits to accomplish political goals *reduces revenues* rather than increases expenditures. Thus, the subsidy is obscured from the voter's view. The chief distinguishing characteristic of a tax credit is that it is a direct reduction of taxes, whereas a tax deduction merely reduces taxable income and is therefore worth only 34 percent as much.

General Business Credit.   The general business credit is a group of tax credits that include:

- Low-income housing
- Energy investment (solar, ocean thermal, biomass, and geothermal)
- Certain rehabilitation expenditures
- Employee stock ownership plan (ESOP)
- Targeted jobs
- Research and development

Until the beginning of 1986, the investment tax credit (ITC) was a part of the general business credit and a major cause of effective tax rates on corporations well below the statutory rate. Repeal of the investment tax credit is expected to increase corporate taxes by $119 million over the 1987–1991 period, an average increase in corporate taxes of about $24 billion per year. Transition rules will permit certain types of property to receive the credit through 1991 if ordered before January 1, 1986. Farmers and the steel industry are allowed a 15-year carryback of the ITC. The ITC is not repealed for reforestation expenses, thereby aiding timber companies.

Importance of Investment Tax Credit.   Prior to 1986 the investment tax credit was given to corporations for acquiring qualified plant and equipment (but not land). The credit was given at the time the plant and equipment were first used. The amount of general business credit that can be taken is limited—85 percent of the income tax for the year. Any unused investment tax credit can still be carried forward for the subsequent 15 years. However, the amount of the carryforward is reduced to 82.5 percent in 1987 and 65 percent in subsequent years. For many companies, the investment tax credit was the major cause of the reduction of the effective tax rate.

Example. In 1985, Georgia Pacific Corporation had an effective tax rate of 33 percent. Ten percentage points of the reduction from the then 46 percent statutory rate were due to the investment tax credit, 10 percentage points for application of the capital gains rate to timber appreciation, and seven percent were increases due to state income taxes and other causes (46% − 10% − 10% + 7% = 33%).

Foreign Tax Credit. The foreign tax credit allows a corporation to subtract the amount of foreign income taxes paid from its U.S. income tax obligation. This credit is not available to foreign sales corporations (FSCs). The amount of foreign tax credit is limited by formula to the ratio of foreign income to total income multiplied by the U.S. income tax payable (with certain adjustments to the latter). Application of the formula has been made much more complicated by the 1986 tax bill. Foreign income must now be divided among a number of "baskets," each subject to a separate foreign tax credit limitation. These baskets include passive income, financial services income, oil and gas, shipping income, domestic international sales corporation income, foreign sales corporation income, and so on. This prohibits a company from "averaging" lowly and highly taxed income to maximize the foreign tax credit.

The new U.S. tax rate of 34 percent now places our rate among the lowest of the following corporate tax rates:

Australia	46 percent
Brazil	35 percent
Canada	46 percent
France	45 percent
Germany	56 percent
Italy	36 percent
Japan	43 percent
Korea	33 percent
Mexico	42 percent
Spain	35 percent
United Kingdom	35 percent

As a result, many companies will pay foreign income taxes in excess of the amount they can take as a credit against the U.S. 34 percent tax rate.

Allocation of U.S. Interest Expense.   The 1986 tax law called for a new set of rules in the allocation of U.S. interest expense between U.S. and foreign income, based on the ratio of U.S. assets to foreign assets. These new rules were phased in over four years for debt incurred on or before November 15, 1985, the rule becoming applicable in 1987. Obviously, some companies must shift debt to their foreign subsidiaries by 1987 to avoid a potential double taxation of a part of their foreign earnings.

Foreign Remittances.   The 1986 tax act also called for new "look-through" rules that will look to the earnings source of moneys transferred from the foreign subsidiary to the domestic parent or subsidiary. This emphasis of substance over form may cause problems for some companies.

Possessions Tax Credit.   Corporations operating in U.S. possessions, including Puerto Rico and the Virgin Islands, may take a Section 936 credit in lieu of the foreign tax credit. The credit is the portion of the U.S. tax attributable to taxable income earned in the possession. The rules are complex, and some companies have found the benefits may be somewhat offset by (1) a lack of reinvestment opportunities in those locations and (2) inability to withdraw funds from the possession except under harsh conditions.

Net Operating Losses.   Net operating losses usually may be carried back 3 years or forward 15 years. When a net operating loss occurs, it must be applied first to the earliest year of the previous three in which a taxable operating profit occurred, and then to the next succeeding year, and so on. Foreign expropriation losses cannot be carried back but can be carried forward either for a 10-year or for a 20-year period, depending on the country. Some financial institutions are permitted 10-year carrybacks. A substantial change of ownership may result in the disallowance of net operating loss carryforwards.

The 1986 tax law made major revisions in the rules for carrying over net operating losses and tax credits and deductions after a major ownership change (generally 50 percent or more over a three-year period). A Section 382 limitation may be applied, determined by multiplying the fair market value of the aggregate equity interest in the loss corporation immediately prior to the ownership change by the "long-term tax exempt rate." Potentially, a very large portion of tax benefits and deductions could be disallowed by this complex set of rules. Disallowance in full is also possible. Thus, the acquisition of a company to capture the value of its tax credits and tax loss carryforwards has become much more difficult and will be particularly risky in the second half of the 1980s during which the rules of the game are not well known or understood.

Recognition of Benefit.   Accounting has taken a stern position on recognizing the benefits of tax loss carryforwards as assets or reductions in liabilities. In order to be in a carryforward position, a company must either (1) have had such a large loss in the current year that it exceeds the profits of the previous three years or (2), more often, have shown persistent losses for a number of years, and therefore have no profits from earlier years to offset with the current year's loss. As a result, the accounting rule demands that the realization of the tax loss carryforward be "assured beyond any reasonable doubt" for the benefit to be booked. When the benefit of an operating loss is realized, it must be reported as an extraordinary item.

Example. In 1984 Aetna Insurance Company had large underwriting losses. In the previous three years the company had little or no taxable income because of heavy investments in tax-exempt bonds. The SEC took the position that Aetna could not book the tax loss carryforward because it was not "assured beyond any reasonable doubt" that it would be able to realize the carryforward benefit. Yet, it was obvious that all Aetna needed to do was to sell its tax-exempt bonds, purchase higher-yielding taxable corporate bonds, and it would then have taxable income which it could use to gain the benefit of the operating loss carryforward. In fact, Aetna did so. An analyst who was familiar with the facts of the situation would accept the tax loss carryforward as a valid asset, properly belonging on the balance sheet, and thereby reduce the year's reported loss.

Match Operating Loss Against Deferred Taxes. Given that today's tax laws allow a 15-year carryforward period (versus much shorter periods at various times in the past), an analyst who has any confidence in the future of a company at all will probably conclude that some or all of its tax loss carryforwards are assets that will be realized.

Operating loss carryforwards, investment tax credit carryforwards, and foreign tax credit carryforwards can be realized and considered to be assets when the company has large deferred income tax liabilities on the balance sheet. In such cases, those book-tax timing differences which will reverse and trigger taxable income during the carryforward period—that is, the deferred taxes that will come due— should be offset by the various carryforward assets. Effectively the liability has been eliminated, for (1) if taxable income occurs, the carryforwards can offset it and eliminate the payment of taxes, or (2) if there is no taxable income after the timing reversal occurs, there will be no tax liability for it. In either event, having a carryforward assures that the reversing book-tax timing difference will not result in the payment of taxes.

Example. The 1985 Acme-Cleveland Corporation Annual Report's income tax footnote states "At September 30, 1985 the corporation has available for federal income tax purposes a net operating loss carryforward of $640,000 which expires in 1999, investment tax credit carryforwards of $1,300,000 which expire in 1998 through 2000, and foreign tax credit carryforwards of $1,160,000 which expire in 1986 through 1990." The amounts of carryforwards for financial statement purposes totalled nearly $25 million. However, the September 30, 1985, balance sheet showed a deferred income tax liability of $382 million, so there could be little question that the $3.1 million carryforwards of losses and credits could be used to reduce tax payments that might otherwise occur. The book carryforwards in excess of amounts available for income tax purposes should not be used to reduce real deferred tax liabilities, because they do not exist for tax accounting purposes.

Move Carryforward Benefit to the Loss Years. There is no justification for considering the tax saved by reason of a past loss or tax credit as part of the current year's earnings. The carryforward portion of reported income does not reflect in any sense the "normal results" of the year; obviously it cannot be projected indefinitely into the future as part of the company's earning power. The security analyst should treat such a tax saving as a nonrecurring item which should be excluded from the current year. To straighten out matters for purposes of projecting trends and the like, the loss carryforward or carryback should be applied to the year in which the loss occurred, not when the benefit was realized by offsetting impending tax payments.

Ignore Carryforwards in Projecting Earning Power. The loss and tax credit carryforwards remaining available at any date do, of course, have significance in the analysis, but not really as part of the future earning power. They represent a special or "windfall" value factor, which can add no more than the discounted present value of the *total possible tax saving* to the value found without benefit of such saving. In other words, the earning power should be projected without any credit from the loss carryforward, and the windfall value of the credit then should be added to the "ex-carryforward" value of the earnings.

Percentage Depletion. Percentage depletion is discussed in Chapter 6. The difference between annual report depletion and income tax depletion does not call for study and possible correction by analysts. They may be concerned, however, by the possibility of some adverse change in this tax privilege.

Portability of Tax Benefits. The tax deductibility of depreciation and amortization and the tax benefits of investment tax credits are transferable under certain circumstances. Transferability of tax benefits played a major role in the growth of the leasing industry, since these tax benefits can be kept, transferred to others, or used as a reduction in the rent charged the lessee.

Example. In 1985, Armco, Inc., sold certain investment tax credits and ACRS depreciation deductions for about $120 million at a profit of about $33 million. The sale complied with the rules for a "safe-harbor" leasing transaction and was therefore presumably structured as a sale and leaseback for tax purposes. The annual report referred to the transaction as a "sale of tax benefits," which is all that actually was sold. The related assets were oil field equipment, computers, steel equipment, and the Ashland caster, which remain on the books and will be depreciated for stockholder reporting purposes. Since Armco already had tax loss carryforwards of $775 million, taxes are not likely to be a problem for the company over the near term. Thus, the tax benefits of depreciation are not currently needed.

Transactions of this sort have been criticized, particularly when the lessor ends up paying little or no income tax. For example, General Electric (GE) has been criticized for "not paying its fair share" of taxes. Yet, the economics are that the lessor is often paying taxes through a conduit— the lessee. If the lessor takes the depreciation, the lessee will have increased taxable income because of the absence of the depreciation tax deduction. Perhaps GE is criticized for its tax planning because it is so good at it.

Industries with a Special Tax Status. The advantages of percentage depletion and other special tax treatment to certain industries have already been pointed out. Certain other industries also have been subject to special provisions in the tax law. Examples include: savings and loan companies, commercial banks, property and casualty insurance companies, and regulated investment companies.

Savings and Loan Companies. Savings and loan companies and certain other thrift institutions are allowed to deduct from income for tax purposes the dividends paid to depositors or holders of accounts. These thrift institutions also are allowed a reserve for bad debts based on (1) the experience method, (2) the percentage-of-loans method, such as commercial banks with assets under $500 million, or (3) the percentage-of-taxable- income method. For the reserve on their mortgage portfolio, they may use 8 percent (40 percent before 1987) of taxable income.

Savings and loans are not allowed to deduct the special premium reserves paid to the Federal Savings and Loan Insurance Corporation (FSLIC), although these reserves look remarkably like insurance premiums that should be expensed. Beginning in 1987, interest on borrowings to carry tax-exempt bonds is no longer deductible.

Commercial Banks. Prior to 1987, reserves for bad debts could be

- 0.6 percent at year-end, or
- The highest level previously reached, or
- A five-year moving average of the bank's own experience

Excess loss reserves are tax preference items for purposes of applying the minimum tax. Beginning in 1987, loss reserves are no longer permitted for banks with $500 million or more in assets. The specific charge-off method must be used. Interest expense for carrying tax-exempt bonds is no longer deductible. Prior to 1987, 80 percent was deductible.

Property and Casualty Insurance Companies. Property and casualty insurers were permitted, before 1987, deductions for increases in unearned premium reserves. Beginning 1987, only 80 percent of the increase will be deductible. In addition, income for the years 1986 through 1991 must include a ratable portion of an amount equal to 22 percent of the balance of the unearned premium reserve at the beginning of 1987.[1] The Tax Reform Act of 1986 also substantially changed the handling of loss reserves, including a requirement to discount loss reserves and loss adjustment expenses and to reduce the deduction for increases and loss reserves by 15 percent of tax-exempt interest and 15 percent of the dividends-received deductions, applicable to stocks and bonds acquired after August 7, 1986.

Regulated Investment Companies. A regulated investment company whose gross income is at least 90 percent dividends, interest, security gains, and the like, and which distributes 97 percent of its ordinary income and 90 percent of capital gains to its shareholders, and meets certain other requirements, is free from income taxes, except on its retained income. Like individuals, regulated investment companies will be able to deduct certain investment expenses (using the criteria of Section 212) only to the extent that they exceed 2 percent of adjusted gross income. The 30 percent limitation on profits from securities held less than three months was liberalized by the 1986 tax law to permit hedging with options, futures, and forward contracts. Real estate investment trusts (REITs) may also be taxed as a regulated investment company, but with a number of special rules and restrictions.

Oil and Gas Companies. Percentage depletion is permitted to small independent oil and gas companies but denied to the large integrated

---

[1]Apparently Congress adopted analysts' old practice of recognizing some profit when the policy is sold rather than waiting for underwriting results to confirm that a profit did indeed exist. Most insurance analysts have repudiated this practice in recent years, and we ardently hope that insurance companies will not adopt such a practice for accounting purposes.

companies. The 1986 tax law eliminated percentage depletion for lease bonuses, advance royalties, and certain other payments. The large integrated companies are required to capitalize 30 percent of domestic intangible drilling costs and amortize them over five years, straight-line, beginning 1987. The figure was 20 percent under the prior law. Intangible drilling costs incurred outside of the United States must be capitalized even by small independent producers and amortized over 10 years straight line, or alternatively, amortized as ordinary cost depletion. Oil and gas companies are subject to the windfall profits tax, which is technically an excise tax rather than an income tax. However, the tax is structured so that the rates apply entirely to amounts that are taxable income. Large oil companies are subject to taxes at rates varying from 30 to 70 percent of the excess of the price received for "old oil" over the base price for the class, with a limitation of 90 percent of net income attributable to each barrel sold. In 1980, when the law became effective, the base prices were far in excess of production costs, so the dollars exposed to this tax represented pretax income. Analysts interested in these companies should acquire IRS forms 720, 6047, and 6458, along with the related instructions.

Taxation of Specialized Industries.   Specialized industry tax advantages and penalties of the type described above are extremely important to the companies and industries involved. Companies that enjoy a favorable tax environment are always subject to the hazard of adverse changes in the law or the regulations in the future, whereas companies bearing what seems an unfair burden of taxation may have more cheerful prospects that the levy may be reduced. Logically, the outlook for a change in the taxation of a company should be included in an appraisal of the value of its earnings. The analyst must read political trends as well as economic ones and may wish to incorporate in longer-term projections those tax changes that are deemed to be highly probable.

Difference Between Taxable and Reported Income

Management may at its option produce a difference between reported income and taxable income in a variety of ways. Other differences are mandated by differing treatment in the tax code and in the accounting rules. Some of the tax material is summarized here to present a unified survey of the tax consequences of corporate accounting methods.

Depreciation.   The differences between reported and tax-return depreciation have been an important element in income account analysis. Formerly they were due to a variety of arbitrary practices by corporations, but at present they are pretty well confined to the use of the straight-line method in published figures versus tax reporting using these methods:

- Modified ACRS after 1986
- ACRS for assets acquired from 1980 to 1986
- Other permitted accelerated methods for pre-1981 assets
- 200 percent and 150 percent declining balance for qualifying assets acquired after 1986

This subject was discussed extensively in Chapter 6.

Unremitted Foreign Earnings. Earnings of foreign and U.S. possession subsidiaries ordinarily are not taxed until effectively remitted to the United States. Chapter 8, in its section on foreign earnings, recommends a method of dealing with the deferred tax provision for such earnings.

Amortization. Chapter 6 discussed the tax effect of various amounts amortized on tax returns but capitalized on the statements. Examples include: (1) intangible drilling costs of oil and gas producers and (2) exploration and development expenses of mines. First the analyst must see that a deferred-tax equivalent is set up against a benefit so obtained, and second, that the company's accounts are made comparable.

Capitalization of Interest. Interest costs incurred in acquiring plant and equipment that require a long acquisition period must be capitalized and amortized over the life of the asset. Companies have flexibility in determining the amount of interest capitalized. Current tax rules require that the capitalized interest be expensed over the shorter of 10 years or the life of the assets acquired. In a number of cases the period over which the company amortizes the capitalized interest for stockholder reporting purposes differs from the period over which the interest is amortized for tax deduction purposes. Therefore, there are deferred tax effects caused by these book-tax timing differences. There are currently no disclosure requirements for the pattern of amortization of capitalized interest. As a result, the analyst may seek that information by direct inquiry to the company.

From the analyst's viewpoint, capitalized interest and its counterpart, allowance for equity funds used during construction (AFUDC), should both be removed from the books, along with their tax effects.

Installment Sales.   An important source of deferred profits for tax purposes has been installment sales. Prior to the 1986 act, the law permitted the profit to be taken in proportion with the receipt of payments; but, almost invariably companies report the full profit in their financial statements at the time of sale, and the difference between indicated and actual tax was disposed of by the standard deferred tax procedure. The 1986 act eliminated the use of installment sale reporting for tax purposes for publicly traded companies and for property sold on a revolving credit plan. The discontinuation of the installment method is a change in method of accounting for tax purposes with the resulting profit spreads over four years—15 percent in the first year, 25 percent in the second, and 30 percent in the third and fourth years. Certain installment sales of personal or real property by dealers and casual sales of real property fall under a *proportionate disallowance rule.* Analysts viewed most installment sales as true revenue all along, with certain exceptions such as abusive real estate transactions.

Bad Debt Reserves.   The 1986 law (1) repeals the bad debt reserve method, which tended to smooth earnings, and (2) substitutes the specific charge-off method. Unless the accounting rules change, most companies will probably continue to use the bad debt reserve for stockholder reporting. We favor retention of the bad debt reserve because the receivables could not be sold without some discount for expected losses. However, in most cases adjusting the accounts will not be worthwhile.

Completed Contract Accounting.   In the past, most contracting companies used percentage-of-completion accounting for stockholder reporting purposes and the completed contract method for tax reporting, thereby creating book-tax differences and the resulting deferred tax effects. The 1986 tax law allows 60 percent of income to be calculated on the completed contract method, subject to the alternative minimum tax, and sets up stricter cost capitalization rules, which will create a modified percentage-of-completion method for tax purposes. However, if the companies continue to report on their traditional percentage-of-completion bases, large book-tax differences will persist.

Analysts have never been entirely comfortable with percentage-of-completion accounting, since the profits reported depend so heavily on estimates, some of which are little better than guesses. Bad guesses and occasional manipulation have resulted in too many large write-offs, which raises the question whether companies using the method can be considered of investment quality.

Capitalization of Production Costs.   The Tax Reform Act of 1986 brought a host of accounting changes for tax purposes. The new rules are being phased in over four years, beginning with 1987. GAAP accounting requires that at least some factory overhead be included in the cost of inventories. Most analysts feel that inventory costs already include too many period and overhead costs, thereby smoothing earnings unjustifiably. Congress seized the "full absorption" concept and raised it from a bad habit to the law of the land. For example, the following items must now be included in inventory:

- Excess of tax depreciation over book depreciation
- Warehousing costs
- General and administrative costs incident to the taxpayer's activities as a whole
- Property taxes and insurance
- Strikes, rework labor, scrap, and spoilage

We fervently hope that these items will continue to cause tax timing differences and not be adopted for financial reporting purposes. The analyst would have few tools to put companies' accounts in order, since little is revealed about what goes into inventories even today. Estimates are that these and other tax accounting changes will result in $60 billion of additional revenue over the period from 1987 to 1991.

Write-downs.   Major write-downs and restructuring of unprofitable segments and product lines usually cause large book-tax differences. For example, in 1985 Mobil Corporation made a $775 million provision for restructuring its retail subsidiary Montgomery Ward. In connection with that transaction, the deferred tax liability was reduced by $227 million. The amounts suggested that part of the loss was expected to be ordinary income and part a capital loss. Under the new act both will be treated as ordinary income.

LIFO Pools.   Timing differences arise when companies use different pools for LIFO inventory in reporting on the tax form and reporting to shareholders. This results in a tax timing difference that ultimately will reverse. If the difference is significant, the footnote reconciling the effective tax rate to the statutory rate should show a specific line item with an appropriate caption, such as "difference in inventory accounting."

Excessive Contributions.   Similar timing differences arise when a company makes contributions to a pension fund or to charities in excess of IRS limitations.

Goodwill.   Amortization of purchased goodwill is not tax deductible, but the goodwill is part of the tax cost basis when the subsidiary is sold or liquidated. Chapter 11 includes recommendations for removing goodwill and its amortization from the accounts for purposes of security analysis.

Early Extinguishment of Debt.   A gain on the extinguishment of debt is ordinary income, but solvent corporations can normally avoid the income by electing to reduce the tax attributes of depreciable assets. Thus, the tax is deferred but comes due through lower depreciation deductions in subsequent years. Losses on extinguishments are usually taken at once on the tax form.

Unexplained Discrepancies—Ask the Company.   Every now and then the analyst will find a discrepancy between reported income and the tax deduction for which no ready explanation is at hand. The effective tax rate will be clearly out of line with expectations based on the U.S. statutory rate and other rates of taxation to which the company is subject. In theory, at least, footnote disclosure will provide the explanation, but the analyst is unable to find an answer there. In such cases, the analyst interested in a thorough presentation should ask the company. An explanation will usually be forthcoming.

Deferred Income Taxes

Deferred Tax Deduction

Some argue that deferred income taxes are not liabilities, because they are taxes on taxable income that has not yet been earned and that therefore there should be no deferred tax liability or expense. However, failure to provide for deferred income taxes is inconsistent with modern accounting. Today's accounting model (sometimes imprecisely called "historical cost" accounting) has a fundamental tenet that the carrying amount of an asset must be a *recoverable amount* and that the carrying amount of a liability must be an amount at which the liability ultimately can be settled (ignoring accrual of future interest).

It can be demonstrated mathematically that if all the assets and liabilities of the company are collected or settled in cash *at their carrying amounts*, the deferred tax liabilities will at that point come due (that is, all book-tax timing differences will reverse). To say that the deferred tax is not a liability is to say that assets are being carried at amounts above the cash that will be recovered from them or that liabilities are being carried at amounts less than the amount necessary to settle them.

The Deferred Taxes Do Come Due.   The taxable income will occur! For an example, see Chapter 6, Table 6.2, at the end of the third year: The recovery of the $150 carrying amount of the asset ensured that the $51 in the deferred tax account would become payable. Since no tax depreciation is deductible for the final three years, the entire $150 carrying amount, when realized, would become taxable income.

Most Tax Adjustments Are Made at the Ordinary Statutory Rate.   In adjusting the income statement of a company for purposes of putting depreciation and other amortization expenses on a common basis, read the footnotes on income taxes carefully for any particular problems in calculating the related deferred tax provision. If the depreciation timing differences are only domestic, the analyst can approximate the related tax effect by multiplying the adjustment to depreciation by 34 percent, plus a bit more if necessary for state and local income taxes. (Calculations for years prior to 1988 would usually be made at the rate prevailing during that year. In the case of 1987, a blended rate of 40 percent would be used, with the 34 percent rate applying after June 30 and 46 percent before July 1.) The tax *expense* calculated by this method may call for an adjustment of deferred taxes in the income statement and the balance sheet, since the taxes paid remain unaffected.

Deferred Tax Liability

The provision for deferred taxes is a real liability, but it continues to be a source of problems for the security analyst. Some discomfort arises because deferred taxes seem to be liabilities that never require a cash outflow. Most companies are growing and regularly add new plant and equipment to replace the old. These new acquisitions create new tax timing differences to replace the old ones that are reversing. The result is that no cash outflow for taxes need occur. The deferred tax balance on the right side of the balance sheet continues to grow, and its nature is puzzling.

A Matter of Perspective.   One problem is the way deferred taxes are measured. Most long-term receivables and payables that bear no interest, or bear an unreasonably low interest rate, must be discounted to their present value at the time they are placed on the books. Interest is accreted thereafter, resulting in either interest income or interest expense. But, for practical reasons, discounting is not required for deferred taxes.

Deferred Tax Issues for the Analyst.   If no cash outflow will occur for many years—perhaps many decades—the analyst must wonder whether:

- The deferred tax account really is a liability with a present value near zero
- The tax deferred represents an interest-free long-term loan from the Treasury Department
- The deferred tax account is any different economically from retained earnings; it should be a part of the equity account

   Clearly, capital is working for the benefit of the stockholders and not for bondholders or trade creditors. For purposes of comparison between companies, include deferred taxes in equity in calculations of return on invested capital and return on equity.

   A final issue that the individual analyst must decide is whether deferred tax liabilities are sufficiently similar to shareholders' equity that *changes* in the deferred tax liability should be part of income in calculating those ratios.

Taxes and the Investment Overview

Concentrate on the Transaction

The frequency of tax changes may mesmerize the analyst into an attitude that the only problem is to make sure that the proper tax rate is used in making adjustments to the financial statements. This attitude carries two dangers. The most obvious is that concentration on the nature of the transaction may be subsumed or even lost. Yet, the centerpiece of financial statement analysis is the identification of the true nature of transactions. Without that, analysis becomes a mechanical and unthinking process that is unlikely to contribute much to investment success.

People Pay Taxes—Not Corporations

The second and more important danger is viewing tax changes as simple additions to or subtractions from the bottom line. That perspective says, in effect, that *corporations* pay taxes. But corporations are merely structures of human conception—a simple way for groups of people to act and organize. The analytical question when there is a tax change is *who will pay* the tax or receive the benefit of the reduction. There are only three choices—the shareholders, the employees, and the customers. One or more of these groups will reap the rewards or suffer the burden of a tax change. For example, the Tax Reform Act of 1986 eliminated the investment tax credit, reduced the benefits of accelerated depreciation, and lowered the rate on ordinary income. The simplistic view is that plant-intensive companies would suffer while companies paying the full rate, for lack of tax credits and deductions, would be the beneficiaries. The analysis must go much further. If the plant-intensive company is suffering stiff foreign competition, it will not be able to pass the tax on to customers. However, depending on its labor position, it may be able to shift part of a tax increase on to its workers. If it cannot, all the burden will go to the bottom line, and the stockholders will carry the full burden. If a company has an oligopoly position due to, say, patents and inelastic demand for its products, it may be able to pass all tax burdens on to its customers and retain all benefits for its stockholders. Admittedly, many companies will suffer a time lag before the tax burdens or benefits are shifted to specific groups of people—owners, workers, or consumers, but a good analysis of the relative bargaining position of each group will reveal the most likely ultimate taxpayers. *People* pay taxes, not legal fictions such as corporations.

10
Balance Sheet Analysis

The Balance Sheet

The balance sheet deserves more attention than Wall Street has been willing to accord it for many years. Following are six types of information and guidance that the investor may derive from a study of the balance sheet:

1. Information on how capital is invested and how the capital structure is divided between senior issues and common stock
2. Strength or weakness of the working-capital position
3. Reconciliation of the earnings reported in the income account
4. Data to test the true success or prosperity of the business, the amount earned on invested capital
5. The basis for analyzing the sources of income
6. The basis for a long-term study of the relationship between earning power and asset values and of the development of the financial structure

Presentation of the Balance Sheet

The conventional balance sheet lists all assets on the left side and the liabilities, capital, and surplus on the right. (In England the two columns are reversed.) Alternative and sometimes more informative methods of presentation are found occasionally in corporate statements, which seek to develop the figure for capital and surplus by subtracting the liabilities from the assets; they also supply a better picture of the working-capital position by listing current liabilities directly below current assets. In some corporate reports this presentation appears under the title of Statement of Financial Condition and is given in addition to the conventional balance sheet.

Although format is a matter of personal preference, we recommend that the analyst experiment with the one presented in Figure 10.1. We shall illustrate the method by restating the December 1985 balance sheet of Bristol-Myers Company, including therein our recommended elimination of $163.9 million of goodwill and restatement of the liability of preferred stock from the $1 par value to a more reasonable $50 liquidation value. Detailed items in the various categories are aggregated.

Capital funds:		
Funded debt		$ 114,200
Other liabilities		77,300
Deferred income taxes		81,700
$2.00 conv. preferred, par $1.00		
165,143 shares valued at $50		8,300
Total senior claims		$ 281,500
Common stock (138,048,132 shares outstanding)		2,278,800
Total funds		$2,560,300
Represented by:		
Current assets	$2,502,200	
Less current liabilities	997,000	
Working capital		$1,505,200
Intermediate assets, net		129,300
Fixed assets, gross	$1,482,400	
Less depreciation	(556,600)	
Fixed assets, net		925,800
Total		$2,560,300

Figure 10.1 Recast balance sheet of Bristol-Myers Company, December 31, 1985 (in thousands of dollars).

Current Assets and Liabilities

Since the reader is assumed to be familiar with accounting, we shall not discuss all the items in the balance sheet in detail but shall consider merely those aspects that may require special knowledge or, more often, a special viewpoint by the analyst.

The Definition of "Current"

Manufacturing, distributing, wholesaling, retailing, and some service companies have "classified" balance sheets, that is, assets and liabilities are classified between "current" and "noncurrent." Normally, electric utilities, banks, insurance companies, and other financial companies do not have a classified balance sheet. The word *current* encompasses assets and liabilities that are expected to be converted into cash or paid with cash within 12 months or over the operating cycle, whichever is longer. For example, cigarette tobacco is usually aged for about three years before sale. Thus tobacco inventories would be classified as "current." Similarly, wines and liquors that have to be aged, long-term construction projects, and the like, result in current assets that are not subject to conversion into cash in 12 months, but rather over some longer period. However, the prevailing practice is to use only the 12-month criterion for classifying liabilities, even when the liability is clearly a part of the operating cycle. For example, a liability for prepayment or deposit on a long-term construction contract would typically be classified as noncurrent.

Current Assets and Duration. The classification of assets as current and noncurrent serves in a general sort of way to identify the speed with which the asset can be expected to be converted into cash in the ordinary course of business. Duration is a measure of risk, somewhat akin to maturity. The duration of accounts receivable may be a matter of days or a very few months. The duration of inventory may range from months to even several years. For fixed assets and long-term debt, duration is obviously measured in years and decades.

Duration and Risk. The riskiness of long duration assets is obvious in the case of a holding of bonds, since the longer the bond the greater the price fluctuation resulting from a given change in interest rates. Although that risk may be less obvious in the case of plant and equipment, it is equally present. Plant and equipment sell at prices which tend to reflect the average discounted present value of future cash flows, just as a bond does. Current assets contribute to liquidity. The ratio of current assets to total assets is clearly a measure of risk. The longer the time before an asset will reappear in the form of cash, the greater the probability that something will go wrong. The analyst will therefore examine current assets, the ratio of current assets to total assets, and the current ratio from the viewpoint of risk evaluation as well as liquidity evaluation.

Current Assets

Cash Items. Current assets include cash and cash equivalents, receivables, and inventories. Certain cash items, usually in the form of government bonds, are sometimes segregated by the company and shown elsewhere than in current assets. On rare occasions they are being held to meet liabilities not shown as current.

Example. At year-end 1985, IBM Corporation's balance sheet showed noncurrent "Investments and Other Assets." A footnote revealed that $503 million were U.S. fixed-income securities. Maturities were not given.

Include Portfolio Cash Items. When companies have a portfolio of investment securities, cash items may exist as part of the portfolio and be classified as noncurrent. There is no formal definition of the term *cash items*. We believe it is helpful to present as current assets actual holdings of cash, and the temporary investment of cash in high-quality, short-maturity investment media (so-called cash equivalents) if they are within the company's control.

Exclude Pension Assets. However, even if we had consolidated the company's pension fund into the company's balance sheet for purposes of certain calculations, we would *not* classify the cash items of the pension fund as current. Although a company could accomplish an "asset reversion" from excess pension fund assets, the process is complex, requires approval by the Pension Benefit Guaranty Corporation, and is subject to potential long delays. Because of this lack of ready access to these cash items, we do not believe that it would be helpful to include them with the company's other cash.

Compensating Balances May Be Unavailable. The analyst should be aware that cash in the bank is not always "available." Some bank loans include an agreement that the company maintain *at all times* "compensating balances" equal to, say, 10 percent of the line of credit plus an additional 10 percent of the actual amount of borrowings. The bank may even insist that these funds be kept in a non-interest-bearing certificate of deposit. In other cases the compensating balance requirement is merely that the company's average working balances remain at a certain level. In any case, cash that represents compensating balances cannot always be drawn upon for payment of obligations. Disclosure of the amounts and terms of compensating balances is improving.

Cash Value of Life Insurance. Cash surrender value of life insurance policies—at times a sizable item—was formerly shown as a current asset in most cases, but now it is almost always shown as noncurrent. The analyst may properly include such an amount, if important, in the current assets for the purpose of certain calculations, e.g., to find the current asset value of the stock.

Receivables. Trade or customer receivables, less allowances for losses, are shown as current assets, even though the period of payment may run well beyond a year, for example, in the case of installment notes. Such installment notes are often sold to finance companies, factors, or banks on a full or partial recourse basis, that is, the seller is, to some degree, responsible for nonpayment. The amount of such repurchase obligation and, if known, the uncollected balance will be shown in a footnote. Some analysts favor adding these amounts to both the receivables and the current liabilities, to get a clearer view of the company's financial position. Assume these circumstances:

1. The recourse provision is limited to, say, 10 percent of the receivables.

2. The bad debt loss experience of the company has been far less than 10 percent.

3. The owner of the receivables has no right to force the seller to repurchase them.

In this situation, we believe that only the expected recourse losses, or at most the 10 percent, should be recorded as an asset and a liability. Conservatism does not demand that liabilities be recorded when they can be avoided by simply saying "no."

But Never Show a Loss. Still other transactions are designed not to remove assets and liabilities from the balance sheet, but rather to *keep them on* to avoid recognition of a loss. Since transactions of this sort are designed to conceal rather than reveal, making appropriate adjustments for them should be considered an analytical triumph.

Adequacy of Loss Reserves. Where receivables play a large part in the company's business, special care should be given to the examination of the reserve for losses and collection expense. If the annual report provides inadequate information, the analyst should look to Schedule VIII of the 10-K. Comparisons should be made with other companies in the same field. In extreme cases, the true value of the receivables may prove to be badly overstated. Remember that credit losses are cyclical and that the losses will probably increase when a receivable comes due at the bottom of a recession and decrease in a business boom.

Example. Hilton Hotels Corporation, in its 10-K Schedule VIII, *Valuation and Qualifying Accounts*, showed the following information on its allowance for doubtful accounts:

Year	Charged to expense	Deductions from reserves
1985	$4,716,000	$2,679,000
1984	2,037,000	3,080,000
1983	2,055,000	4,856,000

The company's volatile collection experience was generated primarily by its casino operations. The company's expense understated its actual loss experience by significant amounts in 1983 and 1984 and partly made up for it in 1985. The expense number shows exactly the opposite trend from the actual pattern of losses, which was sharply downward. However, given the experience of rather large losses in 1983, the analyst would probably question whether the balance of the account at the end of 1984 (in the amount of $3,139,000) provided a safe margin. Apparently the company reached the same conclusion. At the end of 1985 the allowance for doubtful accounts had been raised to $5,174,000.

Inventories. Inventory amounts are increasingly being broken down into raw materials, goods in process, and finished inventory. This additional detail permits the application of new analytical techniques, including determination of the following:

- Turnover of finished goods (the only ones that are ultimately sold!)
- The company's raw materials acquisition policy
- The company's ability to anticipate price changes of raw materials
- Production economies or problems

Include the LIFO Reserve for Most Ratio Analysis.   If inventories are carried on the LIFO method, the LIFO reserve should be added back for calculating such ratios as current assets per share, return on equity, return on invested capital, and physical turnover of inventory. However, in projecting a profit margin for next year's sales, or the effect of layer invasion on reported net income, the analyst will find it more helpful to keep the inventories on a LIFO basis.

Questionable Current Assets
The rules for classifying assets as current should be tightened up to exclude some of the more dubious items. For example, depreciable fixed assets such as bulldozers sometimes appear as current assets because they are being used on a long-term construction project, or a traditionally noncurrent asset will appear as a current asset because the company "intends" to sell it in the coming 12 months. If being part of the operating cycle is to continue to be one of the criteria for currentness, more specific guidance is needed on exactly what the operating cycle is. Obviously, many different cycles of varying lengths are going on at the same time. A defense contractor should not be allowed to keep the operating cycle open for 30 years just because it is continuing to sell spare parts for an airplane or a submarine!

Example. Tonka Corporation, in its annual report for the year ended December 29, 1984, reported in current assets "Assets Identified for Sale (Note 7) . . . $4.4 (million)." Note 7 said, in part, "During 1984, the Tonka Corporate Offices and Manufacturing facilities located in Spring Park and Mound, Minnesota were identified for sale." The buyer had a conditional right to rescind the transaction for a period of up to three years. The properties were, in fact, sold in February 1985 for approximately $5 million.

Off-Balance-Sheet Financing. Companies prefer to get debt off the balance sheet. To do so, they must also remove assets. Be alert to a variety of structured transactions whose purpose is to remove debt, but which may also remove inventories or accounts receivable in the process. This activity has become so widespread that a whole new accounting vocabulary has grown up, including the following:

- Nonsub sub
- Tax-deductible preferred
- Collateralized mortgage obligations (CMOs)
- Collateralized automobile receivables (CARs)
- Nonsale sale

Current Liabilities

Current liabilities include all liabilities due within a year and, in theory but not in practice, those falling due during the operating cycle. They include the current year's maturities of a serial bond or note issue and, in some cases, the portion of a long-term bond issue due to be retired by sinking fund operation within the year. Certain intermediate term and off-balance-sheet liabilities should be reclassified as current by the analyst, if they are likely to be paid in a year or less.

Sinking Funds and Mandatorially Redeemable Preferred Stock. Mandatory sinking fund payments on preferred stock represent the same probable cash outflow as bond sinking funds and maturities. If the amount is significant, the amount of preferred stock redeemable within 12 months should be added to current liabilities and subtracted from the preferred stock outstanding. Although the legal claim of a sinking fund preferred ranks far below that of debt maturities or taxes, the usefulness of the current classification of liabilities is enhanced by inclusion of all known cash outflows of the coming 12 months. If the cash outflow is probable, show the economic substance rather than the legal form.

Offsetting Taxes Payable with Tax Anticipation Notes. The large size of income tax liabilities gives rise to a device, designed partly to improve the current ratio and partly to help finance the usual Treasury deficit. Companies purchase large quantities of U.S. Treasury tax anticipation notes which bear below market rates of interest when held to maturity. The notes may be used at par for payment of federal taxes due on a date somewhat earlier than maturity, thereby providing a higher effective yield. As a result, corporations do not purchase tax anticipation notes unless they intend to use them for payment of income taxes. The notes are exact and legal offsets to the tax liability, and the tax notes must be used for payment of taxes to maximize the rate of return. However, the analyst should reverse the offsetting of the notes and the taxes due to enhance consistency through time and comparability of the current ratio of companies that do and do not use tax anticipation notes. The treatment suggested is controversial among analysts.

Noncurrent Assets

Plant, Property, and Equipment

Usually Carried at Conservative Figures. Fixed assets are referred to as the "plant account," "plant, property, and equipment," "PP&E," or the "property account." In nearly all companies they are now carried at a conservative figure. The usual basis is actual cost less depreciation. In view of the large inflation effect on the current cost of plant and equipment, the depreciated amounts of older plant and equipment are usually far below the cost of replacing the same equipment with used equipment—the depreciated replacement cost at current prices. This partially explains the willingness of acquiring companies to pay even 1½ or 2 times the book value for an acquiree company. Where the purchase method of accounting is used for the acquisition, the fixed assets of the acquired company are given a new carrying amount equal to "fair value," and in most cases the fair value turns out to be far above the previous carrying amounts.

Current Value Information. The changing prices information which was required of some 1200 companies, and provided voluntarily by many others, provides a current cost number that constitutes a measure of the degree of conservatism in the carrying amount of fixed assets. Long before that information was available, security analysts would make inquiries to management about the amount of fire insurance carried on plant and equipment. If the number of facility locations is small, tax assessments can be obtained and used to estimate the value of land and buildings.

Leaseholds. A leasehold is a right to the quiet enjoyment of premises for a stated period of time subject to payment of rent therefor. Such a right may be considered a valuable asset if the current rental value of the leased property is much greater than the rent called for in the contract. In past years, companies have sometimes set more or less arbitrary figures on such leasehold values and carried them as assets. In times of financial stress, the tenant's rights are usually limited to out-of-pocket damages. An asset of that type must of course be considered entirely intangible.

Leasehold Improvements as Tangible Assets. In many cases, however, companies have erected buildings on ground leased to them for a long period. At the expiration of the lease (and stipulated renewals) the building becomes the property of the lessor (the owner of the land). Technically, tenants (the lessees) do not own such buildings; they are part of the leasehold interest. To that extent such buildings, often designated in the balance sheet as "leasehold improvements," might accurately be called intangible assets; but it is more in accordance with substance to consider them as a tangible investment by the lessee and therefore as a tangible asset.

Intermediate and Longer-Term Assets

Intermediate-Term Assets. Intermediate-term items in general consist of noncurrent receivables, investments not treated as current marketable securities, and deferred assets. Claims for tax refunds may be intermediate assets or current receivables, depending on the expected date of their receipt. Some noncurrent receivables are due from officers, employees, or affiliated companies.

Long-Term Assets.

Investments. Most investments in subsidiaries are eliminated from the balance sheet by the use of a consolidated statement, but various types are exceptions to this rule. Some companies do not consolidate all their foreign subsidiaries; others do not consolidate subsidiaries of which less than 100 percent is owned. Most do not consolidate finance and leasing subsidiaries. These investment items may represent the ownership of a substantial amount of current assets. Advances to affiliates are usually eliminated in consolidation if the affiliates are consolidated. If not, they should be combined as "investments in and advances to subsidiaries" so that the dividends or equity earnings from those affiliates can be related to the total amount invested in them. The fact that interest is estimated on loans to equity method investees and disclosed as a related party transaction with affiliates carried on the investment method, permits the analyst a reasonable picture of the profitability of the relationship.

Marketable Securities. The *liquidity* of the company is enhanced by a portfolio of marketable securities, where the sizes of the holdings do not limit liquidity. Such securities may properly be included in current assets. For some purposes, such as determining the normal working capital requirements to support a dollar of sales of a manufacturing company, the portfolio of marketable securities should properly be excluded from current assets. In either case, analysts must decide whether to carry the marketable securities at market or at cost. Obviously, for purposes of determining liquidity, market value is more relevant. For purposes of calculating a return on investment that does not include in the numerator the market fluctuations of the securities portfolio, the lower of cost or market would seem more appropriate.

Where working control is involved, it is doubtful whether the market value of the shares should enter directly into a balance sheet analysis of the owning company. In effect such a procedure would substitute earning power value for asset values with respect to an important part of the company's business and thus vitiate the purpose of balance sheet analysis, which deals with asset values as a separate factor in a company's valuation. An allocation of the underlying asset values—corresponding to an allocation of the controlled companies' earnings—seems more logical.

Example. Seagram Company, Ltd., owned 22.5 percent of E. I. Du Pont de Nemours & Company at 1985 year end. On March 29, 1986, a "standstill agreement" was signed which amended a 1981 agreement. The new agreement provides that Seagram will not purchase more than 25 percent of Du Pont except under certain dilutive conditions. Seagram will be permitted proportional representation on the Du Pont board of directors and its finance committee, to be accomplished by 1990. Du Pont will have the right to nominate two Seagram directors. The agreement extends to 1999, when it can be terminated with two years' written notice. Seagram carries the Du Pont holding on the equity method. The investment accounts for the majority of Seagram's earnings. Analysis of Seagram from the viewpoint of an asset play would surely suggest the use of the market value of the investment.

Prepaid Expense and Deferred Charges

Prepaid Expense. Prepaid expense represents amounts paid to other parties for services to be rendered by them in the future—rent and insurance paid in advance, for instance. The AICPA has suggested that such prepaid expense items be included in the current assets as the equivalent of accounts receivable, and they are now treated largely in this fashion. The analyst's view would be influenced by the nature of the company—an ongoing firm versus a liquidation.

Deferred Charges. Deferred charges, in contrast to prepaid expense, represent amounts paid or payable for which no specific services will be received in the future but which are considered properly chargeable to future operations. These include tax assets, some intangible operating rights, certain start-up costs, and other items. The cost of tools and dies for models not yet on the market, for example, is sometimes carried in this account. Companies usually charge off such items rather rapidly against actual sales. The analyst would consider many of these items doubtful for purposes of balance sheet analysis. In sum, the prepaid-expense and similar items are extremely varied in their character and their validity. The analyst may fortunately ignore most of them as unimportant. The larger ones may require rather careful scrutiny.

Concepts Statement 6, *Elements of Financial Statements,*[1] requires that all assets have "probable future benefits." Conceptually, this rejects the notion that assets are merely past expenses awaiting some future revenue to be attached to. We would anticipate a reduction in the more questionable deferred charges, some of which have been little more than dangling debits.

Example. IBM's 1985 annual report showed a somewhat condensed balance sheet which included a line item "Investments and other assets . . . $6,884 (millions)." Further on, a table provided a breakdown of this category into seven subcategories for the years ended December 31, 1984 and 1985. One of the lines could be described as a deferred charge. It was "program products, less accumulated amortization . . . $1,964 (millions)." Analysts (and accountants) are divided on whether computer programs should be capitalized or expensed. Another line item was goodwill, which nearly all analysts would write off. Still another line was U.S. Treasury securities, which everyone would agree are very solid assets. The analyst will need to do a good deal of searching simply to find the deferred charges and then must use judgment to decide whether they are real assets or items that should be charged to the income statement.

---

[1]Financial Accounting Standards Board, Statement of Financial Accounting Concepts No. 6, *Elements of Financial Statements,* December 1985, pp. 10–12, Stamford, Conn.

Intangible Assets.   The familiar types of intangible assets include

- Goodwill
- Patents
- Copyrights
- Trademarks
- Franchises
- Licenses
- Organization and development expense

These items are discussed in Chapter 11.

The Growing List of Intermediate Liabilities

In the past, few liabilities failed to fall in the categories of (1) current liabilities or (2) funded debt. Those that were of a general reserve nature belonged in surplus. The remainder were so small in amount that they could simply be added to current liabilities. The current situation requires the analyst to address a different set of problems. A sizable body of liabilities refuse to fall neatly into merely two classes. At least three areas need to be assessed:

- Off-balance-sheet financing
- Deferred taxes
- Preferred stock

Off-Balance-Sheet Liabilities

Off-balance-sheet liabilities include

- Operating leases
- Product financing arrangements
- Related party transactions
- Unconsolidated affiliates and related parties that are carrying parent company debt
- Contingent litigation liabilities
- Liabilities for pension and other postemployment benefits

The analyst must decide how to treat these liabilities. Those which properly belong on the balance sheet should be classified as current liabilities,long-term debt, or equity. For example, deferred nonrefundable fee income is not a liability and is best considered equity for purposes of calculating return on equity.

Operating Leases. The preference for *operating leases* over capital leases has two financial reporting reasons. First, operating leases are not shown as assets and liabilities on the balance sheet. In contrast, under a *capital lease*, the books show that an asset was acquired and a borrowing incurred. Second, the expense of an operating lease is simply the rental amount spread evenly over the life of the lease.

Expense under a Capital Lease. Under a capital lease, the asset is depreciated, usually using straight-line method. The interest component of the borrowing is reflected using the mortgage method. In the early years the interest component of a mortgage consumes almost all the payment, while in the later years the payment is practically all principal with very little interest. Thus, the total expenses under a capital lease (depreciation plus interest) are higher than an operating lease's rent in the earlier years and lower in the later years. Use of capital leases reduces the early years' net income and increases income in the later years of the lease.

Capital Leases Are Easily Avoided. The accounting rules to distinguish between capital and operating leases use arbitrary criteria, such as a requirement that the term of the lease not exceed 75 percent of the estimated economic life of the leased property or that the present value of the minimum lease payments at the beginning of the lease shall not exceed 90 percent of the fair value of the property. It is quite simple to convert a capital lease into an operating lease by structuring the terms appropriately. Thus two companies may operate precisely the same in economic terms, but the one with an operating lease will show fewer liabilities and earlier earnings than will the other that has a capital lease. The various ratios of profitability, stability, and financial risk will look better for the former company than for the latter. Yet the economic substance is identical.

The Old Rules-of-Thumb. Historically, most leased assets were real estate. Lease terms were long with extensive renewal options. The practice was for analysts to capitalize the lease by multiplying the annual rent by an arbitrary number such as 10 times or, somewhat later, 8 times. This technique solved a difficult analytical problem for those studying retail chains, in particular, but applied elsewhere. The calculation provided a good approximation of the value of real estate in those days of relatively low interest rates and permitted valid comparisons between those companies that owned their own properties and had debt on the balance sheet with those that rented and showed little or no debt outstanding.

Today's Leases—Shorter Term at Higher Interest Rates. Today, a much higher percentage of leases are short term in nature, covering computers, automobiles, machinery, and similar items having short useful lives. Thus, a multiplier of 8 or 10 times may overstate the asset and liability significantly. Fortunately, companies are required to disclose minimum lease requirements for each of the succeeding five years and the total for all subsequent years in a footnote. Many companies show the longer rentals in five-year brackets. This permits the analyst to estimate the asset and liability with more precision.

Two Leasing Disclosures. Table 10.1 provides a schedule of operating lease rentals for two companies—the data needed to capitalize the leases.

Tonka Corporation. The data clearly show that Tonka Corporation leases relatively short-lived items, and that some of the leases are expiring rather quickly. There is no difficulty in determining the present value of the Tonka leases, other than selecting an interest rate, since projecting future payment dates is unnecessary. All the payments are shown in the table. If an interest rate of 15 percent were selected, and the rental payments are made at year's end, the equation that follows

Table 10.1 Future Minimum Annual Rentals on Operating Leases
(In Millions of Dollars)

Year (ending December 31)	Tonka Corporation	Mead Corporation
1986	0.6	28.9
1987	0.4	25.4
1988	0.4	17.8
1989	0.2	13.3
1990	0.1	10.5
Later years	0.0	285.6*
Total	1.7	381.5

* Through 2057.
Source: From 1985 Annual Report.

would give the present value of Tonka's operating lease obligations at the beginning of 1986. The calculated value of the operating leases would be $1.301 million—about 3.7 times the average annual rental for the next five years and about twice the 1986 rent. Clearly, a multiplier of 8 or 10 would have severely exaggerated the liability and asset (figures represent millions of dollars):

$$\frac{0.6}{(1.15)} + \frac{0.4}{(1.15)^2} + \frac{0.4}{(1.15)^3} + \frac{0.2}{(1.15)^4} + \frac{0.1}{(1.15)^5} = 1.301$$

Mead Corporation. In the case of the Mead Corporation, long-term leases are involved, and at least one of them appears to have had a life of 72 years, since the payments continue through the year 2057. How should the analyst estimate the value of the Mead Corporation leases? First, the analyst would observe that some maturing leases or short-term leases (we don't know which) exist because the minimum annual payments drop fairly rapidly from almost $29 million in 1986 to a little over $10 million in 1990. As a rough estimate, the analyst might divide the number of years between 1991 and 2057 into the total lease payments for those years, giving an average annual rental of $4.26 million. An alternative is to divide the most distant known annual rent, 1990's figure of $10,500,000, into the total remaining rent of $285,600,000, which implies that payments would be completed in the year 2017. That would expire about 40 years too soon. Thus, as a compromise estimate, the analyst might decide to allow the annual rental to continue declining about $3 million a year for another two years, and then calculate the fixed amount that would equal the remaining rent from 1993 to 2057. Thus, the estimated schedule of remaining rent payments for Mead Corporation (in millions of dollars) would be as follows:

1991	10.5 − 3.0	= 7.5
1992	7.5 − 3.0	= 4.5
1993–2057	$\dfrac{285.6 − 7.5 − 4.5}{65}$	= 4.209 annually

Using our assumed maturity schedule and a 15 percent interest rate, the present value of Mead's leases would be $84.3 million. Assumption of a 12 percent interest rate would increase the present value to only $94.8 million, so our projection of Mead's pattern of interest payments does not result in a present value that is highly sensitive to changes in the assumed interest rate. Either number is only about one-fourth of the total operating lease rental payments ($381.5 million) for Mead. Assumption of a different pattern of rental payments could make a significant change in the number. Obviously, obtaining further details of the scheduled minimum rental payments from the company would give analysts more confidence in their calculations.

The Mead calculation illustrates that the old traditional multipliers of 8 and 10 times do not seem to give a very good answer in these times of high interest rates. The average annual minimum rental on operating leases for the first five years is $19.2 million, and a multiplier of 10 times would yield an estimate almost double either of the numbers that we calculated using a discounting technique. Our calculations came out with a multiplier of about 4 times.

Interest Component of Operating Leases. If the analyst capitalizes Mead's operating leases, both the asset and the liability must be shown on the balance sheet. To avoid distorting return on investment, an interest component of the rent must be added to the numerator to balance the presence of the lease liability in the denominator. What portion of the rent should be considered the interest component? We suggest that a reasonable solution is found in the present value calculation. Mead's total rental payments are $381.5 million. The present value is, say, $94.8 million. That is the principal part of the payments. The rest is interest. Thus, the fraction

$$\frac{381.5 - 94.8}{381.5} = 75.15\%$$

might be applied to the five-year average rent as an average interest component. If that figure seems unreasonable as a return on the lease liability, an up-to-date interest rate could be applied to the present value of the earlier expiring leases and an interest fraction, calculated as above, applied to the longer maturity leases.

Should Operating Leases Go on the Balance Sheet? The question remains whether the analyst should put these calculations on the balance sheet. For certain purposes, our answer is yes. Ideally, for calculating such ratios as return on investment, debt to equity, debt to plant, and plant turnover, both the asset and liability should be reflected in the balance sheet. In a liquidation study, operating leases should be excluded from the balance sheet. This asset is available only if the rent is paid, and the liability could be settled for far less than the present value of the asset.

Practical Difficulties. However, some difficulties may persuade the analyst that including operating leases on the balance sheet is not worthwhile. To be perfectly consistent with capital leases, the liability should be reduced each year using the mortgage method and the asset depreciated, probably using straight-line calculation. The calculations for a single lease would be extensive. In the typical case some leases expire each year and new ones are made. Calculating a reasonable depreciation number would require at a minimum viewing each year's expiration as a separate asset with its own useful life. That would require a great deal of labor, and (1) acquisition of information that is seldom available or (2) use of vulnerable assumptions.

The "One-Third of Rent" Rule Is Questionable. Since the interest and depreciation calculations would be complex, and probably subject to an uncomfortable amount of error, some authorities suggest the use of *one-third of the rental payment* as an estimate of the interest component. We are not entirely satisfied with that ratio for long-term leases in the early years. Rent for a lease on a building with a 50-year expected life will be largely interest, since straight-line depreciation would only be 2 percent a year.

What Method Should the Analyst Use? There is no altogether satisfactory solution to the problem of operating leases. Among the issues are the following:

Operating Lease Discounting Rates. Any estimate of the value of the asset and lease obligation will require an interest rate for discounting the stream of payments. Over the life of a lease, a calculation of the interest rate imbedded in the stream of payments will simply generate the interest rate that was assumed. Thus, when the interest rate is used as part of the return on investment, a high estimate of interest will result in a high return on a smaller amount of investment. A lower rate of interest will provide low return on a higher amount of investment. Some comparability could be achieved by using the same interest rate for all companies, but this may result in misleading return comparisons, since it provides the same answer for situations that are probably different.

Operating Lease Depreciation. Calculating a depreciation estimate requires assumptions about the *original* useful life of the asset. Large errors could occur in the depreciation estimate for long-term assets.

Rent as a Proxy. Use of the rent as a proxy for the sum of interest plus depreciation would not provide comparability with companies that lease property using capital leases. However, if the company has many leases that were initiated at various times, the rent may reasonably be assumed to be approximately the correct total of interest plus depreciation. In addition, this approach uses the interest rate assumption only for the allocation of the rent between the two expenses. Long-term leases are not terribly sensitive to moderate changes in the interest rate assumption, and short-term leases have a relatively small interest component in comparison to the amount of depreciation. Thus, a calculation of predepreciation return on capital using rent as the sum of depreciation and interest probably gives an answer that the analyst can live with.

Rules-of-Thumb Must Be Kept Up-to-Date. Use of rules-of-thumb is probably acceptable, although rough approximations of the interest component. We would suggest that if the analyst follows this route, the appropriate rules today are to use:

- One-third of the current year's rental payment for short leases
- One-half for leases in the 12 to 20 year range
- 60 percent for leases over 20 years

We suggest these numbers because they are in line with the interest component of a sample of capital lease disclosures where the length of lease and type of property were disclosed. These rules-of-thumb are based on interest rates inherent in leases that were outstanding in 1985 and the first half of 1986. These rules-of-thumb should be changed as interest rates change. We suggest that analysts who decide to use rules-of-thumb observe the interest rate component of capital leases, particularly of companies in similar industries.

Exclusion of Operating Leases from Return Calculations. An alternative is not to capitalize operating leases at all for purposes of calculating any return number. This approach uses the estimated lease obligation only in studies of the capital structure, the equity ratio, and similar calculations, but does not use the operating lease as part of the denominator of any calculation of return. However, treating operating leases differently from capital leases will often result in identical assets being treated differently. Many capital leases, after passage of a few years, would no longer qualify as capital leases if they were reclassified. They would be operating leases because the lease's life was no longer 75 percent of useful life, nor was present value any longer 90 percent of fair value. Conceptually, there is a good case for putting all these similar assets on the balance sheet.

Other Off-Balance-Sheet Liabilities

Most other types of off-balance-sheet financing require analysts to use judgment rather than fixed rules.

Product-Financing Arrangements

Return of Goods versus Goods on Consignment. Magazines are often sold to newsstands with an agreement to take back any unsold copies when the next issue comes out. In most industries, these would be considered goods on consignment, and the cash received from the customer would be considered a deposit rather than revenue because the returns are not readily estimable. However, those are not the product-financing arrangements that are a problem for analysts.

Inventory Parking. The more difficult inventory transactions are arrangements where inventory is "parked" with another party with the expectation that the buyer will exercise an option to return the goods and receive the original money back with interest. In effect, that is a secured borrowing transaction and should be accounted for as such.

Related Party Transactions. Many related party transactions do involve borrowing and lending between the reporting company and a related party. Related parties include people and organizations that often do not qualify for such terms as subsidiary or affiliate:

- Grantor trusts
- Nonsub subsidiaries whose stock is nominally owned by a third party or that essentially have no economic substance
- Joint venture partners
- Officers and directors
- Principal stockholders and their relatives

Such relationships are sometimes used to borrow in behalf of the company, without the borrowing appearing on the balance sheet. Even worse, the borrowing may show up on the balance sheet of the reporting company as preferred stock, common stock, or some other subordinated security. More often, nothing appears on the balance sheet, but the company has guaranteed the loan or offered other credit assurances through such devices as insurance or letters of credit. Unwinding and understanding some of these complex transactions can be a major task for the analyst.

Contingent Litigation Liabilities. Many contingent liabilities that involve litigation are excluded from the balance sheet on grounds that no reasonable estimate can be made of the outcome or that the outcome would be prejudiced by making such an estimate. These contingencies are usually revealed in footnotes, even though no estimate of the amount of loss may be given.

Is There an Asset?   The economic substance of some hidden liabilities is that the reporting entity is the primary obligor and prime beneficiary of a borrowing or guarantee. The analyst may conclude that a liability and possibly an asset should be placed on the books. Since the liability is usually well hidden, the analyst may uncover such situations more easily by finding the asset from which the company is benefiting.

Other Liabilities

Funded Debt

The characteristics of funded debt are discussed in depth in Chapters 23 and 24.[2]

Pensions and Other Postemployment Benefits

These obligations were discussed in Chapter 4.

Pension Liabilities on the Balance Sheet

Sometimes a pension liability is shown on the balance sheet when in fact none exists economically. This may arise because the company has reached the limit of tax deductibility and chooses not to make further contributions to the pension fund until they become deductible. This can build a sizable liability on the balance sheet even though the pension plan itself may be significantly overfunded and no economic liability exists. The analyst should take the liability off the balance sheet and adjust pension expense, taxes, and equity over the years the overfunding occurred.

Pension Plan Terminations

Another complex pension situation has begun to arise recently. A company discontinues its old defined-benefit pension plan and replaces it with a new defined-benefit plan after purchasing annuities for all the obligations of the old plan and withdrawing cash from it. Any assets remaining in a plan that has satisfied its liabilities might properly be treated as an asset of the plan sponsor—the prepayment of pension expense, and certainly any liability remaining on the plan sponsor's books should be removed from the balance sheet.

"Book Reserve" Pension Liabilities

Most German subsidiaries did not until recently place money in trust for the payment of pension obligations. Instead, they merely showed a liability on the balance sheet—the "book reserve" method of pension accounting.

[2] See the unabridged fifth edition of Sidney Cottle, Roger F. Murray, and Frank E. Block, *Graham and Dodd's Security Analysis*, McGraw-Hill, New York, 1988

Deferred Taxes

The largest intermediate class of liabilities in terms of dollars must surely be the deferred tax liability. Deferred taxes were discussed in detail in Chapter 9; their cash flow effects were discussed in Chapter 7.

Preferred Stock Liability

Until recently, conventional balance sheets showed preferred stock as part of capital and surplus. Thus it was placed with the common stock, as if sharing in the ownership of the business, and was sharply separated from funded debt and other liabilities. (In 1985 the SEC began to require that mandatory redeemable preferred stock be shown outside of stockholders' equity.) The most useful balance sheet analysis will place preferred stock with the funded debt as making up the total prior claims against the capital fund. Bonded debt and preferred stocks may be designated together under "senior issues." However, in analyzing senior claims, the subordinate position of the preferred should be recognized. The proper carrying amount for the preferred stock liability is discussed in Chapter 11.

Preferred Stock Dividend Arrearages

When unpaid preferred dividends have accumulated, this amount should be shown clearly in the balance sheet and not be buried in a footnote. A good arrangement is to place the amount of such accumulation in parentheses immediately below the earned surplus figure, or else to add it to the preferred stock liability. From the viewpoint of the common stockholders such claims are liabilities.

11

Asset Values in Balance Sheet Analysis

Relation of Assets to Securities and Other Claims

The discussion of balance sheet affairs continues, giving attention first to asset values and their relationship to securities and other claims.

Asset Values

The Going Concern

The correct calculation of the asset values and their relationship to securities or creditors' claims depends on the purposes of the analyst. The novice investor is sometimes startled to learn that, say, the book value or net asset value for the common shareholders might legitimately be calculated several ways, depending on the question asked. We shall examine such a set of calculations shortly. Asset values are ordinarily not a critical "going concern" matter, because the assets are expected to be used, not sold. Analysts who are examining a company as a going concern are trying to determine the aggregate investment value of the firm. The earning power of the *assets in use* determines their investment value. Yet, asset values do play a role in analysis of going concerns because they are a measure of the capital employed. The various return-on-capital ratios are very powerful, for they indicate the efficiency with which capital is used.

Asset values may exceed the value based on earning power of some going concerns. In those cases the asset value represents a potential for favorable future developments and provides a margin of safety if earnings collapse. Even below investment value, the asset value is a definite positive factor that may limit the investor's potential loss if earnings fail.

Collateral Value

Viewed as collateral, the pertinent value of an asset is its potential sales price. Claimants and security holders are interested in the collateral and liquidating values of companies, particularly when full or partial liquidation is likely to take place or when there is some question about payment from earning power.

Merger and Acquisition Values

Companies with high liquidating values are often attractive acquisition candidates. Part of the acquisition price can be financed by borrowing against collateral value of the assets. Sometimes assets can be sold for amounts sufficient to repay the entire acquisition cost, leaving assets and earning power for the acquiror. Companies with large amounts of assets are more attractive purchase acquisitions, because there is less goodwill, which analysts ignore as an asset.

Companies that can be bought for substantially less than their asset values may be attractive acquisitions even though they are currently unprofitable. Some of or all the assets can be sold and the capital redeployed in other activities, one hopes in a fashion that will increase the investment value and ultimately the prices of securities.

As a Measure of Capital

The assets of a company are its true capital. Most security analysis tends to use the word *capital* to refer to the claims and interests of debtors and owners—those whose interests appear on the right side of the balance sheet. The right side of the balance sheet tells the *source* of the capital. The left side shows how that capital is allocated among types of investments, generally presenting those assets at the unrecovered amount invested in them.

As a Measure of Safety for Each Security Issue

One of the measures of safety of securities and the claims of creditors is the amount of assets, after deducting all prior claims, available for the particular security or class of claimants. A number of coverage ratios are calculated for purposes of determining the excess asset protection.

The Amount of Equity Claim

Shareholders are entitled to the residual assets after all prior claims have been satisfied.

Computation of the Equity or Book Value per Share

The book value per share of a common stock is found by adding up all the assets, subtracting all liabilities and stock issues ahead of the common, and then dividing by the number of common shares. Our balance sheet presentation of Bristol-Myers for 1985, as given in Figure 10.1 in Chapter 10, will lead readily to the book value per share. All that is necessary is to divide the number of shares into the indicated equity. In the case of Bristol-Myers, the figure is $16.51 per share.

Consider the Effects of Dilution

Dilution of book value should be examined if the analyst is looking to the book value per share in terms of

1. The company's potential for liquidation, sale of assets, acquisition as an asset play
2. Any fashion in which book value is considered a viable alternative to measuring value by capitalization of earnings

The analyst should calculate on a worst-case basis the various combinations of exercise of conversion privileges of convertible issues and of warrants and options so that dilution of book value per share may be assessed.

Treatment of Intangibles in Computing Asset Values

It is customary to eliminate intangibles in the computation of the net asset value, or equity, per share of common stock. The phrase *book value* is a little ambiguous; sometimes it means to include all the assets shown on the books, and, at other times, it means to exclude the intangibles.

When excluding intangibles entirely from book value, analysts often use the expression "net tangible assets per share." That phrase is not accurate for the book value number that we recommend, since we encourage the inclusion of any intangible assets which have a known or estimable market value or which have a direct stream of revenue, such as royalty income.

Example. The 1985 annual report of Philip Morris Companies, Inc., reported goodwill and intangibles of $4.457 billion. About $4.3 billion was goodwill which is being amortized on a straight-line basis over 40 years. About $3.9 billion of the goodwill came about as a result of the acquisition of General Foods. The net worth of Philip Morris at year-end 1985 was $4.757 billion. An immediate write-off of goodwill would virtually eliminate stockholders' equity.

Example. The proper treatment of a particular kind of intangible asset can change. Prior to the Motor Carrier Act of 1980, interstate operating rights were exclusive assets of motor carriers, originally acquired from the Interstate Commerce Commission or other licensing agency. Those operating rights could be sold to another trucking company. Prior to the act, transactions in motor carrier operating rights were frequent and at reasonably predictable prices. The Act deregulated the industry and made the operating rights worthless, since anyone could obtain identical rights at no cost beyond minimal paperwork. A previously valuable right had suddenly become worthless, wiping out the net worth of a number of the weaker trucking companies.

The intangible assets often seen on the balance sheet include such items as patents, franchises, operating rights, and purchased goodwill (the cost of acquisition of another concern in excess of the fair value of assets minus liabilities). Purchased goodwill acquired on or after November 1, 1970, is written off-in installments over not more than 40 years. Purchased goodwill that was acquired before November 1, 1970, need not be written off. That goodwill remains subject to management judgment about whether to amortize and over what period of time. A number of companies continue to carry their pre-1970 purchased goodwill and other intangibles at historic numbers and make no effort to amortize.

Example. The 1985 annual report of ITT Corporation describes its $51,788,000 of pre-November 1, 1970 purchased goodwill as "unamortizable," which is not accurate, and carries it in the plant, property, and equipment account.

Alternative Computation of Book Value

In most cases the book value may be computed readily from the liability side of the conventional published balance sheet. It is sufficient to add together common stock, at par or stated value, the various surplus items, and the translation adjustment. (Most intangibles must be subtracted from this sum.) This will give the total common stock equity, which is then divided by the number of shares. Adjustments may be desirable, to correct the stated liability for preferred stock, and to adjust the carrying amounts of any assets and liabilities that are improperly stated or are known but absent from the balance sheet.

Asset Values and Investment Values

Book Value Is Not Intrinsic Value

The calculation of an equity's book value is not intended to show the "true value" of the shares; if it were, the intangibles of many companies would have to be appraised at a very high figure. Book value is only one of many "values" that the analyst must deal with, and it clearly is not the market value of the stock, nor its intrinsic value, nor the liquidating value. It is, instead, accounting's net asset value, adjusted in a variety of ways by the analyst. It is but one step along the way to determining investment value or "intrinsic value." The very large premiums over book value paid in the acquisition of certain food companies, such as Nabisco and General Foods, is evidence enough that well-established brand names are true economic assets of considerable value. That value can be preserved by advertising, promotion, maintaining product quality, and other actions. The value may continue or even increase over the years. The *book value, asset value,* or *net worth,* discussed in this section, is merely a single factor in the entire value picture. For this limited purpose, we confine ourselves to the various categories of tangible assets and the few intangibles that have liquidating value or other measurable value. *The true value of goodwill, trade names, customer relations, and similar intangible assets is indistinguishable from the value of the earnings which they produce.*

Practical Significance of Book Value

The financial services regularly calculate from the published balance sheets the book value of common stocks, but it is seldom used in a direct way to measure value. This book value is limited to a few important generic situations:

- *Public utilities.* In the field of public utility stocks, the rates allowed by regulatory bodies, and the resultant earning power, may be largely governed by the assets, to the extent that they are included in the rate base. They are usually calculated at original cost, although in a few jurisdictions "fair value" is used.

- *Financial companies.* The assets of financial companies, such as banks, insurance companies, and investment companies, are nearly all so liquid that their value enters—to a varying extent—in investment decisions relating to their shares.

- *Return on equity.* Book value is useful in calculating the return on equity. To the degree that this is a stable number through time, the ratio, combined with the payout ratio, can offer some indications about the amount of growth that can be financed internally.

- *Asset plays and liquidating values.* Identifying takeover candidates known as "asset plays," and estimating liquidating values of companies requires use of book values to some extent. However, since the book values are largely based on recoverable investment on a going-concern basis, the book value is merely a first approximation. In addition to security analysts' usual adjustments, estimates of the current values of individual assets would be needed to improve the accuracy of the numbers.

- *Common-stock valuation models.* There are limited mechanical uses of book value in a few price models for common stocks, although the models are not widely used.

Asset Value and Earning Power Apparently Unrelated. For the great category known as "industrial companies" and for the railroads, book value does not appear to be widely used for direct valuation. Common stocks sell freely either at high multiples or at small fractions of book value and garner little notice. For example, Marion Laboratories, Inc., sold at 63 in April 1986, when its most recent recorded book value was $4.17 a share. At the same time, Datapoint Corporation was selling at 5½ with a book value of $14.92.

We agree with the prevailing viewpoint that asset values are not the primary factor in determining investment values. But this does not mean that it is wise or safe to lose sight completely of this element in the analytical picture. For discussion of this point, see Chapters 23 and 24 on bond and preferred stock valuation and Chapter 34 on the asset value in valuation of common stocks.[1]

Preparation of Balance Sheet for Asset Value Analysis

Table 11.1 shows the adjusted capitalization of American Brands, Inc., at the 1985 year end.

---

[1] See the unabridged fifth edition of Sidney Cottle, Roger F. Murray, and Frank E. Block, *Graham and Dodd's Security Analysis*, McGraw-Hill, New York, 1988.

Table 11.1 Adjusted Capitalization of American Brands, Inc., as of December 31, 1985

	Dollar value (millions)	Percent
Notes payable to banks...	243.2	6.6
Commercial paper	138.7	3.8
Funded debt...	748.7*	20.4
Operating leases...	95.7†	2.6
Total debt...	1,226.3	33.4
Deferred income taxes	323.5‡	8.8
$2.75 Preferred stock, no par, stated at mandatory redemption price of $30.50 (4,507,528 shares)..	137.5	3.8
$2.67 Convertible preferred, no par, stated at $30.50 (preference amount in liquidation) (1,552,328 shares)............................	47.3	1.3
Common stockholders' equity after subtracting $641.8 million goodwill...	1,930.0‡	52.7
Total capital structure...	3,664.6	100.0
Other current liabilities	1,074.1¶	
Total capital and other liabilities.......................................	4,738.7	

*Includes $8.2 current portion of debt and capital leases.
†Present value of minimum operating lease payments using a 12 percent discount rate. The pattern of payments beyond five years was estimated.
‡Adjusted to eliminate the effects of foreign currency translation adjustment losses arising from noncurrent items.
¶Not considered a part of capital structure but required for calculating coverage ratios.

Elimination of Intangibles

The company showed $641.8 million in goodwill resulting from business acquisitions. Net worth was reduced by that amount in full. No adjustment was made to the deferred tax account in this case because the company was considered to be an ongoing firm, the goodwill amortization is not tax deductible, and no tax benefit will be obtained from it until subsidiaries which gave rise to the goodwill are sold or liquidated. However, had we removed other intangibles which were deductible for income tax purposes, we would have reduced equity by only *1 minus the tax rate* times the amount of those intangibles and reduced the deferred tax liability by the remainder. In the case of a company that was expected to be liquidated soon, or which was expected to liquidate its investment in a subsidiary that had given rise to purchased goodwill, it would have been proper to make the tax effect adjustment.

Gains and Losses on Securities

The common stockholders' equity in the table included unrealized appreciation on investments in marketable equity securities of the

Franklin Life Insurance Company in the amount of $4.1 million. The Franklin Life Insurance Company is carried under equity method and is 100 percent owned; the latter fact justifies the inclusion of the $4.1 million in common stockholders' equity. If that unrealized gain represented American Brand's proportional interest in results of a 25 percent–owned affiliate carried on the equity method, the gain should not be used in a calculation of assets available to protect debt and preferred stock, because ready access to the unrealized gains would not exist.

Equity Method Investees

Similarly, one could argue that the *retained earnings* of a 25 percent–owned investee accounted for using the equity method should properly be excluded from this sort of calculation because the retained earnings are not readily accessibile.

Foreign Currency Translation Adjustments

For the reasons discussed in the foreign currency translation section of Chapter 4, stockholders' equity and the deferred tax liability were adjusted to reflect only that portion of foreign currency translation adjustment gains and losses that resulted from the effects of rate changes on working capital.

Carrying Amount of Preferred Stocks

American Brands has two preferred stocks outstanding, both without par value. Both are stated at a carrying amount of $30.50 per share. In the case of the $2.75 preferred, $30.50 is the mandatory redemption price. Both preferreds are entitled to $30.50 per share in liquidation. The $2.67 convertible preferred stock ranks equally with the $2.75 preferred, although the dividend amounts are slightly different. There is also a modest difference in the voting rights of the two preferred stocks, but neither has a prior claim over the other as to payment of dividends or payments in liquidation. As a result, we believe that they should be treated equally and carried at the $30.50 stated value, which is the best for both preferred stocks.

Deferred Taxes

The table shows that American Brands has accumulated a deferred income tax liability of $323.5 million, after our adjustment of foreign currency translation losses. That tax is not currently owed and will not be until certain book-tax timing differences reverse in future years. We have discussed deferred income tax items as a source of capital that works for the common stockholders. However, deferred taxes should not be ignored in calculating the asset protection for the long-term debt or the preferred stocks of American Brands. If the carrying amounts of the preferred stocks and common equity were realized, say in liquidation, the deferred income taxes would become payable and have a claim that would take priority over many debt issues. As a result, in calculating the coverage for the funded debt or the preferred, the deferred income tax liability must be covered too.

Pensions

The 1985 annual report of American Brands showed a modest deficit in its pension fund valuation as of January 1, 1984. The pension liability was $505.9 million versus net assets available for benefits of $484.2 million—a normal situation requiring no adjustment to net worth. However, if the company were in financial difficulty, we would be inclined to show the pension shortfall as a liability. Similarly, if American Brands had a large pension surplus, and it was deemed probable that the company would discontinue its pension plan to obtain the asset reversion, the net pension asset should be added to equity, after adjustment for deferred taxes at the ordinary income tax rate.

Operating Leases

For the reasons discussed in Chapter 10, operating leases were capitalized, using a 12 percent discounting rate.

The Structure of the Balance Sheet

The Capital Structure

Table 11.1 shows the major categories of the capital structure of American Brands:

- Short-term borrowings
- Current and noncurrent funded debt, including capital leases
- Operating leases
- Deferred taxes

- Preferred stock
- Common-stock equity

Ordinarily, those current liabilities other than the current portion of funded debt, notes payable, bank loans, and commercial paper are not considered a part of the capital structure. In some cases, the term *capital structure* is used to refer to long-term sources of capital only. To avoid confusion, use the term *permanent capital* or specify *long-term capital*, if that is what is meant. The treatment of other liabilities is situational. Capital leases would normally be included with the funded debt, but for non-interest-bearing liabilities, for which no interest rate can be assumed or calculated, the liabilities are best excluded from the capital structure to avoid distortions of the return on invested capital calculations. The treatment of deferred taxes varies depending on the objectives of the analysis; for discussion of the reasons to exclude deferred taxes from the capital structure for certain analytical purposes, see Chapter 9. The capital structure or capitalization structure is usually summarized by stating what percentage of the total each category represents.

The Working-Capital Position

Careful buyers of securities scrutinize the balance sheet to see if the cash assets are adequate, if the current assets bear a suitable ratio to the current liabilities, and if there is any indebtedness near maturity that may develop into a refinancing problem.

Cash Shortage Can Be Offset by a Strong Working-Capital Position. Nothing useful can be said here about how much cash a corporation should hold. The investor must decide what is needed in any particular case and how seriously to regard a deficiency of cash. A real shortage of cash rarely occurs unless the working-capital position as a whole is poor. With a good ratio of current assets to current liabilities a corporation can get the cash it needs by bank borrowing or sale of receivables.

Industry Current Ratio Standards. On the subject of the working-capital ratio, a minimum of $2 of current assets for each dollar of current liabilities was formerly regarded as a standard for industrial companies. In more recent years bankers have tended to deviate from the traditional 2-to-1 current ratio, because statistics are now available for individual industry averages. Those statistics indicate significant industry and company differences in the current ratios required for effective operations and reasonable conservatism. Such tables are published regularly by Robert Morris Associates and others, giving industry averages in total and by size of firm.

Bankers' Credit Standards. Analysts should be acquainted with the banking industry standards for credit decisions so that they can be alert to the possibility that a company may have its credit withdrawn. Because of defects in the definition of *current*, many accountants and others think the current ratio is meaningless. They are wrong on two counts:

1. Significant empirical evidence indicates that the current ratio, in combination with others, is highly predictive of bankruptcy and financial stress.[2]
2. Bank credit officers do think current ratios matter, and their decisions have practical consequences.

A Below-Average Ratio Does Not Mean Unsatisfactory. Some tend to believe that a company falling below the current ratio average of its group should be viewed with some suspicion. This logical fallacy necessarily penalizes the lower half of any group, regardless of how satisfactory the showing may be considered by itself. We are unable to suggest better figures than the industry average to use as a definite quantitative test of a sufficiently comfortable current ratio. Naturally the investor would favor companies that well exceed minimum requirements, but the problem is whether a higher ratio must be exacted as a condition for purchase, so that an issue otherwise satisfactory would necessarily be rejected if the current assets are below standard. We hesitate to suggest such a rule, nor do we know what new figure to prescribe.

Quick Ratio and Cash Ratio Standards. In earlier times, the "acid test" was the same as the "quick ratio": the ratio of current assets excluding inventories to current liabilities. With the passing of time, the term *acid test* gradually came to mean the *cash ratio*—that is, the ratio of cash and equivalent to current liabilities. Given that potential for confusion, we will use the expressions *quick ratio* and *cash ratio*. The accepted standard for quick ratio is that current assets exclusive of inventories must at least equal current liabilities. The cash ratio is not a very useful test: no universal standards exist to use as a guide, and the ratio itself is quite volatile.

Failure to Meet Either Current Ratio or Quick Ratio Criteria. Ordi-

[2] E. I. Altman, "Financial Ratios, Discriminant Analysis and the Prediction of Corporate Bankruptcy," *Journal of Finance*, September 1968, pp. 589-609; there is a good discussion of Altman's studies and similar studies by others in George Foster, *Financial Statement Analysis*, Prentice-Hall, Englewood Cliffs, N.J. 1978, pp. 460-480.

narily the investor might well expect a company to meet *both* a current ratio test and the quick ratio test. The failure to meet either of these criteria would in most instances reflect strongly upon the investment standing of a common-stock issue—as it would in the case of a bond or preferred stock, and it would supply an argument against the security from the speculative standpoint as well.

Large Bank Debt. Financial difficulties are almost always heralded by the presence of bank loans or other debt due in a short time. In other words, rarely is a weak financial position created solely by ordinary trade accounts payable. Bank debt is not, however, inherently a bad sign; the use of a reasonable amount of bank credit—particularly for seasonal needs—is not only legitimate but even desirable. But, whenever the statement shows bank loans or notes payable, the analyst will scrutinize the financial picture somewhat more closely than when the balance sheet is "clean."

Bank Loans of Intermediate Maturity. Since the early 1940s, the *term loan* has developed as an important medium of financing by corporations. In general, such loans run from 3 to 15 years, and they are usually repayable in installments over their life—often with a larger than average maturity at the end (called the "balloon"). The lender is usually a bank, but sometimes is an insurance company. These term loans have been made for a variety of purposes:

1. To retire bond issues and even preferred stock
2. For additional working capital
3. To finance acquisitions of property or stock control
4. To finance a project or asset acquisition that will expire over the intermediate term

Debts Covenants and Dividend Restrictions. In most term loan agreements, as well as other forms of borrowing, the borrower promises to maintain working capital at a prescribed figure and not to pay dividends except out of future earnings plus some limited figure. In effect, the greater part of the earned surplus is frozen until the loan is paid off. During that period, before the company has built up a cushion of retained earnings, company stockholders may face at least a temporary loss of divided income.

From the standpoint of security analysis, term loans resemble the short-term notes that used to be sold to the public as a familiar part of corporate financing. They must be considered somewhat equivalent to both current liabilities and early maturing debt. They are not dangerous if either the current asset position is so strong that the loans could readily be taken care of as current liabilities or the earning power is so large and dependable as to make refinancing a simple problem. But if neither of these conditions is present, the analyst must view a substantial amount of intermediate bank debt as a potential threat to dividends or even to solvency.

Covenants in Term Loan Agreements. Term loan agreements are usually sensitive legal instruments because they often pick up both the normal protective provisions of an ordinary bank loan agreement and the traditional protective covenants of a long-term bond. The analyst should be familiar with the typical loan restrictions that exist on short-, intermediate-, and long-term borrowings and should assess the probability that any one of the three types might trigger a default, which in turn would probably trigger cross defaults, which, in theory, make all the debt payable immediately.

Current, Quick and Cash Asset Values per Common Share

In addition to book value per common share, we wish to suggest three other per share numbers of similar character: current asset value, quick asset value, and cash asset value.

Current Asset Value of a Common Stock

The current asset value of a stock consists of the current assets alone, minus *all* liabilities and claims ahead of the issue. This value excludes not only the intangible assets but also the fixed and miscellaneous assets. An occasional practice in Wall Street is to state the net current asset value of a common stock without deducting the senior securities from the working capital. We consider such a figure to be relatively meaningless and potentially misleading.

From time to time, when the market is deeply depressed, a large number of stocks will be available in the market at prices below their net current asset values. In effect, an investor can buy the company for its working capital, with the fixed assets thrown in for nothing. These conditions can exist for companies that are still profitable and for which no visible disaster lies ahead. A diversified portfolio of such companies will usually work out very well because of the low risk in the market price and the likelihood that sooner or later management will make the assets more productive. Also, such portfolios typically become available only in eras of extreme pessimism when stock prices in general are deeply depressed.

Cash and Quick Asset Values of a Common Stock

The quick asset value per share is the sum of cash and receivables, less all claims prior to the common, divided by the number of common shares outstanding.

The cash asset value of a stock consists of the cash assets alone, minus all liabilities and claims ahead of the common. Cash assets include:

- Certificates of deposit
- Call loans
- Commercial paper
- Bankers' acceptances
- Marketable short-term fixed income securities at market value
- Cash surrender value of insurance policies
- Cash itself

A somewhat more stringent calculation includes only the high-quality short-term fixed-income portion of the marketable securities.

Free Cash Asset Value

An alternative calculation of the cash asset value assumes that the current assets other than cash items are applicable to meet the liabilities ahead of the common. The cash assets are then reduced only by the amount needed to meet the balance of senior claims. The remainder of the cash may be considered as available for the common stock. This remainder may be called the "free cash," and the amount thereof per share of common may be called the "free cash asset value" of the common.

Table 11.2 shows an example of the computation of the 1985 asset values for Guilford Mills common stock. Guilford Mills's current assets should be increased by the amount of cash surrender value of life insurance. The analyst might estimate that at, say, $4 million. Thus,

Table 11.2. Guilford Mills, Inc. Condensed Balance Sheet
as of June 30, 1985
(In Thousands of Dollars)

Assets	
Cash items..	$ 2,286
Accounts receivable	79,903
Inventories..	58,258
Prepayments..	3,303
Current assets...	$143,750
Net plant account	68,382
Goodwill...	7,122
Other, principally cash value of life insurance	5,680
Total assets...	$224,934

Liabilities	
Current liabilities...	$ 50,267
Long-term liabilities...	11,860
Deferred income taxes	6,464
Other deferred liabilities...	5,515
Stockholders' investment (7,858,442 shares)........................	150,828
Total liabilities..	$224,934

working capital would be $143,750,000 plus $4 million less $50,267,000
current liabilities, or $97,483,000. From this must be subtracted the
intermediate liabilities, which total $23,839,000, leaving $73,644,000
available for the common stock. This equals $9.37 for each of the
7,858,442 shares outstanding. To determine the amount of quick assets
available for the common, the inventories of $58,258,000 must be
deducted, leaving $15,386,000, or $1.96 of quick assets a share. Subtracting the $79,903,000 of accounts receivable produces a negative
number, so there is no net cash and equivalent per share.

Calculations of Earnings via the Balance Sheet

An All-Inclusive Income

In some cases the true earnings over a period of years may be established
more reliably by comparing the change in common-stock equity than by
adding up the reported profits. These cases usually involve cases of
foreign companies that send items directly to equity or an accounting
change that has the same effect by adjusting the opening balance of the

earliest year presented. The following equation may be used, when there are no complexities:

Earnings for period = Increase in earned surplus
+ gain on marketable securities
+ current portion of foreign currency translation adjustments
+ dividends paid

In an uncomplicated case, an equivalent calculation may be made by comparing the net assets per share at the beginning and end of the period and adding back the dividends paid. However, a balance sheet approach can become somewhat complicated in any of the following situations or circumstances:

- Mergers and acquisitions taking place during the period studied
- Dispositions of subsidiaries occurring, which remove a previously consolidated portion of earned surplus and replace it with a gain or loss in earned surplus resulting from the disposition
- Sale or repurchase of shares of stock by the company
- Extraordinary write-downs or write-ups of assets if they affect the earned surplus
- Stock dividends which may be charged to earned surplus in whole or in part
- Transfers from the earned surplus account to the capital account resulting from, say, an increase in the par value of the outstanding common stock

In all balance sheet comparisons over time, the analyst must trace through the charges and credits to earned surplus to see what items, if any, are to be excluded from the record of overall earnings.

Some Aspects of Stock Sales and Purchases

A basic tenet of accounting is that a company does not make money dealing with itself. As a result, sale or repurchase of stock does not result in income being reported. Yet, from the viewpoint of the long-term holder of the stock, judicious purchases and sales by the company of its own stock can result in increases in the book value per share. For the ongoing stockholder, a dollar of increase in book value per share that arises from the company's trading in its own stock is worth just as much as a dollar of retained earnings. It is simply one more dollar of capital working for each of the shares. It is true that such advantageous trading by the company must be disadvantageous for those investors on the other side of the company's transactions, since they must lose money in the aggregate in order for the remaining shareholders to gain anything.

Stock Repurchase Programs Can Help Long-Term Investors

The fundamental investor usually has a long-term horizon and is concerned with personal gains and losses—not those of other stockholders who come and go. Thus, a company which buys and sells its stock advantageously, thereby increasing both the book value per share of the remaining shareholders and, in particular, the earnings per share, has an attraction that goes beyond the basic earning power. In recent years many companies, such as Teledyne, Inc., General Foods, Washington Post, Ford Motor, Exxon, and Schlumberger have improved their per-share earnings by judicious purchases of their own shares, and in a number of cases they increased book value per share also. Usually, the announcement of the share purchase program by itself will result in an immediate upward move in the stock's price.

Not All Share Purchases Are Advantageous

If the share purchases are made when the stock is unduly high, perhaps to get rid of cash and discourage an unfriendly takeover offer, the analyst is given several incentives to recommend sale.

Long-Term Studies of Income and Balance Sheet Position

Chapter 12 considers the key relationships among invested capital, earnings, dividends, and market price that underlie our judgments as to the quality of a company's performance and the attractiveness of its securities. A comprehensive study of a common stock might well include comparisons of absolute amounts and key ratios that go back many years. Figures of this sort can give the analyst a long perspective and an adequate conception of both the company's vicissitudes and its rate and direction of change. Balance sheets and income accounts for selected years, spaced, say, 10 years apart, will do this job quite well for most purposes, especially when two or more enterprises are compared. A more complete study would include the aggregate earnings for the decades between the balance sheet dates, so that a few key ratios can be computed on the basis of successive 10-year performances rather than for the single years a decade apart.

12
Ratio
Analysis

The study of a given company's financial statements should proceed in the following logical sequence (chapter discussions are given in parentheses):

1. The analyst should make all adjustments to the financial statements needed to present true figures from an analyst's viewpoint and to make them comparable to other companies (Chapters 2 to 11).

2. True operating earnings and cash flows for the period under review should be determined (Chapters 2 to 9).

3. The analyst should examine the balance sheet and establish the working-capital position, the capital structure, and the amount of invested capital per share (Chapters 10 and 11).

4. The analyst should then develop a number of key ratios, which will throw light on the company's overall performance, the safety of its senior securities, and the attractiveness of its common stock for investment.

This chapter covers many of the more important ratios used in the analysis of financial statements. Some special ratios for analysis of senior securities are discussed in Chapters 25 and 26.[1] Many other ratios are used by analysts when appropriate.

There are peculiar aspects in the use of ratios by security analysts. First, because various ratios can often be grouped together as essentially similar, within each group several may tell much the same story. Thus the analyst may pick one of several similar ratios and discard the others,

[1] See the unabridged fifth edition of Sidney Cottle, Roger F. Murray, and Frank E. Block, *Graham and Dodd's Security Analysis,* McGraw-Hill, New York, 1988.

depending largely on convenience and personal preference. For example, a calculation of return on assets tells essentially the same story as one of return on invested capital, because very little of the total assets is not funded by invested capital, and the two ratios tend to move up and down together. However, the analyst must use the same ratios, calculated the same way, for consistency through time and for comparisons between companies.

A peculiar aspect of ratio analysis is that the analyst may calculate a certain ratio one way for one purpose and another way for a different purpose. For example, the analyst may treat the deferred tax liability as part of equity for purposes of calculating return on equity but as a prior claim for purposes of calculating the book value of the common shares. These different uses merely reflect the analyst's attempt to answer different questions, using familiar terminology, such as "the common equity," but with different meanings for different purposes. As familiarity is gained with the use of the security analysts' terminology, the meaning usually becomes clear from the context of the analysis.

In our discussion of ratios throughout this chapter we will refer to the formulas in Figures 12.1, 12.2, and 12.4 through 12.7. The formulas are presented in a simplified form, referring to common terms such as *earnings* or *book value*. Since we assume that the analyst has already made all the appropriate adjustments to those items, we avoid long formula lines that would result if we were to express, say, earnings plus a long list of upward adjustments minus a long list of downward adjustments. Thus, our formulas are misleadingly simple for one who has not read Chapters 2 through 11.

Per-Share Figures and Related Ratios

The Per-Share Ratios

In Wall Street, it is customary to sum up the statistical data about a common stock in three salient figures: the earnings per share, the dividend rate, and the price. Although the price per share is a per-share ratio, it is not thought of as such because it is normally obtained directly from the market. Some analyses also include sales, cash flow, book value, and other items on a per-share basis.

Figure 12.1 shows formulas for calculating eight frequently used per-share ratios. These calculations are fairly straightforward. The numerator is whatever the ratio purports to show on a per-share basis. Where that item represents the results for the year, such as earnings, dividends, or cash flow, the denominator is the weighted average number of common shares outstanding. Where the ratio has a balance sheet figure in the numerator, representing the position on a particular date, the denominator is simply the number of common shares outstanding as of that balance sheet date.

1. Earnings per share = $\dfrac{\text{Earnings available for the common shares}}{\text{Weighted average common shares outstanding}}$

2. Dividend per share
$= \dfrac{\text{Total annual dividends paid to common shareholders}}{\text{Weighted average common shares outstanding}}$

3. Sales per share = $\dfrac{\text{Sales}}{\text{Weighted average common shares outstanding}}$

4. Cash flow per share (Chapter 7)
$= \dfrac{\text{Cash flow from operations after taxes}}{\text{Weighted average common shares outstanding}}$

5. Book value per share (Chapter 11)
$= \dfrac{\text{Book value of common equity } - \text{ goodwill } - \text{ most other intangible assets}}{\text{Common shares outstanding at balance sheet date}}$

6. Current assets per share (Chapter 11)
$= \dfrac{\text{Current assets } - \text{ all claims prior to common}}{\text{Common shares outstanding at balance sheet date}}$

7. Quick assets per share (Chapter 11)
$= \dfrac{\text{Cash } + \text{ receivables } - \text{ all claims prior to common}}{\text{Common shares outstanding at balance sheet date}}$

8. Cash per share (Chapter 11)
$= \dfrac{\text{Cash } - \text{ all claims prior to common}}{\text{Common shares outstanding at balance sheet date}}$

Figure 12.1 Suggested formulas for calculating per-share ratios.

The meaning of each of the per-share ratios should be fairly straightforward, and we shall not dwell on them individually. Experience with calculating and using the ratios, detecting trends and variances, making comparisons, and similar analyses will give the analyst a "feel" for the numbers of the company under study and, over the years, greater depth of understanding of each of the ratios' meanings and limitations.

Per-Share Data Are Defective in Two Ways

Loss of Focus on the Company. The convenience of per-share earnings figures leads inevitably to their widespread use. They have two drawbacks, however, which make them somewhat of a hindrance to serious analysis. The lesser defect is that they draw the investor's attention away from the enterprise as a whole involving magnitudes of

- Sales
- Profits
- Invested capital
- Aggregate market value of the firm

and concentrate it too much on the single share of stock. The greater defect is that a figure of earnings per share, accepted and emphasized without regard to the details of the income account from which it is derived, may easily give rise to misinformation.

Accountants Warn Against Per-Share Emphasis. A significant statement on the dangers of a per-share emphasis was made by the Committee on Accounting Procedure of the AICPA:

> In its deliberations concerning the nature and purpose of the income statement, the committee has been mindful of the disposition of even well-informed persons to attach undue importance to a single net income figure and to "earnings per share" shown for a particular year. The committee directs attention to the undesirability in many cases of the dissemination of information in which major prominence is given to a single figure of "net income" or "net income per share." However, if such income data are reported (as in newspapers, investors' services, and annual corporate reports), the committee strongly urges that any determination of "income per share" be related to the amount reported as net income, and that where charges or credits have been excluded from the determination of net income, the corresponding total or per share amount of such charges and credits also be reported separately and simultaneously. In this connection the committee earnestly solicits the cooperation of all organizations, both governmental and private, engaged in the compilation of business earnings statistics from annual reports.[2]

A Technical Problem of Per-Share Figures. A share is not a constant yardstick. That is, it does not necessarily represent a fixed percentage of the ownership of a company, nor is this year's share the same as last year's

---

[2]AICPA, *Accounting Research Bulletin No. 32*, December 1947, para. 32.

share in economic terms. As a result, a time series of per-share statistics can be subtly misleading if it is not examined thoughtfully and knowledgeably.

No similar objection applies to the use of per-share figures for the cash dividends paid in a given year. This can hardly be open to any misconception. There is frequently some doubt as to what the current dividend rate really is—mainly because of variations between regular and extra disbursements, but that is a difficulty of another sort.

Reported and Restated Earnings per Share

The analyst's intensive study of the income account will lead to occasional *restatement* of the reported profits to reflect the "true" operating earnings. These adjusted earnings will lead to a corresponding adjustment of the per-share earnings. Where the difference between the two amounts is substantial, analysts must point out that their corrected calculation presents a more serviceable picture of the results from operations. In the presentation of tables of historical per-share data, per-share columns can be shown both "As Reported" and "Adjusted," with footnotes explaining the types and amounts of adjustments for each year presented.

Allowances for Changes in Capitalization

Calculations of Earnings per Share (Ratio 1).   Ratio 1 in Figure 12.1 shows the common method of calculating earnings per share for purposes of measurement and communication. Some of its complexities are discussed below. Like most other analysts' ratios, the calculation of earnings per share may be affected by what question the analyst is asking. Although the formula given is satisfactory for measuring the past, when estimating future earnings-per-share, the analyst would make the calculation based on the number of shares expected to be outstanding in the year for which the earnings per share estimate is being prepared. This same caveat applies to all other estimates of future per-share numbers.

Splits and Stock Dividends.   In dealing with the past record, when data are given on a per-share basis, the analyst must follow the elementary practice of adjusting the figures to reflect any important changes in the capitalization which have taken place during the period. In the simplest case the changes will be only in the number of shares of common stock resulting from stock dividends, splits, etc. All that is necessary, then, is to restate the capitalization throughout the period on the basis of the current number of shares. For example, if the stock has been split 2 for 1, all previous per-share data must be divided by 2. (Some statistical services make such recalculations.)

Rights and Conversions. When the change in capitalization results from sale of additional stock at a comparatively low price (usually through the exercise of subscription rights or warrants) or to the conversion of senior securities, the adjustment is slightly more difficult. Rights may be to purchase additional shares of the same issue, to purchase convertibles which may be exchanged for shares of the same issue, or to purchase other securities.

A Simple Method of Rights Adjustment. To make a relatively simple adjustment that is applicable to all of these types of rights, simply obtain the market price of the stock and of the right to which it was entitled immediately after the stock went "ex-rights." The price of the rights is then divided by sum of the rights price plus the ex-rights price of the common stock to get a percentage that is the equivalent of a stock dividend. The per-share figures for all prior periods are then divided by 1 plus the percentage, just as they would be in the case of a stock dividend. This method is the same as used in apportioning the tax cost basis between the stock and the right by the Internal Revenue Service, and therefore historical data are available from the various published tax services, saving the analyst from doing all the individual calculations.[3]

Adjustment for Conversions. When bonds or preferred stocks have been converted into common, the interest or dividend formerly paid, less any related tax credit, is added back to the earnings. The new earnings figure is then applied to the larger number of shares.

The Problem of Earnings Dilution

Analysis of Earnings Dilution

For the investor, three issues are raised regarding earnings dilution and its effects:

- The probability of dilution
- The timing of dilution
- The degree of dilution

---

[3] H. Levy and Marshall Sarnat, *Investment and Portfolio Analysis,* John Wiley & Sons, New York, 1972, pp. 39-44.

This is an area for specific analysis rather than broad and somewhat arbitrary rules. We will contrast the accounting rules with some hypothetical situations to highlight the complexities.

Reported Earnings per Share

Primary Earnings per Share. The financial statements may present two earnings-per-share numbers; one is called "primary earnings," and the other "fully diluted earnings." The calculations use the concept of *common-stock equivalents.* Warrants and options are always considered to be common-stock equivalents. Convertible securities issued after February 28, 1982, are common-stock equivalents if at the time of issuance the convertible security had a cash yield (coupon divided by issue price) less than two-thirds of a certain interest rate—currently, the yield on Aa-rated corporate bonds. (The previous cash yield test had been two-thirds of the prime rate.) The accounting rule may be applied retroactively to convertibles issued prior to that date. Those convertible issues considered common-stock equivalents are treated as if they had been converted into common stock, with appropriate adjustments for the interest or preferred dividends and tax effects made to the earnings available for the common shares considered then to be outstanding. Warrants and options are assumed to be exercised, and the proceeds of exercise used to purchase treasury stock, thereby reducing the number of shares outstanding. If any exercise or conversion results in an *antidilutive* effect, it is eliminated from the calculation.

The Cash Yield Test Doesn't Work. It is interesting to note that articles in the academic literature have revealed that the cash yield test actually tends to identify the securities that will *not* be converted rather than those that will!

Fully Diluted Earnings per Share—A Valuable Warning. Fully diluted earnings is a calculation of the effects of full exercise and conversion on a worst-case basis, that is, the combination giving the greatest possible earnings dilution. If the number is much below primary earnings per share, it stands as a warning that there *may* be danger of dilution.

The Analytical Problem. One would not exercise a right to buy common stock at $40 a share when it could be bought in the market for $20. However, one may have expectations that the right will someday be exercised. The analyst's first step must be to evaluate the company and its prospects for growth to determine whether the future stock value will be greater than the $40 exercise price before the exercise privilege expires. The right will be exercised only when one of the following occurs:

1. The stock price is so far above $40 that the option value has

essentially disappeared, and the dividend from the common stock exceeds the cost of borrowing the $40 to exercise the right.

2. A valuable option is about to expire.

Estimating the Timing of Dilution. To estimate the timing of exercise of such a right, one must estimate that point in time when the dividend would exceed the cost of borrowing and when the stock would be selling at a sufficient premium over $40 so that the option value had essentially disappeared. As long as there is option value, it is more advantageous to sell the right and purchase stock at the market than to exercise. Thus, the analyst must estimate future price-earnings ratios, growth rates of earnings and dividends, payout ratios, interest rates, and similar elements. In the case of convertibles, the likelihood of the company calling the convertible instrument to force conversion has to enter into this enormous calculus. Two-thirds of a past interest rate is not a likely filter to capture such complexities.

What Gets Diluted—Earnings? Once the timing of the conversion or exercise has been estimated, how should this information be interpreted? What is it that gets diluted? Between today and the date that exercise or conversion is expected to occur, the company will pay dividends to its existing shareholders. Since the shareholders will not be expected to return any of those dividends, that part of earnings is not diluted.

Are Retained Earnings Diluted? Are the *retained earnings* diluted? Retained earnings, of course, become a part of book value. If the book value is projected to be $20 a share at the time of exercise or conversion, then we must compare this $20 per share with the dollars per share that the company will receive. If the company will get more than $20 for each new share created, the book value per share will rise rather than decline, that is, the effect would be antidilutive rather than dilutive. Thus, retained earnings may or may not suffer dilution!

Future Dividends? Perhaps the subsequent stream of dividends will be diluted by exercise or conversion. Dilution of future dividends will depend on the incremental rate of return earned on the funds acquired as a result of exercise or conversion, resulting in a dilutive or antidilutive effect on the stream of future dividends.

What Is the Price of Dilution? Assume, finally, that dilution of earnings per share will be 10 percent, beginning 10 years from now. How much does that change the price of the stock today? Assuming an earnings and dividend growth rate of 8 percent and a discount rate of 15 percent, the present value of the stock would be reduced by about 5 percent: 10 percent × $(1.08/1.15)^{10}$ = 5.3 percent. Thus the analyst must remember two important rules:

1. Dilution may not matter much if it is not going to take place for a long time.

2. Even if one expects immediate exercise or conversion, the results may be either antidilutive or dilutive.

What Steps Should the Analyst Take?

Determine If There Is a Problem—Then Calculate the Magnitude. First, the analyst should always look at the fully diluted earnings per share to see if there is a *potential* problem. If the fully diluted earnings are only 5 or 10 percent below reported earnings, there is no immediate problem. If the dilutive effect is greater, then the analyst must determine the timing, probability, and degree of dilution and discount the effects back to present value for a downward adjustment in the intrinsic value of the stock.

Normally Use Average or Projected Shares Outstanding. For the ordinary calculation of earnings per share, we recommend the use of (1) the weighted average number of shares outstanding for analysis of *past* results or (2) the number of shares expected to be outstanding for *prospective* calculations such as future earnings per share.

Adjust for Expected Conversion, If Significant. If there is an expectation of significant dilution from conversion, the analyst should calculate that per-share dilution on a worst-case basis for those issues which are expected to be transformed into shares of common stock.

Allowance for Outstanding Warrants and Stock Options

Use the Treasury Stock Method. In projecting future earnings, the *treasury stock method* normally should be used for any new funds expected to be received, that is, the cash proceeds of exercise are assumed to be used to purchase shares, and adjustment is made for the elimination of the interest or preferred dividends, with tax effects where appropriate.

Alternatively, Estimate the Return on the Proceeds of Exercise. The alternative to the treasury stock method is to estimate the earnings on the additional capital brought in by exercise of rights, warrants, or options. This is a more complicated procedure, but it may be justified if the expected incremental rate of return on investment is significantly higher or lower than is being earned currently by the company.

Formulas for Valuing Options.   Stock options granted to company employees and others have the same theoretical consequences as the warrants just discussed, but they do not have a market price. Their market price can be estimated using Black and Scholes's model or a variation thereof [4] or the *minimum value model.* The analyst can determine thereby roughly how much the option value exceeds the exercise price. That relationship is useful information on the *probability* of exercise, since a premium over exercise value inhibits exercise.

Minimum Value Formula.   The value of an option is never less than the current price of the underlying stock minus the present value of the exercise price and minus the present value of all dividends to be paid by the exercise date.[5] This is the *minimum value model,* and it is easily implemented by selecting a borrowing rate for discounting purposes, if the analyst has a satisfactory projection of future dividends.

Observe the Premium over Exercise Price.   At the same time, a fair sense of the likelihood of exercise is gained simply by observing the premium, if any, of the exercise price over the market price of the underlying stock. If they are far apart, the price of the stock must rise a great deal to trigger exercise. If they are close, say within 25 percent, applying the treasury stock method will give a quick picture of the seriousness of the dilution threat. Our 5 percent of net income rule should be used to judge whether the *cumulative* dilution effects require an adjustment of per-share numbers.

Conversion of "Class B" into Publicly Held Shares

A considerable number of privately owned companies have gone public through the sale of "Class A" common stock, whereas the interest of the former sole owners has been vested in "Class B" (sometimes plain "common") shares. Though the respective dividend rights of the two classes vary from company to company, they usually give some priority to the public shares. However, in virtually all cases the other issue has the

[4] Fischer Black and Myron Scholes, "The Pricing of Options and Corporate Liabilities," *Journal of Political Economy,* vol. 81, no. 3, May–June 1973, pp. 637–654.

[5] William F. Sharpe, *Investments,* Prentice-Hall, Inc., Englewood Cliffs, N.J. 1978, pp. 364–365.

right of conversion—share for share—into Class A stock. Occasionally, the conversion right is immediate and complete, but more often it can be done only in blocks over a period of several years.

In most cases, analysts make their calculations on the basis of full conversion, that is, assuming only one class of stock outstanding. In a few cases, when the analyst must decide about the Class B stock, the assumption would not be helpful.

A General Rule for Participating Interests

In calculating the earnings available for the common, the analyst must give full recognition to the rights of holders of participating issues, whether or not the amounts involved are actually being paid. Various types of bonds and preferred stocks have features which permit them to receive a share of income or a share of dividends paid on the common stock. These issues usually have claims to fixed payments which are made before the calculation of their participating or variable payments. The consequences of their existence are similar to those of convertibles and options, and thus the analyst must make appropriate adjustments to reflect in the per-share figures the claims of these instruments on the residual earnings of the company. In most cases the adjustment by the analyst will result in a hypothetical fixed-income security plus a number of shares of common-stock equivalents. Normally, the fully diluted per-share earnings shown in the annual report will signal the need for investigation of dilution.

Dividends per Share (Ratio 2)

Dividends per share qualifies as a ratio, but it is practically never calculated in any fashion other than to add the total dividends per share paid over the period in question, since dividends are normally declared on a per-share basis. Ratio 2 in Figure 12.1 would require that the shares outstanding be weighted by the dividends paid which is a fairly complicated way of calculating something that is available directly. Naturally, historical dividends per share would be adjusted for splits, stock dividends, rights, and the like.

Sales per Share (Ratio 3)

As shown in Figure 12.1, sales per share are calculated simply by dividing sales by the number of shares outstanding.

Cash Flow per Share (Ratio 4)

Cash flow per share is a useful measure of a company's general ability to leverage itself, to pay dividends, to convert "book earnings" into cash, and to enjoy financial flexibility. However, the cash flow does not "belong" to the equity holders in the same sense that earnings do. It may be committed to debt service or some other prior claim, such as rent. A ratio of "discretionary" cash flow per share requires making provision for these committed cash outflows.

Book Value, Current Assets, Quick Assets, and Cash per Share

Balance sheet data, when calculated on a per-share basis, are always the amounts outstanding as of the balance sheet date divided by the shares outstanding on that date. The common balance sheet per-share ratios are numbered 5 through 8 in Figure 12.1.

Price Ratios

A basic principle of finance is that no investment decisions regarding a common stock can properly be made except in the light of a specific price, which is usually the current market but may be some anticipated or calculated figure. The security analyst should compare the price with earnings, dividends, asset value, and—for a valuable additional insight— sales. Thus, the price ratios in Figure 12.2 are as follows:

Ratio 9 —price-earnings ratio

Ratio 10—earnings yield (the reciprocal of the price-earnings ratio)

Ratio 11—dividend yield

Ratio 12—sales per dollar of common, at market

Ratio 13—price-to-book value

These ratios are ordinarily calculated on the basis of the last full year's results or the latest balance sheet. However, the earnings may be an average for some suitable period of years. The earnings used for a price-earnings ratio may be for the trailing 12 months, the current fiscal year, or an estimate of the forthcoming 12 months. Some brokerage house letters give two price-earnings ratios, one using estimated current fiscal year earnings and the second using the ratio to the subsequent fiscal year's estimated earnings. One investment service publishes price-earnings ratios based on the latest three quarters of reported earnings plus an estimate of the earnings for the first unreported quarter. Since year-to-year earnings changes can be quite large, it is important that the earnings be identified as to the time period used and as to whether the figures are actual or estimated. The price may be a recent price, end-of-period, an average, anticipated, or a calculated price. These same problems can apply to other price ratios, and therefore the analyst must be aware what price and time period are being combined in any ratio. The analyst preparing a written report should take care that all ratios are properly explained, either in the text or in footnotes.

9. Price-earnings ratio (Chapter 11) $= \dfrac{\text{Price per share}}{\text{Earnings per share}}$

10. Earnings yield $= \dfrac{\text{Earnings per share}}{\text{Price per share}}$

11. Dividend yield $= \dfrac{\text{Dividend per share}}{\text{Price per share}}$

12. Sales per dollar of common at market value

$= \dfrac{\text{Sales}}{\text{Weighted average shares outstanding} \times \text{stock price}}$

13. Price-to-book value $= \dfrac{\text{Price per share}}{\text{Book value per share}}$

Figure 12.2 Suggested formulas for calculating price ratios.

Price-Earnings Ratios

Market Ratios and Multipliers

The main purpose of calculating earnings per share, aside from indicating dividend protection, is to permit a ready comparison with the current market price of the stock. The resultant *price-earnings ratio*, or *P/E*, is a concept that the working analyst will have to deal with extensively. The question of what price-earnings ratios are, and what determines them, must now be considered. Our treatment of the subject will fall into two parts. The first deals with the actual behavior of the market, that is, of investors and speculators, with respect to price-earnings ratios. The second part, reserved for a later chapter on valuation methods, will explore what the price-earnings ratio or multiplier *should be*.

Confusion Over Earnings Used

The statement that a common stock is selling at "N times earnings" is not without some ambiguity. The earnings referred to may be from the past year, from the current year, partly estimated, or next year's earnings, or even from the latest three months multiplied by 4. The phrase is sometimes amplified to read "N times anticipated earnings" for a stated period in the future, or "N times average earnings" for a stated period in the past, or even "N times trailing 12-months earnings." For the most part, however, the concept of the price-earnings ratio is applied to what is considered a current or quite recent full year's figure.

Diversity of P/E Ratios

When faced with a large assortment of price-earnings ratios, the analyst is likely to be bewildered by their diversity and inconsistency. Stock prices fluctuate over a wide range within a single year, which means that their ratios will vary correspondingly in that year. The average annual ratio for nearly every stock is likely to differ widely from one year to another. Finally, the ratios of different stocks when observed at the same moment cover a wide range. For example, in February 1987, Wheeling-Pittsburgh Steel sold as low as 1.3 times and International Banknote as high as 85 times the then current estimates by Value Line of earnings for the year ending March 1987. Surely, only price divided by normal earnings has any meaning or constancy.

Are There Any Understandable Patterns?

It seems almost impossible to make any degree of order out of this chaos. Nevertheless, one may discern some fairly well-defined and not irrational patterns in the price-earnings ratios, when they are viewed from the proper vantage. An effective method is comparing average price over a representative period of years with the average earnings during the same time. In Table 12.1 we show the resultant ratios for each of the 30 stocks in the Dow-Jones industrial average, taking the two 5-year periods, 1975 to 1979 and 1980 to 1984, and 1985.

Quality of Earnings.   For the vast majority of common stocks, the average relationship between price and earnings—as shown by this kind of computation—reflects the views of investors and speculators as to the quality and growth of the issue. A strong, successful, and promising company usually sells at a higher multiplier of current or average earnings than one that is less strong, less successful, and less promising.

Table 12.1 Average Earnings per Share, Prices, and Price-Earnings Ratios of Individual Stocks Constituting Dow-Jones Industrial Average (1975–1979, 1980–1984, and 1985)

Common stock*	1975 to 1979 Average			1980 to 1984 Average			1985		
	Earnings	Mean price**	Price-earnings	Earnings	Mean price	Price-Earnings	Earnings	Mean price	Price Earnings
Allied-Signal	$2.41	$33.9	14.1×	$4.88	$30.9	6.3×	$3.40	$41.0	12.1×
Aluminum Co.	3.48	23.8	6.8	3.18	33.6	10.6	1.32	35.3	26.7
American Can	5.51	36.2	6.6	3.50	37.4	10.7	5.02	56.6	11.3
American Express	1.79	17.7	9.9	2.75	27.3	9.9	3.55	45.5	12.8
American T & T	na†	na	na	na	na	na	1.43	22.2	15.5
Bethlehem Steel	2.12	25.6	12.1	(2.53)	22.9	nmf‡	(2.45)	16.8	nmf
Chevron	3.26	19.9	6.1	5.62	38.1	6.8	4.19	35.1	8.4
Du Pont	4.08	41.1	10.1	4.98	43.2	8.7	5.04	58.5	11.6
Eastman Kodak	3.15	50.0	15.9	4.14	48.1	11.6	1.46	47.2	32.3
Exxon	3.29	24.3	7.4	6.06	34.8	5.7	7.43	50.2	6.8
General Electric	2.37	25.0	10.5	4.09	40.4	9.9	5.13	64.8	12.6
General Motors	8.86	60.3	6.8	5.14	56.9	11.1	12.28	75.2	6.1
Goodyear	2.59	19.0	7.3	3.28	23.8	7.3	2.81	28.1	10.0
Inco	1.75	23.4	13.4	(2.10)	17.0	nmf	0.28	12.9	46.1
IBM	4.48	63.5	14.2	7.79	85.1	10.9	10.67	138.1	12.9
International Paper	6.28	51.0	8.1	5.28	46.3	8.8	1.61	51.1	31.7
McDonald's	1.51	21.8	14.4	3.38	34.6	10.2	4.99	66.3	13.3
Merck	1.94	33.0	17.0	2.93	41.9	14.3	3.79	57.5	15.2
Minnesota M&M	3.84	55.5	14.5	5.77	66.8	11.6	6.02	82.6	13.7
Navistar	7.04	32.1	4.6	(13.48)	14.3	nmf	0.77	15.9	20.6
Owens-Illinois	3.56	23.2	6.5	3.76	29.6	7.9	5.23	46.9	9.0
Philip Morris	1.43	15.1	10.6	3.13	28.0	8.9	5.08	25.6	5.0
Procter & Gamble	2.77	42.7	15.4	4.57	46.6	10.2	3.80	61.1	16.1
Sears. Roebuck	2.38	28.1	11.8	2.86	26.0	9.1	3.53	36.0	10.2
Texaco	3.86	26.4	6.8	6.28	37.3	5.9	4.62	33.7	7.3
Union Carbide	2.27	16.6	7.3	2.15	17.3	8.0	.36	18.2	50.6
United Technologies	2.13	17.4	8.2	3.63	28.4	7.8	4.58	40.5	8.8
U.S. Steel	2.60	34.8	13.4	2.01	25.3	12.6	1.71	28.7	16.8
Westinghouse Electric	1.50	9.1	6.1	2.61	18.1	6.9	4.30	36.5	8.5
Woolworth	2.36	10.8	4.6	1.88	13.6	7.2	2.75	24.8	9.0

*Adjusted for splits and stock dividends through 1985.
**Average of annual mean prices.
†na: Not available on a comparable basis.
‡nmf: Not a meaningful figure.

Certain Key Influences of P/E. The chief analytical elements governing the price-earnings ratio include

1. Those factors that are fully reflected in the financial data (tangible factors):

   - Growth of earnings and sales in the past
   - Profitability—rate of return on invested capital
   - Stability of past earnings
   - Dividend rate and record
   - Financial strength or credit standing

2. Those factors that are reflected to an indefinite extent in the data (intangible factors):

   - Quality of management
   - Nature and prospects of the industry
   - Competitive position and individual prospects of the company

The Intangibles Influence the Tangible Record. The five tangible factors may be studied by the analyst in the financial statements. The three intangibles do not, of course, admit of the same type of definite, quantitative calculation. Bear in mind that, typically, the incalculable factors have already exerted a strong influence on the reported results. In other words, the figures themselves will show, fairly clearly and comprehensively, how good a business is and how well the company is managed, unless the incumbent management has recently taken over or major new developments in the industry or in the concern make the past results irrelevant to the future. In the early stages of a highly dynamic industry—electronics, communication, semiconductors, computers, genetic engineering, drugs—expectations of future profits are often divorced completely from the actual accomplishments of the past. But those are not the usual cases.

Table 12.1 demonstrates another influence—the *Molodovsky effect.*[6] This is the tendency of a company suffering temporarily depressed earnings to sell at a high price-earnings ratio. The 1985 price-earnings ratios of Aluminum Company, Eastman Kodak, Inc., International Paper, Union Carbide, and Inco may reflect what the market perceives as a nontypical denominator. A casual scanning of the 1985 price-earnings ratios will show that some are two or more times the price-earnings ratios that prevailed in the 1980 to 1984 period. In fact, they look like the highly optimistic price-earnings ratios that are reserved for very high quality fast-growing companies. Examination of the particular companies sug-

[6]Nicholas Molodovsky, "A Theory of Price-Earnings Ratios" *Financial Analysts Journal,* November 1953, pp. 65–80.

gests that most of them are not growth stocks, and the quality of some is not especially high. Beware of using the price-earnings ratio to measure cheapness or dearness of the stock market. The *average* price-earnings ratio in 1985 is 75 percent higher than that of the 1980 to 1984 period, but a scanning of the individual stocks shows that the majority are up only 30 percent or thereabouts. The median of 12.6 times earnings in 1985 would probably give a much better indication of the cheapness or dearness of the market as a whole, and most of the high price-earnings ratio examples in 1985 (but not in the earlier periods) are probably results of the Molodovsky effect.

Key Ratios Pertaining to Tangible Factors

The tangible factors affecting the quality of a company may be measured by the use of key ratios and other calculations. In addition to the per-share and price ratios, five other groups of ratios give insight into the past record or "tangible factors":

Profitability ratios: margins and activity ratios

Growth rate

Stability ratios

Payout ratio (dividend policy)

Credit ratios

The previous section of this chapter discussed some of the shortcomings of per-share ratios, particularly distraction from analysis of the business as a whole. The best discipline is to focus on price and per-share data *last*, after a complete analysis of the above five groups of ratios. These five groups measure the performance and financial strength of the enterprise apart from the market valuation. Let us first discuss these various ratios in their proper sequence and then illustrate their use by applying some of them to a pair of chemical companies in Chapter 13 and to the grocery industry in Chapter 14.

Profitability Ratios
Management's Ability to Use Capital

The broadest measure of profitability is the ratio to total capital of the *final* net profit available for capital funds. The final net profit for capital reflects all recurrent items of profit and loss, including income tax, without deducting interest on funded debt and lease obligations, because interest is a part of return. The fundamental merit of the return-on-invested-capital ratio is that it measures the *basic* or overall performance of a business in terms of the total funds provided by all investors rather than a single class. The ratio is a measure of management's ability to employ assets profitably, independent of the method of funding the assets. The ratio can also be calculated *before income taxes*, which will provide a measure of profitability that is independent of both funding and how the company is taxed. The latter calculation is helpful in certain intercompany comparisons.

Several Useful Variations.   As a group, profitability ratios are perhaps security analysts' most powerful tools. They are calculated in a variety of ways, each telling a slightly different story from a slightly different perspective. Among these ratios are return on:

- Total assets
- Capital (variously defined)
- Long-term investment
- Equity

The latter may be the return on book equity, however stated in the accounts, or the return on net tangible assets attributed to the shareholders—the recommended method. In all cases, the return (numerator) must be consistent with the defined capital (denominator). For example, if short-term borrowings are excluded from capital, their interest should be excluded from return.

Average Capital or Beginning Capital.   A common error is to divide the return by capital as of the end of the period. For example, return on equity might be calculated, incorrectly, as the earnings for the year divided by the book value at the end of the year. The problem is that the capital referred to as "book value" was not at work either at the beginning of the year or throughout the year. It was simply the amount that had been accumulated or remained at the end of the year. The acceptable methods are return divided by (1) the average capital for the year (return on the average capital at work) or (2) the capital that existed at the beginning of the year (return on the beginning investment). Either figure is acceptable for analytical purposes, but the method should be identified and used consistently in comparisons. The first method has the advantage when capital has been infused or extinguished during the year. The end-of-year problem exists regardless of which profitability ratio is being calculated, so the above comments apply equally to return on assets, return on total capital, return on long-term capital, and others.

Return on Capital (Ratio 14). The most comprehensive gauge of the success of an enterprise is the percentage earned on invested capital (ratio 14 in Figure 12.3). The terms *invested capital, capital funds,* and *total capital* may be used interchangeably. Short-term borrowings, such as bank loans and commercial paper, and the deferred tax liability are included in the capital at work. Practice varies on the matter of operating leases, but we prefer to include them in invested capital. In theory, current accrued payables that are not interest bearing should be excluded because their interest component is not observable. As a practical matter, it is often more convenient to include them by calculating the return on (total) tangible assets, including the leased assets under operating leases. Either ratio, if consistently applied, is useful and provides comparability.

Adjustments. Certain adjustments should be made to the equity capital figure. In the case of companies that use LIFO inventory accounting, the LIFO reserve should be added back to equity. Goodwill and any other intangible assets which lack a going market price or an identifiable stream of revenues should be subtracted from the equity capital. Deferred taxes should be considered equity in return on equity calculations (but as debt when calculating capital ratios or book value per common share). The present value of operating leases should be inserted into the balance sheet both as an asset and a liability. This liability, of course, would be part of total capital but not, of course, of equity capital. The liability for other postemployment benefits should be recognized as additional debt, and equity should be reduced by that amount. Other hidden assets and liabilities may need similar treatment. Preferred stock dividend arrearages should be shown either as a liability or as an increase in the preferred stock claim, and an equal amount must be deducted from the common stock equity.

Our formula for the return on capital calculates the denominator from the asset side by subtracting from total assets the goodwill and any intangible assets that need removal, adding an asset for the asset leased under operating leases, and reduces the total by accrued payables. Accrued payables are viewed as current liabilities that do not bear interest, in contrast to bank loans, commercial paper, notes payable, and the like. The denominator could be constructed as easily from the right side of the balance sheet. Judgment may direct the analyst to make various other adjustments to the capital accounts. Similarly, adjustments may be made to the numerator of the equation. For example, if goodwill and other intangibles have been deducted from equity, their amortization, write-offs, and tax effects should be eliminated from earnings. If the present value of operating leases is included in the capital in the denominator, then the numerator must contain the appropriate interest component, tax adjusted, which is a portion of the rental paid.

Ordinarily, the return on capital should be calculated using the average capital at work during the year, which is often approximated by averaging the beginning and ending amounts of capital. Alternatively, the interim financial statements may be included in the average.

To make companies comparable, reduce the interest expense in the numerator by the appropriate income tax rate. This treats the interest as if it were not tax deductible, or the same as the earnings for the common, preferred stock or minority interest. Thus, companies with significantly different capital structures can be compared on a common basis in terms of the profitability of their capital. It also is helpful in presenting the trend of profitability over time for a company whose capital structure changed significantly.

Return on Capital—Indirect Calculation.   Return on capital may be either computed directly as shown in Figure 12.3, ratio 14, or as the product of capital turnover (ratio 15) times earnings margin (ratio 16).

Capital Turnover—An Activity Ratio (Ratio 15).   Capital turnover (ratio 15) is one of a family of ratios that is sometimes called "activity ratios" or "turnover ratios." These ratios are normally calculated as sales divided by the item mentioned. They often provide the earliest signs of change in a company and demand an explanation. This family includes:

• Total capital turnover (ratio 15)

▪ Asset turnover

• Inventory turnover (ratio 38)

• Equity turnover

• Plant turnover

▪ Accounts receivable turnover (ratio 39)

▪ Working capital turnover

Earnings Margin (Ratio 16).   Note that the *earnings margin* in ratio 16 is not the same as *margin of profit* as it is ordinarily used in accounting. The latter phrase refers to the direct operating results only and is figured before the income tax deduction and before nonoperating income and

14. Return on capital
$$= \frac{\text{Net income} + \text{minority interest} + \text{tax-adjusted interest}}{\text{Tangible assets} - \text{short-term accrued payables}}$$

15. Capital turnover $= \dfrac{\text{Sales}}{\text{Tangible assets} - \text{short-term accrued payables}}$

16. Earnings margin
$$= \frac{\text{Net income} + \text{minority interest} + \text{tax-adjusted interest}}{\text{Sales}}$$

17. Return on capital before depreciation
$$= \frac{\text{Net income} + \text{minority interest} + \text{tax-adjusted interest} + \text{depreciation}}{\text{Tangible assets} - \text{short-term accrued payables}}$$

18. Return on common equity
$$= \frac{\text{Net income} - \text{preferred dividend requirements}}{\text{Common equity} - \text{goodwill} - \text{most intangibles} + \text{deferred tax liability}}$$

Figure 12.3 Suggested formulas for calculating profitability ratios.

charges. Our figure is the ratio to sales of the *final* net profit and tax-adjusted interest available for the capital funds.

Turnover and Margin and Return on Capital. The turnover of capital and other activity ratios are very sensitive to changes in operations and the financial structure of a corporation. Examination of ratios 15 and 16 may offer a ready explanation for a change in the return on capital and an incentive for further investigation of the specific causes of the change.

Allowing for Differences in Depreciation Policy. The importance of depreciation has increased significantly in the postwar period, and at the same time marked differences in depreciation policies exist among companies. (See Chapter 6.) Thus, a comparative analysis of a number of corporations within an industry should consider the depreciation factor. This may be done in a number of ways, such as the ratios of depreciation to sales or to gross plant. In Table 6.4 of Chapter 6 an example of the latter sort of adjustment to the depreciation expense was shown for selected airline companies.

Return on Capital before Depreciation (Ratio 17). Return on capital before depreciation (ratio 17 in Figure 12.3) simply compares companies' returns on capital after eliminating the effects of different depreciation policies. Several warnings are in order in the use of this ratio. First, it represents neither a calculation of true return nor of cash flow. It is merely a ranking system that eliminates the effects of differences in depreciation. An assumption that the depreciation should be the same, relative to capital, is inherent in the ratio. Therefore, its use in comparing companies that are not relatively homogeneous is potentially misleading.

Return on Common Equity (Ratio 18). The second most significant profitability ratio to investors is return on equity—ratio 18. Its fascination is proportional to the market's preference for common stocks over fixed-income securities. However, it is an important ratio with respect to management's use of the common stockholder's capital and the ability of management to leverage the rate of return on equity by incurring debt. The injection of financial leverage has the undesirable effect of increasing the variability of earnings for the common stock. Analysts use the trade-off between higher earnings and the increased variability of earnings to determine whether management has chosen the optimum amount of financial leverage.

Deferred Taxes as Equity Capital. An area of some potential controversy is our decision to include the deferred income tax liability as a source of capital—particularly of equity capital. Although it is not "invested" capital in the usual sense, there is little doubt that when Congress creates rules that defer the payment of income taxes to a later date, the effect is the same as giving the company an interest-free loan. The absence of any capital cost (interest) causes the profits of using the assets funded by that loan to flow directly to pre-tax income, so the return on that capital is ultimately reflected as a part of the return on equity. Some companies have very large deferred income tax liabilities. For example, Exxon had over $11 billon of deferred tax liabilities at the end of 1985. Other companies have only trivial amounts. To compare Exxon's return on equity with a company that has no deferred tax liability or even has only deferred tax assets, would lead to an overly favorable assessment of the relative efficiency of Exxon's use of equity capital in comparison to the other company. Thus, to exclude the deferred tax liability would substantially destroy the comparability of return on equity calculations and convey a misleading impression to the user of such a ratio.

Are Deferred Taxes Earnings? What is considerably more controversial in our view is whether changes in the deferred tax liability represent the equivalent of gains or losses that should be included in the numerator of the return on equity equation. The arguments for and against seem somewhat reasonably balanced, and the burden of that decision is placed upon the reader.

Other Quasi-Equity Items. Some companies have a significant amount of long-term liabilities that do not have financing characteristics and may be thought of in the same fashion as deferred taxes—that is, capital that is working essentially for the common shareholder. Most items that would qualify for that view are really deferred income and deferred gains. Unlike a true liability, these will not require a cash outflow. They are simply credits which accrual accounting is not yet ready to call income or gain. The best treatment is a matter for the individual analyst's judgment, since the choice of an appropriate method is a matter of some controversy. To think symmetrically, the issue should also arise on deferred losses which are carried as assets. No benefit will ever arise from them, and it can be argued that deferred losses should be subtracted from equity.

Profitability for Periods and for Individual Years. The profitability ratios should be examined in terms of both period averages and individual years. Thus the year-by-year fluctuations as well as the level of performance over a span of time may be appraised.

Growth Rates, Stability, and the Payout Ratio

Growth Rates

Ratios and Compound Annual Rates. The figures most frequently compared over time for company growth rates are sales, total return and earnings per share (ratios 19 through 21 in Figure 12.4). Although our suggested ratios merely compare levels, expressed as a percentage, many analysts express growth in compound annual growth rates by determining the number of years between the midpoint of the base period and the midpoint of the final period and using that as the exponent by which to reduce the overall change into an annual rate of change.

Many other growth rates are calculated by analysts, using both gross and per-share figures. They include:

- Cash flow
- Dividends
- Book value
- Plant account
- Physical data (such as units produced or capacity)
- Retained return on equity (a proxy for growth)

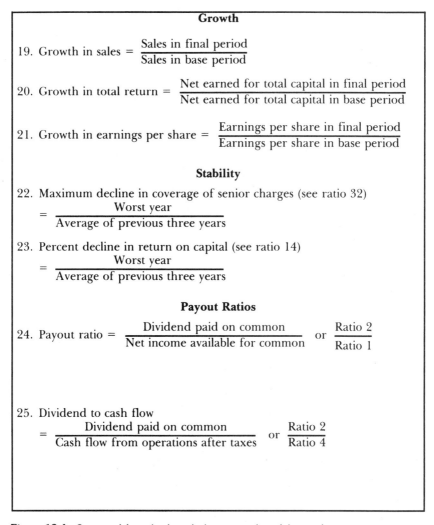

Growth

19. Growth in sales $= \dfrac{\text{Sales in final period}}{\text{Sales in base period}}$

20. Growth in total return $= \dfrac{\text{Net earned for total capital in final period}}{\text{Net earned for total capital in base period}}$

21. Growth in earnings per share $= \dfrac{\text{Earnings per share in final period}}{\text{Earnings per share in base period}}$

Stability

22. Maximum decline in coverage of senior charges (see ratio 32)
$= \dfrac{\text{Worst year}}{\text{Average of previous three years}}$

23. Percent decline in return on capital (see ratio 14)
$= \dfrac{\text{Worst year}}{\text{Average of previous three years}}$

Payout Ratios

24. Payout ratio $= \dfrac{\text{Dividend paid on common}}{\text{Net income available for common}}$ or $\dfrac{\text{Ratio 2}}{\text{Ratio 1}}$

25. Dividend to cash flow
$= \dfrac{\text{Dividend paid on common}}{\text{Cash flow from operations after taxes}}$ or $\dfrac{\text{Ratio 2}}{\text{Ratio 4}}$

Figure 12.4 Suggested formulas for calculating growth, stability, and payout ratios.

Smoothing Cyclical Effects. The infrequency of *major* cycles since 1949 has often ruled out the smoothing of cyclical effects for analytical work. Instead the analysts have had to make trend comparisons over some conveniently long period, say 10 years. To diminish the effect of single-year variations we recommend that such a comparison be made between several-year averages, for example, 1983 to 1987 versus 1973 to 1977. Another technique uses statistical regression over time to obtain the trend.

Inflationary Growth.   The analyst must consider the source of growth and not be misled by growth caused partly by inflation. A company that shows annual sales growth of 5 percent in an era of 7 percent inflation is not even keeping up with inflation, and the analyst must determine whether the shortfall is due to a decline in units, a squeeze on profit margins, or other specific causes.

Industry Growth Rates.   The annual growth rates of various industries may be compared by this method, using a suitable group of companies as a sample of each industry. One difficulty that arises occasionally is the vast difference in size between the largest one, two, or three companies in an industry where the rest of the participants are relatively small. To get a better picture of the various growth opportunities for the smaller companies in the industry, create growth indices for each company and then average the growth indices so as to give equal weight to all companies. This may reveal that the significant growth opportunities that exist for some of the smaller companies are not large enough markets to make much impact on one of the larger companies. In other cases, where the industry's products are more homogeneous, the analyst may want the growth rate to be weighted by the relative size of the companies—a more conventional approach. Again, we have an example of devising a method of calculation that may depart from custom or the rules, but the analyst does so to find the right answer to the question at hand.

Stability

Treatment of an Earnings Decline.   The analyst can develop arithmetical indexes of the stability of earnings over a given period of years. For instance, select the lowest net income in, say, a 5- or 10-year period and calculate the ratio to the average of the preceding 3 years, as in ratio 22. This will indicate how serious was the effect of any temporary setback. A cumulative decline over several years also could be measured against a previous average period. We believe the effect of a "poor year" on earnings should always be measured against some preceding period and not against an average that includes subsequent years. If the later years show a large increase in profits, they (if used in such an average) would make the earnings appear arithmetically unstable, when in fact they are forging ahead.

Cyclical versus Secular Declines.   The last four decades have not seen a year of general business recession sufficiently marked to test out the inherent stability of all enterprises. In no year-to-year comparison did corporate profits decline as much as 25 percent, although some industries may have had severe changes in profitability. In some instances, a decline represents a drop from unusually high levels; in other instances, it represents a true business cycle decline in demand.

Thus in some companies and industries the postwar fluctuations have supplied a reasonably good test of the relative soundness or competitive position of the individual firm. However, for some companies (and industries) the analyst would need to go too far back in time for a comparable test. The remoteness of figures substantially reduces their usefulness, but in some cases it may not have been destroyed.

Stability and Growth.   Over short periods, say five or six years, stability may be measured by using the standard deviation, but this measure is not satisfactory when growth is rapid. In that case, departures from the trend line can be measured statistically or studied visually on log-linear graph paper.

Safety Considerations (Ratios 22 and 23).   Earning stability plays a large part in determining the quality of a bond or preferred stock. Simply calculate the *minimum* coverage of charges or of prior charges and preferred dividends shown during a substantial number of years in the past. It may be useful to test stability of coverage on a pro forma basis, as if the company had a similar capital structure and level of interest rates to those prevailing now.

In many cases the *minimum dividend* paid on the common stock over, say, a 10-year period will give a valuable clue to inherent stability as well as to management's attitude on this factor—of major importance for all but the acknowledged growth companies. (The dividend paid by a growth company in the past may have little bearing on minimum dividend expectations in the future or other determinants of its value.) Consequently, for the nongrowth company we suggest only two standard measurements of stability:

Maximum decline in coverage of senior charges (ratio 22)

Maximum decline in earnings rate on total capital (ratio 23)

Ratios 22 and 23 may be supplemented by measuring the maximum decline in the return earned on common-stock capital and in per-share earnings.

Payout Ratios (Ratio 24)

The percentage of available earnings paid out in common dividends often has a most important effect upon the market's attitude toward those issues not in the growth category. The payout of earnings may be calculated, quite simply, by dividing the earnings into the dividend (ratio 24 in Figure 12.4).

For issues paying stock dividends as well as cash, only the cash dividend should be included in the calculation of payout ratios. Stock dividends are like stock splits—the investor receives nothing that was not already owned, and the company gives up nothing of value. Some bookkeeping entries are made, and some paper is mailed out, but nothing of economic significance occurs.

Payout of Cash Flow (Ratio 25)

The percentage of cash flow paid out in dividends is a more stable number than the ratio of dividends to earnings. Thus, the past relationship of dividends to cash flow (ratio 25) is more useful in estimating future dividends than the conventional payout ratio (ratio 24).

Credit Ratios

Credit ratios (Figure 12.5) are a diverse group which attempt to capture liquidity, financial flexibility, capital structure, ability to service debt, cash-generating characteristics, and other credit tests.

The Current, Quick, and Cash Ratios (Ratios 26–28)

The significance of these ratios, along with the cash ratio (ratios 26 to 28) was discussed in Chapter 11, under "Working-Capital Position."

Equity Ratio (Ratio 29)

The surplus of assets over the claims of senior securities is indicated by the equity ratio—ratio 29. Essentially the same information is provided in two other ratios. One is the debt-to-equity ratio, also sometimes called the debt ratio. However, the term *debt ratio* is also frequently used for the ratio of debt to total capital. Since all three provide essentially the same information, the analyst or the investment organization should select a standard method and stick to it, with a footnote explanation of the ratio used for the benefit of outsiders and newcomers who might read the analyst's report. Note that deferred taxes are treated as debt in this calculation.

26. Current ratio (Chapter 11) $= \dfrac{\text{Current assets}}{\text{Current liabilities}}$

27. Quick ratio (Chapter 11) $= \dfrac{\text{Current assets } - \text{ inventories}}{\text{Current liabilities}}$

28. Cash ratio (Chapter 11) $= \dfrac{\text{Cash items}}{\text{Current liabilities}}$

29. Equity ratio $= \dfrac{\text{Common equity at book value}}{\text{Tangible assets } - \text{ accrued payables}}$

30. Equity ratio at market $= \dfrac{\text{Common equity at market value}}{\text{Tangible assets } - \text{ accrued payables}}$

31. Coverage of senior charges $= \dfrac{\text{Pretax earned for capital}}{\text{Senior charges}}$

32. Cash flow coverage of senior charges

$= \dfrac{\text{Cash flow from operations after taxes } + \text{ senior charges}}{\text{Senior charges}}$

33. Cash flow to total capital

$= \dfrac{\text{Cash flow from operations after taxes } + \text{ tax-adjusted interest}}{\text{Tangible assets } - \text{ accrued payables}}$

34. Total debt service coverage

$= \dfrac{\text{Cash flow from operations after taxes } + \text{ rentals } + \text{ tax-adjusted interest}}{\text{Interest } + \text{ rent } + \text{ current maturities } + \text{ sinking fund payments}}$

35. Defensive interval (days)

$= \dfrac{(\text{Cash } + \text{ receivables}) \times 365}{\text{Total operating expenses } - \text{ depreciation } - \text{ other noncash charges}}$

Figure 12.5 Suggested formulas for calculating credit ratios.

Equity Ratio at Market (Ratio 30)

The equity ratio at market (ratio 30) is calculated by dividing the total capital fund, at book figure, into the common stock component thereof at market value. That is, the common stock component is calculated as the number of shares outstanding multiplied by the price per share. An alternative method uses the same denominator but averages the market value of the equity, generally over a five-year period. The equity ratio at market indicates the market's view of the goodwill of the company. If the market value of the equity is far above book value, the company apparently could sell additional stock for purposes of reducing debt and not dilute the book value per share. Although investors would rather look to cash flows for payments on fixed-income securities, they may find it reassuring that the equity market offers another method of payment. They will feel less reassured when the market prices the company's asset value lower than the figures on the company's books.

Coverage of Senior Charges (Ratio 31)

Senior charges are defined most commonly as interest expense. The growth of leasing has seen the interest component of capital leases included in the definition, and interest on operating leases, total rentals, and preferred dividends may be included under some definitions.

The coverage of senior charges (ratio 31) is found by dividing the balance available for senior charges by the senior charges, which may be defined as some combination of the following:

- Interest on short- and long-term debt, including capital leases
- Interest expenses plus an interest component for operating leases
- Interest expense on short- and long-term debt plus rentals on both capital and operating leases
- Total fixed charges, rentals, and preferred dividends

Separate ratios may be computed for each type of coverage. These are key figures in determining the quality of a bond or preferred-stock issue. Their calculation and significance will be discussed in detail in Chapters 23 and 24.[7] The quality of a common stock, and its resultant price-earnings ratio, are also influenced strongly by the margin of safety shown for the above senior charges.

It is our recommendation that the analyst define fixed charges to include interest and all rentals but not the preferred dividend requirements when the safety of the interest-bearing debt or the leases is a concern. However, if the issue is the safety of the preferred stock, then the calculation should include all the prior charges, including the preferred dividend. This latter definition is also desirable from the viewpoint of common-stock analysis, since all those claimants have a prior position over the common. The amount available for senior charges includes all the senior charges. For example, if the senior charges include rentals, then rentals should also be included in the numerator.

Most financial discussions assume that a company's credit indexes

---

[7]See the unabridged fifth edition of Sidney Cottle, Roger F. Murray, and Frank E. Block, *Graham and Dodd's Security Analysis,* McGraw-Hill, New York, 1988.

cannot be too strong. This plausible view ignores some real problems relating to the most advantageous corporate policies from the standpoint of its equity owners—the common stockholders. A company may have more cash than it needs, making for an impressive working-capital ratio and for excellent credit but maybe signifying a relatively unprofitable or inefficient use of the stockholders' capital.

Similarly, the best capital structure, in terms purely of credit standing and financial strength, includes no senior securities, that is, the "common-stock ratio" is 100 percent. However, the implication here is that no company should ever willingly issue bonds or preferred stock. This simply is not true. (See Chapter 33 for discussion of the optimal capital structure.[8])

Cash Flow to Senior Charges (Ratio 32)

Chapter 7 discussed methods of calculating cash flow. For purposes of calculating the relationship of cash flow to senior charges (ratio 32), the numerator should be the cash flow from operations less taxes paid with tax-adjusted interest added back.

Cash Flow to Total Capital (Ratio 33)

Cash flow to capital (ratio 33) focuses on the rate at which capital replenishes itself. If the ratio is 0.25, in theory at least, the company sees its capital in the form of cash every four years. In that sense, the figure is somewhat like an activity ratio, and, in every sense, the higher the number the better.

Total Debt-Service Coverage (Ratio 34)

The numerator of debt-service coverage (ratio 34) is the after-tax cash flow plus rentals and tax-adjusted interest. The denominator is the total debt-service requirements. These requirements include all interest, rent, current maturities of debt, and mandatory sinking fund payments. If the company is being studied from the viewpoint of the preferred stock, the preferred dividend requirements and sinking funds would be included with the senior securities' requirements. In general, bank credit officers consider the cash flow coverage of total debt service requirements to be more important than the more conventional coverage calculations that address only interest and rent.

---

[8] See the unabridged fifth edition of Sidney Cottle, Roger F. Murray, and Frank E. Block, *Graham and Dodd's Security Analysis,* McGraw-Hill, New York, 1988.

Defensive Interval (Days) (Ratio 35)

The defensive interval (ratio 35) calculates the number of days of operating expenses that could be paid with only the currently available quick assets. The operating expenses should exclude depreciation and other noncash charges. This ratio is another worst-case test, since it assumes that operations continue at the current level, that no revenues come in, and that the only sources of payment of these out-of-pocket operating expenses are present holdings of cash and equivalent and the proceeds of collecting the accounts receivable. The ratio is best used as a series over time for an individual company and for comparing companies in the same industry.

Other Ratios

A few additional ratios of possible interest are shown in Figure 12.6. The ratio of depreciation to sales and of depreciation to gross plant, property, and equipment (ratios 36 and 37) are used primarily to compare companies in the same industry and with substantially similar property accounts. The ratios are designed to reveal the liberalism of or conservatism of depreciation policies, and in some cases to make adjustments to put the compared companies on essentially the same depreciation basis. In the case of capital intensive companies, depreciation may be a very large portion of total expenses. What seems a modest shift in the estimated useful lives may result in a significant shift in reported net income.

$$36.\ \text{Depreciation to sales} = \frac{\text{Depreciation expense}}{\text{Sales}}$$

$$37.\ \text{Depreciation to gross plant} = \frac{\text{Depreciation expense}}{\text{Gross plant}}$$

$$38.\ \text{Inventory turnover} = \frac{\text{Cost of goods sold}}{\text{Inventory including LIFO reserve (if any)}}$$

$$39.\ \text{Accounts receivable turnover} = \frac{\text{Sales}}{\text{Accounts receivable}}$$

Figure 12.6 Suggested formulas for calculating other ratios.

Inventory turnover (ratio 38) is simply the ratio of cost of goods sold to inventory, with the latter including the LIFO reserve if the company is on that basis. The resulting number shows the number of times the *units* of inventory are "turned over"—that is, sold and then replenished. A popular variation is to use the reciprocal of the ratio multiplied by 365 days. In that case, the inventory on hand is referred to as so many "days" of inventory.

Accounts receivable turnover (ratio 39) is simply the ratio of sales to accounts receivable and is sometimes a useful warning of credit or collection problems. Accounts receivable turnover is also sometimes expressed in days.

The ratios given in this chapter are the common garden varieties that will serve most of the analyst's needs. In a given analysis, the analyst will use only some of them. At times the analyst will run across printouts that may include a hundred or more general purpose ratios. Specialized industry ratios must bring the total available to more than a thousand, with perhaps that many in regulated industries alone (banks, insurance, railroads, utilities, airlines, etc.). Without a sense of perspective, an analyst can drown in ratios and in information overload. We suggest that the analyst stay largely within the 39 ratios suggested here, plus the ratios for senior securities in Chapters 23 and 24. [9] Yet, at times the analyst will find or invent a ratio that gives just the exact answer needed for an important question. The area is one for judgment with an eye on consistency and comparability.

[9] See the unabridged fifth edition of Sidney Cottle, Roger F. Murray, and Frank E. Block, *Graham and Dodd's Security Analysis,* McGraw-Hill, New York, 1988.

13

Key Ratios in Company Comparisons

Calculation of Key Ratios for Two Chemical Companies

To illustrate the key ratio technique, we have selected two chemical companies of roughly equal size but of with somewhat different financial and operating characteristics—Hercules, Inc. (Table 13.1), and Rohm & Haas Company (Table 13.2). The calculations are presented in separate columns, based on the averages of 1975 to 1979 and of 1980 to 1984 and also on the results of the single year 1985. All of the market value ratios are based on an average of the high and low price for each year. Table 13.3 shows separately the comparative market value ratios for Hercules Inc., and Rohm & Haas based on the price prevailing at the end of May 1986. (This date was selected on the assumption that by that time the analyst would have received the annual reports and have had the opportunity of analyzing the data.) For brevity's sake, not all the ratios discussed in Chapter 12 are used in this chapter. The subject here is the process of ratio analysis, not ratios themselves.

The Common-Stock Capital or Earning-Capital Base

In computing the return on common-stock capital, the analyst is concerned with the *earning-capital* as distinguished from the *equity* or *ownership base*. Thus the analyst measures the return on all the capital

Table 13.1 Hercules Incorporated

Data and ratios	1975–1979	1980–1984	1985
Basic data ($ millions)			
Sales	1,799.8	2,659.2	2,587.2
Depreciation and amortization	97.0	113.7	105.7
Tax expense	62.3	46.8	39.0
Net for capital (before tax)[a]	205.4	288.8	245.4
Net for total capital (after tax)[a,b]	123.0	203.7	162.0
Interest expense (including all leases)	40.9	83.8	96.6
Net for common	102.3	158.2	109.8
Common dividends	40.0	62.3	86.5
Total capital book value[c,g]	1,364.7	2,042.4	2,544.3
Deferred taxes[d]	95.3	190.5	212.0
Common-stock equity—book value[d]	794.8	1,218.0	1,496.8
Common stock at market value[e]	992.0	1,244.0	1,943.0
Average shares outstanding (millions)	42.9	46.7	54.1
Current assets (year end)			1,045.8
Current liabilities (year end)			415.9
Ratios (see Chapter 12):			
Profitability ratios			
14. Return on capital	9.0%	10.0%	6.4%
15. Capital turnover	1.3×	1.3×	1.0×
16. Earnings margin	6.8%	5.9%	6.3%
17. Return on capital before depreciation and amortization	16.1%	15.5%	10.3%
18. Return on equity[d]	11.5%	11.2%	6.4%
Growth ratios			
19. Ratio of sales to 1975–1979 base......	100%	148%	144%
20. Ratio of net for total capital to 1975–1979 base....................................	100%	166%	132%
21. Ratio of net per share of common to 1975–1979 base...........................	100%	142%	85%
Stability ratios			
22. Maximum decline in coverage of senior charges—lowest year vs. average of three previous years[f]	−62%	−42%	−30%
23. Decline in return on capital—lowest year vs. average of three previous years[f]	−39%	−14%	−32%
Payout ratios			
24. Percent of earnings paid on common	39%	39%	79%
25. Dividends to cash flow	12%[f]	11%[f]	16%[f]
Credit ratios			
26. Current ratio	2.0×[f]	2.2×[f]	2.5×[f]
29. Equity ratio	59%	59%	58%
31. Coverage of senior charges	5.0×[f]	3.5×[f]	2.5×
31. Minimum coverage of senior charges	2.0×[f]	2.6×[f]	2.5×

Table 13.1 Hercules Incorporated (*Continued*)

Data and ratios	1975–1979	1980–1984	1985
Per-share figures ($)			
Price of common......................................	23.13	26.65	35.94
1. Earnings per share............................	2.38	3.39	2.03
2. Dividend per share	0.95	1.33	1.60
3. Sales per share	41.95	56.94	47.82
5. Book value per share.........................	18.53	26.08	27.67
Market-price ratios			
10. Earnings yield..................................	10.3%	12.7%	5.7%
11. Dividend yield	4.0%	5.0%	4.5%
12. Sales per dollar of common at market	$1.81	$2.14	$1.33
13. Price-to-book value...........................	1.3×	1.0×	1.3×

[a]Includes estimated interest component of rent on operating leases.
[b]Interest return has been reduced by pro forma tax effects, at a 46% rate after 1979 and a 48% rate during 1975–1979, for purposes of intercompany comparison.
[c]Includes deferred tax liability as part of equity.
[d]Based on average book value at beginning and end of years.
[e]Average of annual mean between the high and low prices, adjusted for stock splits, multiplied by average number of shares outstanding.
[f]These figures cannot be calculated from the basic data given.
[g]Includes estimated operating leases. Amounts are averages of beginning and end of year figures.

directly at work for the common stockholder, and whether or not the stockholder actually has legal title to all of this capital is somewhat beside the point. In this sense, the common stockholders' earning-capital base may be defined as total tangible assets less current liabilities and interest-bearing noncurrent debt. (The capital working for shareholders would thus include the reserve for deferred income taxes and similar items.) Approach this calculation from the right side of the balance sheet: Typically, the earning-capital base would consist of the following minus goodwill and other doubtful assets:

• Common-stock equity
• LIFO reserves and any hidden assets actively contributing to earnings
• Deferred tax liability

The computations which follow use this definition of earning-capital base.

Earnings Available for Total Capital

In this analysis, the earnings available for total capital are taken to be:

• Net income after taxes (subject to the analyst's adjustments)
• Interest on both current and noncurrent debt
• Interest on operating leases

Table 13.2 Rohm and Haas Company

Data and ratios	1975–1979	1980–1984	1985
Basic data ($ millions)			
Sales	1,174.1	1,871.2	2,051.0
Depreciation and amortization	77.6	93.9	111.0
Tax expense	37.6	77.0	86.0
Net for capital (before tax)[a]	128.1	234.9	189.1
Net for total capital (after tax)[a,b]	70.7	137.6	159.3
Interest expense (including all leases)	41.2	44.2	64.8
Net for common	49.3	113.7	124.3
Common dividends	18.0	36.1	49.3
Total capital book value[c,g]	972.4	1,254.8	1,490.1
Deferred taxes[d]	52.5	91.6	130.2
Common-stock equity—book value[d]	547.3	811.8	937.7
Common stock at market value[e]	619.4	1,035.5	1,572.6
Average shares outstanding (millions)	25.8	25.8	23.5
Current assets (year end)			924.0
Current liabilities (year end)			444.0
Ratios (see Chapter 12):			
Profitability ratios			
14. Return on capital	7.2%	10.9%	10.7%
15. Capital turnover	1.2×	1.5×	1.4×
16. Earnings margin	6.0%	7.3%	7.7%
17. Return on capital—before depreciation and amortization	15.2%	18.4%	18.1%
18. Return on equity[d]	11.7%	12.6%	11.6%
Growth ratios			
19. Ratio of sales to 1975–1979 base	100%	159%	175%
20. Ratio of net for total capital to 1975–1979 base	100%	195%	225%
21. Ratio of net per share of common to 1975–1979 base	100%	231%	277%
Stability ratios			
22. Maximum decline in coverage of senior charges—lowest year vs. average of three previous years[f]	−54%	−36%	−20%
23. Decline in return on capital—lowest year vs. average of three previous years[f]	−49%	−19%	−25%
Payout ratios			
24. Earnings paid on common	37%	32%	40%
25. Dividends to cash flow[f]	8%	10%	11%
Credit ratios			
26. Current ratio	2.4×[f]	2.6×[f]	2.1×
29. Equity ratio	56%	65%	63%
31. Coverage of senior charges	3.1×	5.3×	4.2×
31. Minimum coverage of senior charges[f]	1.6×	3.4×	4.2×
Per-share figures ($)			
Price of common	24.11	40.17	67.00

Tables 13.2 Rohm and Haas Company (*Continued*)

Data and ratios	1975–1979	1980–1984	1985
1. Earnings per share............................	1.91	4.41	5.29
2. Dividend per share	0.70	1.40	2.10
3. Sales per share	45.51	72.53	87.28
5. Book value per share........................	21.21	31.47	39.90
Market-price ratios			
10. Earnings yield..................................	7.9%	11.0%	7.9%
11. Dividend yield	2.9%	3.5%	3.1%
12. Sales per dollar of common at market	$1.90	$1.81	$1.30
13. Price-to-book value...........................	1.1×	1.3×	1.7×

aIncludes estimated interest component of rent on operating leases.
bInterest return has been reduced by pro forma tax effects, at a 46% rate after 1979 and a 48% rate during 1975–1979, for purposes of intercompany comparisons.
cIncludes deferred tax liability as part of equity.
dBased on average book value at beginning and end of years.
eAverage of annual mean between the high and low prices, adjusted for stock splits, multiplied by average number of shares outstanding.
fThese figures cannot be calculated from the basic data given.
gIncludes estimated operating leases. Amounts are averages of beginning and end of year figures.

The interest on the debt is adjusted for the prevailing income tax rate: 48 percent in the years 1975 through 1979 and 46 percent in 1980 through 1985.[1] The interest expense includes the estimated interest component of rent paid on operating leases. Capitalized interest is also included in the return on capital and the amortization of capitalized interest is eliminated from expense. Interest is, of course, deductible for tax purposes, and earnings for common and preferred shares are fully taxed. To gain reasonable comparability between companies that are capitalized differently and use different instruments among their senior securities and borrowings—for example, operating leases, commercial paper, long-term bonds, and preferred stock—the interest must be reduced by the benefits of its tax deductibility. Using an alternative approach, the return on capital ratios may be calculated on a pretax basis. Both approaches are perfectly acceptable as methods to equalize the different tax treatment of interest and net income, but the after-tax approach has the advantage of treating taxes as an expense, which they are. Certain ratios are also calculated before depreciation in an effort to neutralize differences in companies' depreciation policies under comparison. Remember that depreciation is also an expense, and interpret those ratios accordingly.

The growth factor is measured by comparing 1985 and the 1980–1984 average with the 1975–1979 base. The data and ratios for the full analysis are presented in seven sections. Twenty-four key ratios, distributed in six topical sections, are identified by the ratio numbers used in

[1]The Tax Reform Law of 1986 changed the corporate rate on ordinary income from 46 percent in 1986 to a blended rate of 40 percent in 1987, and 34 percent thereafter.

Chapter 12. Whenever a substantial proportion (say, in the 50 to 60 percent range) of senior securities exists in the capital structure, as is the case in our example, the analyst may well find it desirable to compute all the profitability ratios on a common-stock, as well as a total capital, basis. Both of our sample companies spent at least part of the 1975–1985 period with their equity ratio in that range, but we have omitted those calculations and their discussion for purposes of brevity.

Details of the Adjustments

At the beginning of Chapter 12 we emphasized that the analyst must make all adjustments *before* calculating ratios, trends, averages, and other statistical or arithmetical processing. Thus it seems appropriate to relate here some of the adjustments that were made, some that would have been desirable but were not made, and some unusual adjustments which were based on analytical judgment rather than firm rules.

Eliminating Intangible Assets.   Goodwill was eliminated from the balance sheet, reducing net worth by the full amount. No tax adjustment was made in the case of goodwill. Rohm and Haas had $60 million of patents and trademarks less an unknown amount of amortization. Details of these patents and trademarks were available for only the years 1983 through 1985, and the company was receiving royalties and related fees amounting to about 10 percent of the gross cost of those intangibles. It was decided that those intangibles had a reasonably identifiable earnings stream and that only the goodwill and its amortization should be removed from the accounts.

Other Postemployment Benefits.   Rohm and Haas showed $25 million of expense for health benefits and insurance policies on 3100 retired and 8300 active employees. Since they were covered by a single policy, the company was unable to identify the portion attributable to retired employees. The liability for other postemployment benefits was ignored because (1) data were not available for earlier years and (2) the estimate of the amount of the benefit applicable to the retirees would be unreliable.

Operating Leases.   Operating leases were capitalized for each year, estimating the pattern of rental payments beyond the fifth year, if necessary, and using a 10 percent discount rate. Note that the old rule-of-thumb of "one third of rent" as the interest component would have worked very well for Rohm and Haas. However, for Hercules, particularly in 1980 and subsequent years, when Hercules was leasing a considerable amount of office space, the one-third rule would have been only about half of an appropriate interest component.

Changes in Pension Assumptions and Methods.   In 1985 both companies changed their actuarial cost methods to the projected unit credit method and made changes in certain assumptions. In addition, in 1984 Hercules changed some actuarial assumptions. Rohm and Haas reduced pension expense from previous amounts around the $30 million level to zero for 1985; Hercules reduced pension expense by about the same amount for 1984 and 1985 from the levels which had prevailed over the previous decade. Is is reasonable that Rohm and Haas' workers earned large pension benefits in 1985 but the company recorded no cost for them? A more realistic view would say that pension expense had been overstated in prior years when gains were shown in the company's portfolios and on other actuarial assumptions and that some reasonable adjustment should be made by the analyst. In the case of Rohm and Haas we estimated the correct pension expense at $30 million pretax, reducing 1985 earnings by $16.2 million after tax. The $30 million was then used as a reduction in past pension expense, spread over the previous 10 years in equal amounts. A similar adjustment was made for Hercules, but pension expense was increased in both 1984 and 1985 and the cost thereof was spread over the previous nine years. These steps also required balance sheet and tax adjustments.

LIFO Reserves.   Both companies use LIFO figures for substantial portions of their inventories. For purposes of calculating the capital at work, the after-tax amount of LIFO reserve was added to equity, and deferred taxes for the gain were set up based on the prevailing tax rate for the year. Changes in the LIFO reserve were not added to the income for the year.

Foreign Currency Translation.   Rohm and Haas is unusual in that it uses the dollar as its functional currency for all overseas operations. Thus, no foreign currency translation adjustment arises in its accounts. The gains and losses shown in income are from all monetary assets and liabilities denominated in foreign currencies which changed relative to the dollar during the period. Hercules uses local currency in a number of overseas locations. Information was available in the 10-K to eliminate the effect of foreign currency rate changes on plant and equipment. For comparative purposes, eliminations of the gains and losses from the plant account would put Hercules on almost the same basis as Rohm and Haas, with the exceptions of inventories and a few other minor nonmonetary assets and liabilities. Thus, the gains and losses arising from land, plant, and equipment were eliminated from Hercules accounts, both in the balance sheet and the income statement.

Capitalized Interest.   The effects of interest capitalization on the plant account were removed.

Depreciation and Amortization. Depreciation and amortization were adjusted to eliminate the amortization of goodwill, amortization of capitalized interest, and some other intangibles.

Extinguishment of Debt. In 1982 Hercules recorded an extraordinary nontaxable gain of $11,553,000 as a result of exchange of 2,038,000 shares of common stock for $50 million principal amount of 6½ percent convertible subordinated debentures. This transaction was not a conversion but rather a special exchange offer of about $38 million of stock for the convertibles. We do not believe that an economic gain occurred, and therefore we eliminated this item from the income statement and stockholders' equity. The transaction does have tax consequences, but the amount did not justify making an adjustment.

Estimations. It was necessary to estimate a number of needed figures and, as indicated in the discussion of the pension situation above, to spread certain numbers in an arbitrary fashion. This is a common problem for security analysts, and the only answer is to apply common sense to the facts that are known. Our examples were deliberately based on published information only. In an ongoing analytical situation, the analyst would have frequent contact with the company, permitting more knowledgeable adjustments.

Ratio Comparisons

Note that the figures and ratios in the first five sections of the comparison relate to the performance and position of the two *companies.* Thus they supply indications of the quality of the enterprise as a whole and, presumably, of its management. In nearly all the ratios developed in the first three sections, Rohm and Haas fared better than Hercules, although not by a large margin.

The fifth section, on credit ratios, shows that Rohm and Haas had the better current ratio from 1975 through 1984, and the poorer one in 1985 due to heavy stock repurchases. Rohm and Haas has had a more conservative equity ratio over the past six years and somewhat better interest coverage. With a small edge to Rohm and Haas, the credit standing of the two companies is about the same.

The final section of the tables offers ratios that depend on the market price of the common stock. At its *average price* Hercules has offered more sales, earnings, dividends, and net assets per dollar invested than Rohm and Haas. This correlated with the historical record, which showed the advantage in profitability, growth, and stability to be in favor of Rohm and Haas. Hercules' per-share progress shows the negative effects of dilution, whereas Rohm and Haas benefited from repurchase of shares.

A Comparison at Current Prices

Table 13.3 shows the relations of price to earnings, dividends, and assets of the two stocks, using the end-of-month price for May 1986. The table shows that Hercules' 1985 earnings were sharply depressed from the level of the previous five years. Rohm and Haas's 1985 earnings were off from the 1984 peak but up from the 1980 to 1984 average. Hercules is the cheaper stock in terms of assets, yield, and adjusted earnings for recent years but not in terms of 1985 earnings. Our key ratio technique can carry the analyst to the point of demonstrating that Rohm and Haas has been a more profitable and more dynamic business than Hercules, but this advantage may be offset by Hercules' lower price. Whether the advantage is in fact offset cannot be demonstrated by any mathematical operations. The answer must be given in the form of an opinion emanating from the informed judgment and perhaps the prejudices of

Table 13.3 Market Value Ratios, for Two Companies

	Hercules	Rohm and Haas
Market price on May 31, 1986..	50⅛	100½*
1985 sales per dollar of common at market........................	$0.95	$0.87
1985 earned per dollar of common at market†	4.05%	5.26%
1980–1984 average earned per dollar of common at market†	6.76%	4.39%
Dividend yield..	3.2%	2.4%
Price-to-book value using 1985 year-end net assets.............	1.81×	2.52×

*Before 3-for-1 split payable June 12, 1986.
†Adjusted earnings from Tables 13.1 and 13.2.

the analyst. The determination of the respective merits or attractiveness of the two common stocks *at their prevailing market prices* is the final and most difficult stage of a full-scale comparative security analysis. This is a matter of common-stock valuation, and our observations on the subject belong to a later section of this book.[2] But prior to reaching a conclusion as to value in relation to price, the analyst will draw a number of deductions from the key ratios developed in our comparative table. Let us discuss these in some detail, to illustrate what we may call the "intermediate" or "dissective" state of security analysis.

[2] See the unabridged fifth edition of Sidney Cottle, Roger F. Murray, and Frank E. Block, *Graham and Dodd's Security Analysis*, McGraw-Hill, New York, 1988.

Profitability and Turnover Ratios

Table 13.4 offers a possible explanation of the more rapid growth shown by Rohm and Haas from the mid-1970s to the mid-1980s. The first ratio, capital turnover, is an activity ratio. It shows that Rohm and Haas increased the turnover of its capital significantly from the first period to the second. Hercules did not. Both companies suffered a modest decline in margins before depreciation (but mixed results after depreciation). Those differences were minor. The third line, the return on capital before depreciation, is simply the product of the first two lines. Clearly the factor that increased Rohm and Haas's return was the increased capital turnover. Both companies showed a decline in the ratio of depreciation to sales, but Rohm and Haas's decline occurred in part because sales outgrew capital. When that element is factored in, the two companies' depreciation policies appear roughly the same. The decline in the relationship of depreciation to sales aided the return on total capital after depreciation for both companies.

Table 13.4. Profitability and Turnover Ratios for Two Companies

	Hercules		Rohm and Haas	
	1975–1979	1980–1984	1975–1979	1980–1984
Capital turnover	1.32	1.30	1.21	1.49
Earnings margin before depreciation and amortization	12.2%	11.9%	12.6%	12.3%
Return on capital before depreciation and amortization	16.1%	15.5%	15.2%	18.4%
Ratio of depreciation and amortization to sales	5.4%	4.3%	6.6%	5.0%
Return on capital	9.0%	10.0%	7.2%	10.9%
Return on equity	11.5%	11.2%	11.7%	12.6%

Finally, the difference in the pattern of return on total capital from the return on equity shows that Rohm and Haas used a smaller amount of leverage somewhat more effectively than Hercules did in providing an improved return to the common stockholders.

The numbers in Table 13.4 would lead the analyst to an investigation of segment and product line data to determine what changes over the decade led to Rohm and Haas's improved activity ratio, and whether further improvements seem likely.

Progress Ratios

Each of the three ratios pertaining to growth favor Rohm and Haas by a significant margin. However, the 1985 figures for Hercules are probably not as bad as they seem. High start-up costs, production problems at certain new plants, and a significant strike had a hopefully nonrecurring negative impact on sales and earnings. The sales numbers in 1984 and 1985 were also significantly reduced by the formation of a 50-percent-owned joint venture at the end of 1983 to take over sale and manufacture of polypropylene resin products and certain other lines of business. That joint venture, HIMONT, Inc., had sales of over $900 million in both 1984 and 1985. Since the joint venture is carried on the equity method, some significant amount of Hercules' sales and capital were effectively deconsolidated for the years 1984 and 1985.

A comparison of the return on total capital to the return on equity for Hercules in 1985 demonstrates that company's vulnerability to its relatively larger financial leverage.

Indexes of Stability

The measures of stability in Tables 13.1 and 13.2 tend to give an edge to Rohm and Haas but demonstrate the inherent volatility of the chemical industry. An almost universal law of security analysis is that, within any industry, the units with better profit margins show smaller percentage profit declines in recession years. Similarly, those with the least financial leverage show smaller percentage declines in earnings for the equity. Rohm and Haas has been increasing its margins after depreciation and reducing its financial leverage. Hercules has improved in after-depreciation margins but has not reduced its leverage.

Payout Ratios

Rohm and Haas consistently had lower payout ratios of earnings and cash flow than Hercules. (The figures for 1985 should be considered nonrepresentative, since both companies had depressed earnings in 1985 relative to 1984.) Rohm and Haas's lower payout ratio permitted it to finance a larger portion of its growth from internal sources, and this permitted the company to improve its equity ratio. Hercules, however, was able to maintain its equity ratio only by increasing the number of shares of stock outstanding, thereby diluting the rate of growth of earnings, dividends, and book value per share. Average shares of Hercules outstanding in 1985 were 26 percent more than the average for 1975 to 1979, whereas Rohm and Haas had a 13 percent reduction for the same period.

Credit Ratios

The credit ratios for both companies are in satisfactory condition, and both companies should be considered financially strong. Rohm and Haas has improved its coverage of senior charges and Hercules' coverage has been well maintained. Rohm and Haas has had a slightly superior current position except in 1985. However, most of that reduction in the current ratio is due to repurchase of over 8.5 million shares of common stock in 1984 and 1985.

Per-Share Figures and Price Ratios

Note in Tables 13.1 and 13.2 that the purchaser of Rohm and Haas at the average price from 1975 to 1979 was buying *more* dollars of sales and net assets and *less* earnings and dividends than could have been obtained by investing the same money in Hercules. However, on average during 1980 to 1984 the Rohm and Haas investor's stock was selling at a price 66 percent higher than its purchase price, versus 15 percent for Hercules investors. The Rohm and Haas investor would also have received an average dividend of 5.8 percent in the 1980 to 1984 period, the same as the Hercules investor. If the figures were brought up to date through May 1986, the superior investment results obtained in Rohm and Haas would be even more dramatic, with the common stock increasing from $24.11 to $100.50—a gain of over 300 percent in market price; Hercules slightly more than doubled from $23.13 to $50.12. Hindsight clearly shows that the accolades go to Rohm and Haas in terms of both dividends and price appreciation. The bulk of the explanation is found in the per-share figures, which show far superior growth in sales, earnings, dividends, and book value. The superior return to Rohm and Haas investors is attributable to the substantially greater growth in earnings. It is the earnings growth that permits the growth of dividends and a rising yield on cost. It is earnings that cause the stock price to rise if the multiplier remains constant. And it is superior earnings growth that can justify an increase in the multiplier from the level of the average stock to a level that includes a premium for growth.

Note that an investor who early in 1980 could observe only the figures for 1975 to 1979 in Tables 13.1 and 13.2 might well have chosen Hercules in preference to Rohm and Haas. The profitability numbers gave Hercules better marks on four out of the five ratios shown. The measures of stability, payout, and credit were by and large a standoff for that period of time. The growth in earnings from the previous peak to 1979 favored Hercules, as did the price-earnings ratio and the yield offered. The investor who had a firm conviction that Rohm and Haas was the more attractive stock, would not have been able to make a strong case based on the historical record alone and would have had to justify that position by correctly forecasting a more rapid rate of growth in earning power for Rohm and Haas than for Hercules. The additional information for the years 1980 through 1985 in Tables 13.1 and 13.2 give a clear statistical advantage to Rohm and Haas but pose for today's investor the same question of which stock is more attractively priced, based on such price data as that presented in Table 13.3.

Emphasis Is on Quality

The foregoing analysis of key ratios for the full period from 1975 to 1985 showed that the qualitative factors clearly favored Rohm and Haas and the pricing measures now make Hercules appear the cheaper stock. The comparative investment results for the period of the analysis show that in spite of its higher price Rohm and Haas was by far the better buy. This conclusion confirms the accepted view in the market regarding to the purchase of *quality* shares. Remember, however, that (1) at some point even the best common stock can be overpriced and (2) anticipation of an improvement in the quality of a below-average share can result in an excellent investment opportunity. In the latter instance the investor is certain to enjoy an increase not only in earnings and dividends but also in the multiplier.

Improved quality can be the result of numerous factors; changes in management and in product mix are among the most prominent. At an early stage in the proceedings, anticipating with reasonable accuracy either the results of such changes or the length of time that may be required to bring them to fruition is no easy task. But the rewards for successfully doing so can be substantial.

Analysis Related to Physical Data

Analysis of a company's results should not be confined to dollar figures but should extend to those physical data that lend themselves to analytical study. The material usually considered, whenever it is available, includes the following.

Physical Reserves

The category of physical reserves is significant for all companies dependent on a wasting asset, such as oil and gas producers and mining companies, and possibly also for a transportation concern which depends on the reserves of its main shippers or suppliers, such as a railroad transporting chiefly coal or an oil or gas pipeline.

Metal, mineral, and oil reserves are often found in less developed and/or politically unstable parts of the world. Analysts will typically discount the value of such reserves to reflect expectations of nationalization, oppressive taxation, or wars and insurrection.

Many companies limit their development to only a few years' reserves because local taxes would be greatly increased if they reported that more ore was being developed. In addition, companies with wasting assets generally anticipate the exhaustion of present bodies by property purchases or leases. Thus, it is quite unusual for an important company of that type actually to go out of business because its reserves have been exhausted.

In estimating reserves, the analyst should consider the quality as well as the quantity. If a mining company has mainly low-grade ore in reserve and is presently mining high-grade ore, its future earning power must be viewed conservatively. There is similar significance in the ownership of less valuable oil reserves as against the more valuable high-gravity, low-sulphur oil.

The analyst must treat figures of reserves with circumspection. They do, of course, have some informative value. Other things being equal, a company with large developed reserves is preferable to another with small reserves.

Example. The 1984 annual report of AMAX, Inc., included the data on its molybdenum reserves shown in Table 13.5. Similar details were provided on the company's other major metal and mineral reserves. Detailed production figures for each product were also provided.

Table 13.5. Reserve Data from the 1984 Annual Report of AMAX, Inc.

	Molybdenum (millions of tons)				
	1984	1983	1982	1981	1980
Colorado					
Climax	408	413	413	418	433
(% molybdenum disulfide)	(0.31)	(0.31)	(0.31)	(0.31)	(0.31)
Henderson	240	246	246	230	239
(% molybdenum disulfide)	(0.38)	(0.38)	(0.38)	(0.42)	(0.42)
Canada					
Kitsault	115	115	115	105	105
(% molybdenum disulfide)	(0.19)	(0.19)	(0.19)	(0.19)	(0.19)

Example. Exxon Corporation's 1985 annual report includes required information on the "standardized measure of discounted future net cash flows relating to proved oil and gas reserves." Table 13.6 shows the worldwide figures for 1985 and the causes of changes in the figures. The total disclosure was far more extensive than this sample.

This standardized measure is not an appraisal of the oil and gas reserves. It is simply a calculation, using a discount rate of 10 percent, of the present value of the future net cash inflows from sale of *proven* oil and gas reserves, with consideration given to the costs, taxes, method of production (e.g., secondary or tertiary recovery), and the like. *Probable* reserves are not included, nor is the value of *possible* oil reserves on lands

Table 13.6. Condensed Disclosure on Oil and Gas Reserves from the 1985 EXXON Annual Report

Standarized measure of discounted future net cash flows	Total worldwide ($ million)
As of December 31, 1985	
Future cash inflows from sales of oil and gas	217,131
Future production and development cash costs	84,562
Future income tax expenses	63,843
Future net cash flows	68,726
Effect of discounting net cash flows at 10%	37,904
Standardized measure of discounted future net cash flows	30,822

Changes in the standardized measure	1985 ($ million)
Value of reserves added during the year	
Extensions, discoveries, other additions and improved recovery, less related costs	3,916
Changes in value of previous year reserves	
Sales and transfers of oil and gas produced during the year, net of production costs	(12,065)
Development costs incurred during the year	4,205
Net change in prices and production costs	(3,252)
Revision of previous reserves estimates	831
Accretion of discount	6,268
Other changes	(1,210)
Net change in income taxes	2,180
Total change in standardized measuring during the year	873

NOTE: The complete disclosures included details for 1983–1985 and data for six geographic areas.

held under lease. Interestingly, although the information was not received with much excitement on Wall Street when it first became available, subsequent acquisition prices of oil companies tended to confirm that the standardized measure was not too bad an estimate of the takeover value of oil reserves, and oil analysts began to pay considerably more attention to it.

The calculation of oil reserves (including the liquid content of gas reserves) has made a great deal of technical progress in recent years, and most companies now supply estimates by their own staff or by consulting geologists. Use of reserve figures in analyses and comparisons of oil companies is common—in general a certain dollar value is set on the oil in the ground and then the book figure for the other assets, net, are added to find a total valuation. Observe that, in the field of oil and mining companies, more emphasis is placed on appraised value of the assets than in the case of manufacturing and trading concerns.

Capacity

Most producers and processors of basic materials have a definite capacity expressible in physical units, for example, tons of steel ingots; bags of sugar, both raw and refined; barrels of oil put through refineries; or barrels of cement. The capacity figure changes, of course, through plant additions or abandonments, but it helps describe the position of the company at the time of analysis. How much weight capacity figures deserve will vary greatly with circumstances.

Production in Units

Production in units is a basic figure for intensive analysis; when compared with capacity it indicates

- Possible need for future expansion
- Potential increase in output
- Breakeven point

When a company produces a *homogeneous product*, e.g., copper, sugar, or cement, and when unit figures of production are published, the analyst can calculate

- Selling price
- Cost of production

- Margin of profit per unit
- Share of market

These are useful for comparative analysis and for calculating the effect of price and cost changes on the individual company.

Some productivity ratios and capacity utilization ratios should be used with caution. Capacity utilization figures for the textile industry have long been based on operating two 8-hour shifts, with Sundays and holidays off. In war time, the industry typically operates around the clock, seven days a week, indicating that the true capacity to produce goods is about twice the number normally used for purposes of measuring plant capacity.

In the coal industry, the total of tons produced per worker day was long considered the measure of a coal mine's efficiency. Early in the 1980s an industry group investigated how companies were calculating this number. They found huge disparities. Some companies counted only underground production workers, excluding shift leaders, inspectors, and others. Other companies included anyone vaguely associated with coal production, including those involved in washing, cleaning, sizing, and transporting the coal, overseers, and the like. Recalculations on a common basis established that some mines long considered to be among the most efficient in the country actually had an unenviable standing in the rankings.

For many years the retail trade industry put great emphasis on the statistic "sales per square foot of retail floor space" for comparable stores. Again, there were definitional problems concerning which floor space should be included and which excluded. With some grocery chains now staying open 24 hours a day, seven days a week, comparisons of grocery chains' sales per square foot must be done with a great deal of care.

Production by Divisions

Many manufacturers turn out a variety of products, which fall into several categories or industrial divisions. To study the company from the standpoint of industry analysis, clearly the analyst wants to know how the firm's products are divided, in unit terms and by dollar value. Companies now provide segment data in considerable detail, although the allocation of overhead continues to lack comparability. A typical disclosure would include the following items for each major product group:

- Sales
- Operating profits

- Equity in earnings of affiliates
- Identifiable assets at year end
- Investment in affiliates
- Depreciation expense
- Capital expenditures

Concentration and Geographical Location of Sales

Businesses dependent on one or two major customers are considered somewhat more vulnerable than are those with a large number of less important accounts. The former situation is found often among the makers of automobile parts, defense contractors, and in companies manufacturing almost exclusively for a large mail-order or chain-store organization. A large, successful company normally will have a substantial foreign business in addition to its domestic sales, but a heavy dependence on exports—especially to a single geographical area—must be viewed as an added hazard. Analysts must consider these matters and allow weight in their valuations according to their own judgment.

14

Ratios in Industry Analysis

Comparing Companies with Related Groups

Securities can neither be analyzed nor valued in a vacuum. The analytical function requires that a company be compared both with companies of a similar nature and with stocks in general to determine the characteristics and attractiveness of the individual issue. In general, individual companies are grouped together by

- Traditional industry definitions, such as soft drinks or automobiles
- Economic sectors, such as consumer nondurable goods
- Sensitivity to some economic factor, such as interest rates
- Market sector, such as low-priced stocks or growth stocks

Before making any forecast, the analyst must understand how the company makes money. Profit comes from adding value to the inputs (labor, raw materials, etc.). The value added arises from increasing the utility through changing the form, location, size, convenience, appearance, or some other characteristic of the original inputs in a way that makes the product or service more desirable.

Thus, the analyst must understand the workings of the industry in which the company operates and competes. A company's competitors must be understood, for they are a part of the operating environment. Analysts tend to compare stocks in a "peer group," such as an industry, with others in the group to a greater degree than with the market as a whole.

Before the valuation the analyst will try to determine which companies have done better or worse than the group, and more important, why. It is a great convenience to devise some measure of what has been "normal" or average performance for the group, as a yardstick against which each company can be compared. Because of the difference in the size of the companies, ratio analysis has become the most common tool for measuring the tangible record of the companies and the industry on a basis independent of size. The modest objectives of this chapter are to provide sample displays of industry data, and to discuss some of the uses of averages, indexes, and other techniques, along with some of their disadvantages.

Analysts face many challenges in preparing the data for a company so that its ratios are consistent through time and comparable with other companies under consideration. In addition, preparing an industry "average" or benchmark ratio against which to compare the other companies presents some technical complications.

Seven Grocery Chains

Ratio Tables

To provide a basis for discussion of alternative techniques and their strengths and weaknesses, a number of tables of ratios have been prepared on seven grocery chains. The grocery industry was chosen because of its homogeneity and because all readers should be generally familiar with its retailing activities. The list of companies includes very large and very small companies, some with high profitability and others with low, and companies of disparate qualitative characteristics.

Original Data Adjusted for Operating Leases

In preparing the data for industry ratio analysis, each company was treated in accordance with the recommended adjustments discussed in Chapters 2 through 11. The rent schedules of operating leases were projected and discounted at a 10 percent rate. The resulting present value was capitalized as an asset and a lease liability. The present value is *principal* and the remainder of the operating lease rental payments is *interest.* The ratio of this interest component to the total rental payments was assumed to be constant for all years, and therefore, the interest expense for operating leases for each year was calculated as the interest ratio multiplied by the year's total operating lease rental expense. These steps put the equity ratio and the return on total capital on a more comparable basis than would be the case if the operating leases were not capitalized. Some error is introduced on an absolute basis because of the estimated discount rate, but on a *relative* basis the picture is improved because the bias is in the same direction for all companies.

FIFO Inventories

At the beginning of the 10-year period studied, only a minority of the companies were on a LIFO basis, but at the end of the period all seven companies used LIFO. Because discontinuity would exist if no adjustment were made, and proper information is not available to adjust to LIFO for the early years, all companies were placed on a FIFO basis for the years studied.

Other Adjustments

Where interest had been capitalized, it was expensed, and estimated amortization and tax effects eliminated from the accounts. A few unusual and nonrecurring items along with their tax effects, were eliminated or moved to years other than the ones in which they had been reported. Goodwill was eliminated, along with its amortization. Only one company had foreign currency translation adjustments, but inadequate information was available for the recommended analytical adjustment.

Other than the capitalization of operating leases, most of the adjustments for these companies turned out to be sufficiently small so that they could have been ignored. However, the analyst seldom knows whether the aggregate sum of the adjustments is large enough to make a material difference until the adjustments have been calculated.

The Industry Is Changing

A few decades ago, grocery chains were mostly homogeneous in their activities and characteristics. A variety of standardized ratios for the industry were used to discover the reasons for differences in profit margins, sales growth, and the like. These included such data as sales per store, square feet of retailing space per store, sales per square foot of retailing space on a "comparable stores basis," and the like. In more recent years, nearly all grocery chains have added drugs as a product line; some acquired drug stores and others introduced a drug department into the grocery store. In addition, some have gone for superstore and combination store concepts, handling as many as 20,000 items versus 10,000 three decades ago. The old-fashioned neighborhood supermarket may now have grown to more than an acre of retailing floor space, be located in a huge shopping mall, and offer such durable and luxury goods as lawn and garden furniture, power tools, or several brands of videocassette recorders. Sales per square foot no longer seem to mean very much when one company tends to operate on the traditional Monday through Saturday store hours while another is open around the clock year-round. Although the ratios continue to tell the analyst that something is happening, more digging is required of the analyst today to understand why a grocery chain is successful or not.

Profitability

The Profitability Ratios

Table 14.1 shows the conventional profitability measures of the seven grocery chains. We reemphasize our belief that the percentage earned on total capital is the best measure of the success of any company and should be the starting point for the analysis. Because of our bias favoring investing in common stocks over bonds, the table also includes the return on common stockholders' equity for the seven companies. Five-year averages are also shown for 1976 to 1980 and for 1981 through 1985.

Technical Issues

Weighted versus Unweighted Industry Averages. The table introduces the first of our technical issues in calculating industry averages. The industry ratios could be calculated by setting up an aggregate industry income statement and industry balance sheet, and then calculating the desired ratios for each year. The advantage of this calculation is primarily in comparing the success of one industry with that of another. Such aggregate calculations do a very good job of showing the overall results of the industry, regardless of whether it has many small participants, some small and some large, or only a few large participants.

However, in the case of our seven grocery chains (which represent only a small part of the entire grocery industry) Kroger and Safeway would have accounted for 62 percent of sales and would have a similarly large influence on each of the ratios. For practical purposes, the calculated ratios would essentially reflect what happened to those two companies, and the results of the other five companies would be largely obscured. Comparing the five smaller companies with a weighted industry average would simply indicate how each of the five companies did relative to Kroger and Safeway. This would deemphasize the rankings of performance of the individual companies.

Table 14.1 Profitability Measures

Years	Unweighted industry average	Albert- son's Inc.	Borman's	Food Lion	Lucky Stores	Kroger	Safeway Stores	Super- markets General
			Percent Earned on Capital					
1985	9.9	10.6	8.0	13.3	7.6	7.4	9.4	12.9
1984	9.3	11.2	3.2	13.9	8.1	7.5	8.7	12.8
1983	7.8	11.0	−5.5	12.7	9.0	7.4	8.3	11.4
1982	10.1	11.5	8.0	12.8	8.7	8.2	8.1	13.4
1981	11.0	11.7	1.3	14.9	10.1	8.8	6.9	12.9
1980	10.6	11.9	7.5	13.6	11.1	9.2	7.5	13.5
1979	11.2	11.9	6.7	15.0	13.2	8.5	8.5	14.7
1978	10.9	11.9	9.4	14.6	12.2	7.5	8.9	11.7
1977	9.3	10.4	4.3	12.7	10.7	6.9	7.6	12.4
1976	10.2	9.2	6.6	14.4	9.0	6.4	12.3	13.6
Average								
1981–1985	9.6	11.2	5.2	13.5	8.7	7.8	8.3	12.7
1976–1980	10.5	11.1	6.9	14.1	11.2	7.7	9.0	13.2
Difference	−0.9	0.1	−1.7	−0.6	-2.5	0.1	-0.7	−0.5
			Percent Return on Equity					
1985	15.7	16.7	15.9	22.6	12.4	11.8	12.5	18.2
1984	13.6	18.2	−1.7	24.3	13.9	11.5	11.6	17.4
1983	9.5	18.7	−29.6	23.1	16.6	10.9	12.4	14.2
1982	16.5	20.9	13.6	21.4	16.1	12.8	12.4	18.0
1981	13.9	23.3	10.8	20.1	20.0	15.4	8.7	17.4
1980	18.0	24.8	13.4	16.4	23.1	15.6	10.8	22.2
1979	20.6	26.5	10.8	17.5	29.2	15.2	13.8	31.0
1978	19.6	26.3	19.8	16.4	25.9	14.0	15.2	19.9
1977	15.6	21.3	1.9	15.1	22.9	11.1	11.9	25.0
1976	16.1	17.0	8.8	18.6	19.5	9.5	12.3	26.8
Average								
1981–1985	14.0	19.6	−1.9	22.3	16.8	12.5	11.5	17.1
1976–1980	18.1	23.8	10.9	16.8	24.1	13.1	12.8	25.0
Difference	−4.1	−4.2	−12.8	5.5	−7.3	−0.6	−1.3	−7.9

Thus, for purposes of comparing individual companies, an unweighted industry average was chosen. That is, the ratio was calculated for each company, the ratios for the year added, and the sum divided by 7. These are the columns entitled "Unweighted industry average." Although this method was chosen for its simplicity and because the five-year averages would tend to ameliorate some of the technical problems, the analyst should be aware that the unweighted industry figures for a single year may be misleading. The most obvious example is the industry return on equity for 1983. It includes Borman's negative return of 29.6 percent of equity, which pulls the industry average down sharply, even though

Borman's represents only about 2 percent of the revenues and assets of the seven companies sampled.

Dealing with Outliers.   One technique for handling the Borman's problem is to eliminate the highest and lowest observation in each sample as being atypical, and simply average the remaining five. The elimination of Borman's and Food Lion, the worst and the best return on equity for 1983, would give a more characteristic 14.6 percent average for the industry sample. An objection to that technique is that throwing out the high and low observations each year means that a different mix of companies is represented in the industry average in each year, and therefore not exactly the same companies are being presented through time.

Borman's 1983 loss was so large as to draw the analyst's attention to the possibility that some highly unusual and nonrecurring event had taken place during that year. No other number in the table comes anywhere close to it. The analyst, upon investigating Borman's situation, would find that the company had left itself vulnerable to a price war (initiated by competitors who were enjoying lower labor costs due to protection of the bankruptcy courts), and was exposed because of its geographic concentration in the State of Michigan, circumstances which do not justify treatment of the figures as unusual or nonrecurring.

Averaging Ratios.   Although it is not the common practice, from a mathematical viewpoint the preferred procedure in averaging ratios is to take the geometric mean rather than the arithmetic mean. However, this method does not work where negative numbers may be involved. To use a geometric mean requires that the negative numbers be excluded from the sample or that other techniques be used that are mathematically quite complex. The practical answer seems to be to use the arithmetic mean, perhaps with removal of outliers.

Decomposition of Return on Capital

Table 14.2 shows the return on total capital decomposed into its two components, the earnings margin and capital turnover. The three companies with the highest return on total capital all enjoy superior earnings margins and in general stood up well in capital turnover.

The surprise in the picture is the remarkably high turnover of Borman's, which has suffered a weak and erratic earnings margin. In seeking the explanation for Borman's rapid capital turnover, inventory turnover figures were also included in the table. Unfortunately,

Table 14.2 Decomposition of Return on Capital

Years	Unweighted industry average	Albert-son's Inc.	Borman's	Food Lion	Lucky Stores	Kroger	Safeway Stores	Super-markets General
			Earnings Margin					
1985	1.9%	2.3%	1.0%	3.0%	1.5%	1.7%	1.9%	2.2%
1984	1.9	2.3	.4	3.1	1.6	1.8	1.7	2.2
1983	1.7	2.3	− .6	2.9	1.9	1.7	1.6	2.0
1982	1.8	2.3	.9	2.6	1.7	1.6	1.6	2.2
1981	1.9	2.2	.2	3.4	2.0	1.8	1.3	2.1
1980	2.0	2.2	1.0	3.5	2.2	1.7	1.4	2.2
1979	2.1	2.3	.9	3.7	2.4	1.6	1.6	2.4
1978	2.1	2.2	1.3	3.7	2.2	1.6	1.7	2.1
1977	1.9	2.0	.6	3.3	1.9	1.5	1.5	2.4
1976	1.9	1.8	1.0	3.3	1.7	1.3	1.7	2.7
Average								
1981–1985	1.8	2.3	.4	3.0	1.7	1.7	1.6	2.1
1976–1980	2.0	2.1	.9	3.5	2.1	1.5	1.6	2.3
			Capital Turnover					
1985	5.3×	4.7×	8.1×	4.4×	5.0×	4.3×	4.9×	5.8×
1984	5.5	4.8	8.9	4.5	5.1	4.2	5.2	5.8
1983	5.4	4.7	8.6	4.4	4.9	4.4	5.1	5.7
1982	5.6	5.1	7.6	5.0	5.0	5.2	5.2	6.0
1981	5.6	5.4	7.8	4.3	5.0	4.9	5.3	6.3
1980	5.6	5.3	7.8	3.9	5.1	5.4	5.2	6.3
1979	5.5	5.2	7.5	4.0	5.5	5.2	5.2	6.1
1978	5.4	5.4	7.3	3.9	5.5	4.8	5.2	5.7
1977	5.2	5.3	6.9	3.8	5.5	4.7	5.2	5.2
1976	5.5	5.1	6.8	4.3	5.2	4.8	7.2	5.0
Average								
1981–1985	5.5	4.9	8.2	4.5	5.0	4.6	5.1	5.9
1976–1980	5.4	5.3	7.3	4.0	5.4	5.0	5.6	5.7
			Inventory Turnover					
1985	8.4×	10.3×	9.2×	7.5×	7.7×	7.7×	7.9×	8.5×
1984	9.0	10.9	10.5	8.0	8.8	8.3	8.0	8.3
1983	8.8	10.6	10.4	7.5	7.9	8.7	8.3	8.5
1982	9.4	10.6	10.3	8.0	8.3	10.4	8.4	9.6
1981	9.4	10.9	11.1	8.7	7.9	9.3	8.7	9.3
1980	9.7	11.2	10.1	10.1	8.1	9.3	9.3	9.7
1979	9.7	11.5	10.8	10.0	8.0	8.6	9.1	9.8
1978	9.8	11.3	10.9	10.0	7.5	8.7	9.0	11.2
1977	10.1	12.5	12.4	11.1	8.3	8.4	9.4	8.5
1976	10.1	12.5	12.5	11.6	7.5	8.8	9.7	8.3
Average								
1981–1985	9.0	10.7	10.3	7.9	8.1	8.9	8.3	8.8
1976–1980	9.9	11.8	11.3	10.6	7.9	8.8	9.3	9.5

they do not appear to offer a full explanation of Borman's capital turnover. The analyst would have to look to the company's other assets, probably to the depreciated carrying amounts of the stores themselves, for an explanation of Borman's high capital turnover rate.

The manufacturing of house brands is a significant activity for some but not all grocery chains. Manufacturing, of course, requires capital investment in plant and inventories, and the turnover in manufacturing is far below that of ordinary food retailing. Thus, those companies that are vertically integrated would be expected to have lower turnover rates. The analyst would also investigate whether this would offer an explanation of Borman's high turnover rate in comparison with the other companies.

The Effects of Leverage

Table 14.3 offers some explanation of the difference between companies in bringing down to equity a disproportionately large or small portion of the return on total capital, as found in Table 14.1. Leveraging a company increases the return on equity above what would be obtained if the company did not borrow. The leveraging will work as long as the after-tax cost of the borrowing is less than the return on total capital. In the case of Borman's, the equity ratio was consistently the lowest in the industry sample. However, because, in some years, Borman's did not earn a sufficient return on total capital to cover its interest expense, the heavy leverage served to reduce rather than increase earnings in those

Table 14.3. Equity as a Percentage of Total Capital

Years	Unweighted industry average	Albertson's Inc.	Borman's	Food Lion	Lucky Stores	Kroger	Safeway Stores	Super-markets General
1985	38	50	29	43	36	29	40	39
1984	38	48	25	49	36	33	38	38
1983	37	44	26	42	35	31	41	41
1982	38	43	34	45	34	35	36	41
1981	38	37	30	55	35	32	37	38
1980	40	36	29	71	34	35	40	36
1979	40	33	28	73	36	36	40	33
1978	39	30	30	78	32	32	41	31
1977	39	34	26	76	37	31	40	26
1976	37	30	30	68	33	34	41	24
Average								
1981–1985	38	44	29	47	35	32	38	39
1976–1980	39	33	29	73	34	34	40	30

years. The analyst should examine the interest rates paid by Borman's on short-term bank borrowing, funded debt, leases, and the like to determine whether the company had been paying inordinately high interest rates on some of its debt, and when those high interest rate instruments are due to mature. The effects of leverage are influenced by the ratio of total debt to capital, and by the interest rate paid on debt.

Growth by Leveraging

The relatively modest leverage of Food Lion makes its recent return on equity all the more remarkable. However, the analyst would notice that a significant contributor to Food Lion's high and growing profitability has been the reduction from an ultraconservative 73 percent equity ratio in 1976 to 1980 to a moderate 47 percent ratio in the more recent five-year period. Thus, the increase in the return on equity from the earlier five-year period is in part due to increased borrowing. Although the company's equity ratio remains conservative, one would not expect a great deal more improvement in return on equity once the company's ratio reaches the industry average.

Supermarkets General shows an opposite pattern from that of Food Lion, having moved from a highly leveraged position to a level approximately equal to the industry average. This reduced leverage has been a cause of the company's decline in return on equity from the level of the earlier five-year period.

Although we chose to show only the equity ratio as a measure of leverage, a more detailed industry analysis could include a table of average interest rates on borrowings, including leases. Changes in interest rates may also give useful explanations of changes in the return on equity of leveraged companies.

Indexes—Base Period versus Base Year

The use of indexes is a convenient way to escape the difficulty of comparing trends of companies whose data vary significantly in size. Most government indexes use a single base year, setting the index at 100 at that point. That is workable in economics because most economic statistics on the broader aspects of the economy are fairly stable. Results of individual companies tend to be much more volatile, and therefore, it is usually a better practice to use a period of several years as the base, rather than a single year.

Table 14.4. Growth Indexes, 1976–1980 (Base = 100)

Years	Unweighted industry average	Albert-son's Inc.	Borman's	Food Lion	Lucky Stores	Kroger	Safeway Stores	Super-markets General
			Sales Index					
1985	246	224	123	565	193	214	156	248
1984	220	210	128	445	190	199	156	211
1983	193	190	125	355	172	190	147	171
1982	176	175	125	287	164	184	140	157
1981	148	154	118	202	148	141	131	145
1980	133	135	125	165	133	129	120	127
1979	116	118	113	126	119	113	109	115
1978	98	100	98	91	96	98	100	100
1977	81	80	86	66	80	84	89	84
1976	72	66	78	52	72	76	83	74
Average								
1981–1985	197	191	124	371	173	186	146	186
1976–1980	100	100	100	100	100	100	100	100
			Total Cash Flow before Interest Index					
1985	259	255	139	574	199	200	189	257
1984	219	233	97	422	182	195	188	217
1983	179	203	22	330	175	186	158	176
1982	162	176	139	247	161	128	143	163
1981	161	148	93	213	162	237	125	152
1980	134	132	125	161	130	144	115	133
1979	111	119	93	132	127	102	109	97
1978	105	106	126	96	106	93	105	102
1977	75	79	68	62	75	74	85	85
1976	74	64	89	48	63	87	87	83
Average								
1981–1985	196	203	98	357	176	189	161	192
1976–1980	100	100	100	100	100	100	100	100
			Total Earned for Capital Index					
1985	235	235	129	480	137	237	190	238
1984	200	230	49	390	142	226	164	200
1983	152	205	−84	291	150	206	152	146
1982	161	184	123	207	133	187	139	152
1981	131	156	21	196	141	163	108	129
1980	133	141	126	161	135	140	109	119
1979	121	126	106	133	134	118	112	119
1978	103	104	132	95	100	97	107	89
1977	73	73	56	62	73	80	83	86
1976	69	56	79	49	58	64	89	87
Average								
1981–1985	176	202	48	313	141	204	151	173
1976–1980	100	100	100	100	100	100	100	100

Table 14.4. Growth Indexes, 1976–1980 (Base = 100) (Continued)

Years	Unweighted industry average	Albert-son's Inc.	Borman's	Food Lion	Lucky Stores	Kroger	Safeway Stores	Super-markets General
			Earnings per Share Index					
1985	205	232	157	426	103	137	151	231
1984	160	221	− 15(d)*	363	109	124	129	192
1983	91	195	−311(d)	265	121	104	128	134
1982	151	172	148	196	107	166	121	144
1981	109	161	− 79(d)	191	122	162	83	120
1980	133	144	139	162	123	143	99	123
1979	126	129	107	132	130	123	118	146
1978	109	104	172	93	99	102	118	78
1977	67	71	15	64	82	73	84	78
1976	64	51	67	49	66	59	81	74
Average								
1981–1985	143	196	− 20(d)	288	112	139	122	164
1976–1980	100	100	100	100	100	100	100	100

*(d) = deficit.

In Table 14.4 we have selected the average results for the years 1976 through 1980 as 100, the base for our index. Note that for the sales index, excepting Food Lion, setting the year 1978 as our base year would have made little difference. However, when we create an index for such a volatile number as earnings per share, 1978 would have been a poor one to use as a base for measuring progress.

Several of the companies were very consistent in bringing down a constant portion of sales to cash flow and to the total earned for capital, but some fell considerably short in bringing a proportional amount down to earnings per share. The analyst would investigate the causes of these shortfalls, which could range from dilution due to sale of additional shares, to poor margins, or to high interest rates.

Interest Coverage—Cash Flow Is the Key to Quality

Table 14.5 shows the cash flow coverage of all interest expense. That ratio is one of many used to measure the quality of the company's debt instruments. It is a maxim of this book that if debt of a company is of unsuitable quality for purchase, no one other than a speculator should purchase the equity. Thus, all analytical studies should include at least some measures of the quality of a company's debt.

The reader may be interested in comparing the relative standing of these companies in terms of interest coverage with the Table 14.2 data on capital turnover. In general, rapid capital turnover is viewed as a

Table 14.5. Cash Flow Coverage of All Interest

Years	Unweighted industry average	Albert-son's Inc.	Borman's	Food Lion	Lucky stores	Kroger	Safeway stores	Super-markets general
1985	5.8×	4.6×	3.1×	12.3×	6.4×	6.9×	4.4×	2.8×
1984	5.7	5.0	2.3	11.6	7.6	4.8	5.6	3.1
1983	6.4	5.2	4.0	12.4	6.7	6.3	6.5	3.4
1982	6.3	4.9	2.7	13.8	6.9	5.8	5.8	3.9
1981	6.0	5.0	3.4	12.3	5.9	6.6	4.9	4.1
1980	6.3	5.2	2.7	12.7	6.0	9.1	4.3	3.8
1979	5.6	5.2	4.2	12.2	5.5	3.7	4.5	3.8
1978	4.8	5.7	0.7	8.9	5.2	4.3	4.7	4.1
1977	5.3	6.1	2.9	9.4	5.4	4.4	5.1	4.0
1976	5.6	7.3	3.9	9.0	5.8	4.4	4.6	4.1
Average								
1981–1985	6.0	4.9	3.1	12.5	6.7	6.1	5.4	3.5
1976–1980	5.6	5.9	2.9	10.4	5.6	5.2	4.6	4.8

highly desirable characteristic, but it is sometimes accompanied by low depreciation expense, perhaps because stores are old and have low acquisition costs. This tends to reduce cash flow. Although Food Lion and Kroger had rather unimpressive capital turnover, both had very good cash flow coverage of interest. Food Lion's interest coverage is easily explained by its wide earnings margin and conservative capital structure. The explanation for Kroger's interest coverage is not obvious from these tables, so the analyst would review Kroger's cash flow statement to determine whether the favorable coverage came about from above-average depreciation or perhaps from high deferred taxes. If the answer were not found there, it might be derived from low interest rates. Whatever the answer, the important point is that comparative ratio analysis not only tells a variety of useful stories about companies and industries, it also indicates areas which should be investigated by the analyst. Thus, the anomalies make a unique contribution to security analysis.

Per-Share Growth Rates

Comparisons of Averages

Table 14.6 presents a convenient mechanism for comparing the growth in per-share attributes for the seven grocery chains from the first five-year period to the second. The five-year averages are assumed to represent the normal cash flow, earnings, dividends, and book value for the companies. Thus, the percentage change from the first five-year period to the second five-year period represents the *total* growth from

Table 14.6 Per-Share Growth Attributes

	Unweighted industry average	Albert-son's Inc.	Borman's	Food Lion	Lucky Stores	Kroger	Safeway Stores	Super-markets General
			Cash Flow per Common Share					
Averages								
1981–1985		$ 3.77	$ 2.89	$ 0.93	$ 4.18	$10.57	$ 8.17	$ 3.03
1976–1980		1.96	2.97	0.27	2.67	7.71	5.71	1.60
Percent change 1976–1980 to 1981–1985	80	92	−3	244	57	37	43	89
			Earnings per Share					
Averages								
1981–1985		$ 2.26	$−0.24	$ 0.59	$ 1.94	$ 4.21	$ 3.09	$ 1.32
1976–1980		1.15	1.21	0.20	1.72	3.04	2.52	0.81
Percent change 1976–1980 to 1981–1985	42	96	nmf*	180	12	38	64	63
			Dividend per Share					
Averages								
1981–1985		$0.60	$0.03	$0.05	$1.15	$1.85	$1.44	$0.37
1976–1980		0.26	0.08	0.01	0.86	1.00	1.18	0.17
Percent change 1976–1980 to 1981–1985	87	126	−63	286	34	85	22	117
			Book Value per Share					
Averages								
1981–1985		$12.95	$12.13	$2.46	$11.64	$28.50	$25.40	$7.21
1976–1980		5.23	11.19	1.19	6.69	19.75	18.85	3.23
Percent change 1976–1980 to 1981–1985	77	148	8	107	74	44	35	123

* nmf = not a meaningful figure.

the midpoint of the first five years to the midpoint of the second five years. To obtain the *annual* rate of change, one would add 100 percent and take the fifth root of that sum. For example, the earnings per share growth from the 1976–1980 period to the 1981–1985 period for Albertson's, Inc., was 96 percent. To get the annual growth rate, one would add 100 percent to the total and express the result as a decimal: 1.96. The natural logarithm of 1.96 is 0.673. That divided by 5 is

0.13459, the antilog of which is 1.144. Thus the annual growth rate from midpoint to midpoint was 14.4 percent.

Growth Rates Using Indexes

An alternative measure of the growth in earnings per share would be to use the index shown in the final section of Table 14.4. A simple calculation from the beginning to the end can provide a growth rate estimate. First divide the beginning index of 51 (1976) into the final index of 232 (1985). Using the same logarithmic method described above, the index would give a rate of 18.3 percent growth in earnings per share for Albertson's, reflecting the unduly low index number for the beginning year, 1976. Note that earnings per share doubled from 1976 to 1978 (the index moved from 51 to 104). Which growth rate better characterizes the company's history is a matter for analytical judgment and consideration of many factors. In any event, the important growth rate lies ahead. The central issue of the growth aspect of valuation is whether the future growth of the company will be in some ways similar to that of the past, or in some ways different.

The index numbers can also be used with other techniques to estimate an annual rate of historic growth, e.g., a linear regression of the years versus the index numbers. The values found on that regression line give a compound growth rate of 17.1 percent, whereas log linear regression gives an 18.6 percent growth rate.

With such a large range of calculated growth rates, the analyst must pay close attention to choosing between the use of a series or averages. Averages have the advantage of muting the outliers. Individual years give a longer history, but at the cost of some accuracy. The analyst's judgment will lead to one or the other approach, in a given situation, as having greater potential usefulness in estimating the future growth rate.

Stock Price Comparisons—Attributes per Dollar Invested

Table 14.7 shows certain key data on a basis of the investment of $1 in a stock. The first data line is based on the stock price as of December 31, 1985. Ordinarily we would have selected a date somewhat later—in the year 1986—so that the annual report would be available when the analyst was making the purchase or sale decision. However, in the first half of 1986 three of these grocery chains were rumored to be takeover targets, and the prices reflected that speculative possibility. The dollars of sales, cash flow, earnings, dividends, and book value shown on the

Table 14.7. Stock Data on a Per-Dollar-Invested Basis

| Company | Stock price | Per dollar of market value | | | | |
		Sales	Cash flow	Earnings	Dividend	Book value
Albertson's Inc.						
1985	32.50*	4.69	0.15	0.08	0.02	0.53
1981–1985 Average	22.50	6.32	0.17	0.11	0.03	0.59
Borman's						
1985	12.00*	29.35	0.39	0.16	0.00	1.11
1981–1985 Average	6.93	58.42	0.50	(0.05)	0.01	2.04
Food Lion						
1985	21.75*	1.61	0.07	0.04	0.00	0.17
1981–1985 Average	11.00	2.18	0.09	0.06	0.00	0.24
Kroger						
1985	47.88*	8.19	0.19	0.09	0.04	0.59
1981–1985 Average	35.09	11.99	0.34	0.13	0.05	0.85
Lucky Stores						
1985	25.00*	7.35	0.19	0.07	0.05	0.53
1981–1985 Average	18.10	9.33	0.23	0.11	0.07	0.65
Safeway						
1985	36.88*	8.83	0.24	0.10	0.04	0.77
1981–1985 Average	23.56	14.84	0.36	0.13	0.06	1.13
Supermarkets General						
1985	50.50*	2.81	0.08	0.04	0.01	0.19
1981–1985 Average	11.82	11.34	0.31	0.13	0.04	0.73

*Price as of December 31, 1985; other data on this line are for the year 1985.

first data line are the actual figures for 1985. Since some of those numbers may not have represented normal conditions, most analysts would use an average or an estimate of what was normal rather than the actual figures for the year. The first line is designed to show what the investor could have bought with $1 invested in each of the seven stocks on December 31, 1985. The 1985 data were used in preference to the five-year data because of the strong growth trends of three of the companies.

The second data line shows the average stock price for the period 1981 through 1985 and the average amounts of the various data items for the five-year period from 1981 to 1985, calculated as amounts that would have been obtained by investing $1 in the stock at the average price for the five years. Comparing the two lines gives a notion of what could be bought at the end of the period versus what could have been bought at the average price.

The calculated results, in this case, show that if the 1985 figures are representative, investors would have obtained much less of each attribute at the December 1985 price than they had been able to obtain at the average price for the previous five years. This is not particularly startling, since all the stocks were up sharply from their five-year average price. However, some of the attributes rose sharply also.

Tables such as 14.7 help provide a sense of perspective. They indicate what the analyst can obtain today versus what was obtainable on average over a reasonably long previous period. They bring together the data for a number of companies that are reasonably similar in their business activities. They emphasize how much the investor is giving up to obtain a rapid rate of historical earnings growth and how much can be gained in past attributes for the investor who is satisfied with lower-quality issues.

Although Table 14.7 may help the investor decide which of the seven stocks is the most attractive growth stock and which is the most attractive yield stock *in historical terms*, the industry-oriented table provides no information about whether grocery stocks are cheap or dear relative to the rest of the stock market. This comparison requires industry data and some broad measure such as Standard & Poor's 400 industrials stock index, for which similar data can be obtained.

Table 14.7 is a good example of the techniques of combining ratios to produce new ratios. The sales per dollar of market value ratio is simply the ratio of sales per share to price per share, and the other ratios to market value are calculated similarly.

The examples of useful tables and techniques in this chapter have used only historical data, but a real study of an industry would include projections of the future for both the companies and the industry composite. The orderly comparison of the past record of a homogeneous group of companies is a sound basis for detecting and understanding what is "normal" for or characteristic of that group. Individual companies' departures from the norm tell something of the individual company's characteristics. All that information is good background for forecasting the future.

The reader may find it useful to spend some time comparing the price data of Table 14.7 with the various data found in the other tables. What factors correlate best with the pricing of these stocks at year-end 1985 or during the 1981 to 1985 period? Profitability, growth, stability, leverage, yield, or creditworthiness? How much more important is the current record than the distant past? Which measure of the growth record or of earning power seems the best technique in explaining the stock prices?

Tentative answers to such questions can be formed, but pricing anomalies will continue to leave one with a feeling that the stock prices are not fully explained by the past record, regardless of technique. That feeling is correct. Expectations about the future are the dominant factor in stock pricing. The correlation of stock prices with the past is largely a reflection of the persistence of past company and industry characteristics through time. That continuity exists to a greater degree in stable industries, such as the grocery chains, than in cyclical or technology industries. Even in the stable industries, blind extrapolation of past data is a poor substitute for analysis.

Price comparisons between companies, such as those found in Table 14.7, are among the analyst's most powerful tools for determining relative values. They are used in the final steps of the investment decision, for price is the analyst's greatest ally.

Index

Abbott Laboratories, 48, 75
Accelerated cost recovery system (ACRS), 105
Accelerated depreciation methods, 105–106
Accounting, 31–38
  big bath, 69–70
  conservatism of, 33–34
  consistency of, 32, 44
  contract, 177–178
  income statement analysis, 41, 48
  independence of cash flows from, 133–134
  realization principle, 34
Accounting Principles Board (APB), 77
Accounts payable, 141
Accounts receivable, 139, 253
Accrual accounting, 33
Accrued current liabilities, 141–142
Acme-Cleveland Corporation, 163, 171–172
Acquisition value of assets, 206
Adjustment(s), 26–28, 44
  arising from working capital, 73–76
  for capitalized interest, 109–110
  cash flows, 138–139
  depreciation, 117–118
  of foreign assets, 50
  foreign currency translation, 70–76
  implicit versus explicit, 26
  inventory valuation and, 97–98
  key ratios and, 259–262
  to normalize expense, 87
  profitability ratios and, 241–242
  reasons for, 27–28, 37–38
  reserves and, 63–65
  taxes, 47
  (See also Per-share adjustments)

Aetna Life and Casualty Insurance Company, 47, 171
Affiliates:
  consolidation of, 46, 153–154, 160
  cost methods for, 156–157
  defined, 153
  equity method for, 154–156
  exclusion of results of, 157
  finance and leasing, 157–160
  losses of, 162–164
  minority interest deduction, 154
  (See also Foreign operations)
Airline depreciation rates, 118
Allowance for equity funds used during construction (AFUDC), 108–110
Allstate Insurance, 159
Alternative minimum tax (AMT), 166–167
Altman, Edward I., 215*n*.
Aluminum Company, 238
AM International, Inc., 47
AMAX Corporation, 82, 268
American Brands, 74, 212–213
American Can Company, 50
American Institute of Certified Public Accountants (AICPA), 24, 89*n*., 112*n*., 193, 226*n*.
American Tobacco (*see* American Brands)
Amortization, 102–103, 119–125
  key ratios and, 263
  taxable versus reported income and, 175
Archer Daniels Midland Company, 47
Armco Financial Services Group, 67
Armco, Inc., 67, 173
Ashland Oil, Inc., 48
Asset(s):
  absent, 46

Asset(s) (*Cont.*):
  acquisition value of, 206
  cash, 185–186
  claim on, 207
  current, 184–190
  foreign, 50
  intangible, 123–125, 179, 194, 207–208,
    211, 238–239, 259–269
  intermediate-term, 191
  long-term, 191–192
  merger value of, 206
  noncurrent, 190–194
  receivables, 186–188
  sale of, 48–50
Asset plays, book value and, 210
Asset value(s), 30, 205–213
  of common stock, 217–218
  free cash, 218–219
Auditor's opinion, 34–35
Average cost method for inventory
  valuation, 95
Avis, 50

Bad debt reserves, 60, 177
Balance sheet, 183–203
  affiliates' leases and, 157–158
  for asset value analysis, 210–213
  assets on, 184–194
  capital structure and, 213–214
  earnings calculations via, 219–220
  inventory valuation for, 98
  liabilities on, 189–190, 194–203
  pension plans and, 79–81
  presentation of, 183–184
  reserves on, 59
  working-capital position, 214–217
Balance-sheet analysis, 205–221
Ball, Raymond J., 37*n.*
Banks, special tax status of, 173–174
Barnsdall Oil, 163*n.*
Base stock method, 95
Beaver, William H., 23*n.*, 37*n.*
Berliner, Robert H., 88*n.*
Bethlehem Steel Corporation, 106
Big bath accounting, 69–70
Black, Fischer, 36*n.*, 232
Black, Richard B., 47
Bond(s), income statement analysis for
  selecting, 44–45
Book value, 207–210
Borman's, 277–281
Bristol-Myers Company, 184, 207

Buffet, Warren, 125
Business Conditions Digest, 7*n.*
Business cycle, 246
Butler, W. F., 7*n.*

Capacity, physical, 270
Capital:
  assets as measure of, 206
  average or beginning, 240
  cash flow to, 252
  earning, 255, 257
  earnings available for, 257–260
  equity, 244
  management's ability to use, 239–245
  return on, 240–243, 278–281
  total, 252
  (*See also* Capital maintenance)
Capital consumption adjustment (CCA),
  117
Capital expenditures, 143, 146
Capital gains, 54–55, 168
Capital leases, 122–123, 195
Capital losses of financial companies,
  54–55
Capital maintenance, 133
Capital structure, 213–214
Capital turnover, 242
Capitalization:
  allowances for changes in, 227–228
  of interest, 261
  of production costs, 178
Captive finance and leasing companies,
  158–159
Carnation Company, 160
Carry forward benefits, income taxes and,
  172
Cash, 185–186
Cash cycle, 33
Cash flow(s):
  approximation of, 130–131
  capital maintenance and, 133
  comparison of methods for computing,
    147–150
  confusion between income and,
    150–152
  deferred taxes and, 112
  depreciation and, 133
  direct method of computing, 135–147
  dividends and, 130, 144
  financing activities and, 143–144
  gross, 131–132
  importance of, 129–132

Cash flow(s) (*Cont.*):
  independence from accounting,
    133–134
  indirect computing method, 132–133
  inflows and, 34, 138–140
  interest coverage and, 283–284
  operating, 142
  outflows and, 140–143
  payout of, 248–249
  per share, 234
  restructurings and, 69
  to senior charges, 251–252
  to total capital, 252
Cash inflows, 34
Cash ratio, 215–216
Chase Econometrics, 4
CIT Financial Corporation, 125
Claim(s):
  equity, 207
  in income statement analysis, 47
Class life asset depreciation range
  (CLADR) system, 105, 106, 117
Coldwell Banker, 159
Collateral value, 206
Commercial banks, special tax status of,
  173–174
Common equity, return on, 243–244
Common stock(s), 210, 217–219
  "class B," conversion of, 232
Company(ies):
  capital gains and losses of, 54–56
  comparing with related groups, 273–
    274
  fraudulent, 42–43
  use of income statement for, 41
  [*See also* Industry(ies)]
Comparability:
  of accounting, 32
  affiliates and, 158
  depreciation and, 43–44, 87, 117–118
  of inventories, 43–44, 87, 96–98
Conditional forecasting, 9
Conformity rules for LIFO, 92–93
Conservatism of accounting, 33–34
Consistency of accounting, 32, 44
Consolidated financial reports, 153–154
Consolidation, 46, 153–154
Contingent litigation liabilities, 201
Contract accounting, 177–178
Coopers & Lybrand, 35
Cost layers under LIFO, 92
Credit ratios, 249, 266

Current assets, 184–190
Current cost, depreciation and, 116–117
Current liabilities, 141, 189–190
Current values:
  depreciation and, 108
  for property, plant, and equipment,
    190–191
Curtailments, pension, 82

Data Resources, Inc., 4
Dean Witter, 159
Debt:
  doubtful, 125
  extinguishment of, 179, 262
  of subsidiaries, 158
  working-capital position and, 216–217
  [*See also* Leverage; Loan(s)]
Debt-service coverage, total, 252
Deconsolidation, 160
Deere & Company, 93
Defensive interval, 253
Deferred charges, 193
Deferred taxes, 59, 110–117, 171–172,
  179–181, 213, 244
Depletion, 119–120, 172
Depreciation, 87, 102–118
  cash flows and, 133, 140–141
  comparability of, 43–44, 46, 117–118
  computation of, 85–86, 105–108
  funds flow statement and, 146
  industry characteristics and, 103–104
  intra-industry ranges of, 116
  key ratios and, 262
  as necessary cost, 151–152
  on new utility plants, 107
  profitability ratios and, 243
  taxable versus reported income and,
    175–176
  useful lives, 114, 116
Depreciation to gross plant ratio, 253–254
Depreciation to sales ratio, 253–254
Development items, expensing, 124–125
Dilution of book value, 207
Discontinued operations, 51
Dividend(s):
  capitalization of, 227
  cash flows and, 130, 139, 144
  80% exclusion, 167–168
  per share, 233
  working-capital position and, 216–217
Dividend arrearages, preferred stock, 203
Dividend payout ratio, 130–144, 248, 265

Dollar perspective, foreign currency
adjustments and, 71
Domestic International Sales Corporation
(DISC), 47
Double declining balance method, 105,
106
Drtina, Ralph E., 149n.
Dukes, R. E., 37n.
Du Pont, E. I., de Nemours and Com-
pany, 192

Earning(s):
asset and investment values and, 30
available for total capital, 257–259
calculation via balance sheet, 219–220
decline in, 247
deferred taxes as, 244
foreign, unremitted, 161–162, 176
price-earnings ratios and, 235
quality of, 236
reported, 35–37, 112–113
"true," 35–37
[See also Income; Profit(s)]
Earning capital base, 255, 257
Earning power, book value and, 210
Earnings margin, 242
Earnings per share, 227–234, 266,
284–286
Eastman Kodak, Inc., 238
Economic analysis, 3–19
cyclical and secular forecasts and, 5–
10
security analysis and, 10–17
Economic models, 6–7
Employee Retirement Income Security
Act (ERISA), 76
Equity, return on, 210, 243–244
Equity capital, deferred taxes as, 244
Equity claim, 207
Equity Funding Corporation, 43
Equity method:
for affiliates, 154–156
asset value analysis and, 212
Equity ratio, 249
Excessive contributions, 179
Expenses:
allocation over time, 101–102
cash flows and, 140
prepaid, 141, 193
Exploration costs, 123
Exxon Corporation, 62, 221, 269–270

Fabricant, Soloman, 108n.
Federal Savings and Loan Insurance
Corporation (FSLIC), 173
Finance charges, unearned, 66
Finance companies:
book value and, 210
captive, 158–159
"stand-alone," 159
Financial Accounting Standards Board
(FASB), 24, 33n., 57–58, 61, 77
Financial statement analysis, 23–38
accounting and, 23–26, 31–38
Financing, off-balance-sheet, 189
Financing activities, 128
cash flows and, 143–144
Firestone Tire & Rubber Company, 93
First causes, 14
First-in, first-out (FIFO) method, 89, 90,
96–99
[See also Inventory(ies)]
Fluorocarbon Company, 51
Food Lion, 278–283
Ford Motor, 221
Forecasts, 6–19
Foreign currency translation adjustments,
70–76
asset value analysis and, 212
cash flows and, 142
key ratios and, 261
Foreign operations, 160–162
assets and, 50
exclusion from financial reports, 154
income taxes and, 169
unremitted earnings and, 161–162, 176
Foreign tax credit, 169
Foster, George, 37n., 215n.
Fraudulent companies, 42–43
Funds flow statement, 127–152, 244–245

Gains:
actuarial, 81
allocation of, 67–69
asset value analysis and, 212
cash flows and, 138–140
on company's securities, 53–54
of financial companies, 54–55
insurance, 50–51
translation adjustments and, 70–71
(See also Capital gains)
Gas companies, special tax status of,
174–175

General business credit, 168
General Electric (GE), 173
General Electric Credit Corporation
(GECC), 159
General Foods, 209, 221
General Motors Acceptance Corporation
(GMAC), 158–159
General Motors Corporation, 158–159
General Refractories Company, 35
Generally accepted accounting principles
(GAAP), 23–24
Georgia Pacific Corporation, 169
Going concern, asset values and, 205–206
Goodwill, 125, 179
Graham, Benjamin, 125
Grocery chains, analysis of, 274–276
Growth, 245–249, 281
Growth rates, 245–247
per-share, 284–286
Guilford Mills, 219

Hercules, Inc., 255, 256, 260–267
Hertz, 50
Hickman, B. G., 7n.
Hicks, John Richard, 28
Hilton Hotels Corporation, 187–188
HIMONT, Inc., 265

IBM Corporation, 75, 186, 193
Ideal Basic Industries, 49
Inco, 238
Income:
adjustments from working capital in,
73–76
all-inclusive, 219–220
capital maintenance and, 28–30
cash flows and, 150–152
distributable, 147, 149
estimating, 146–147
from interest, 139
long-term studies of, 221
net, 154
recognition of, 46
[See also Earning(s)]
Income statement, 41, 57–84, 98, 135–144
Income statement analysis, 39–55
Income taxes, 124–125, 165–182
cash outflows for, 142–143
deferred, 59, 110–117, 171–172,
179–181, 203, 212, 244
depletion and, 119–120, 172

Income taxes (*Cont.*);
depreciation and, 103–105
in income statement analysis, 46
(*See also* Tax Reform Act of 1986)
Indexes, 281–283, 286
Industry(ies):
growth rates of, 246–247
with special tax status, 173–175
Industry analysis, ratios in, 273–289
Inflation, 86–88, 245–246
Inflation accounting, 87–88
Infrequent items, 51
Installment sales, 177
Insurance companies, special tax status of,
174
Insurance gains, 50–51
Insurance reserves, 63
Intangible assets, 123–125, 179, 194,
207–208, 211, 238–239, 259–269
Interest:
allocation of, 170
capitalization of, 108–110, 142, 176,
261
cash flows and, 139, 142
operating leases and, 198
tax-exempt, 167
Interest coverage in industry analysis,
283–284
Interests:
minority, 154
participating, 233
Intermediate liabilities, 194–202
Intermediate-term assets, 191
Internal Revenue Service (IRS):
LIFO conformity rules of, 92–93
(*See also* Income taxes)
International Banknote, 236
International factors, economy and, 19
International Paper Company, 111, 238
Inventory(ies), 43–44, 46, 87, 141, 188,
201, 275
Inventory valuation, 85–99
Investing activities, 128
Investment(s), 50, 62, 108–109, 133, 143,
191–192
Investment companies, special tax status
of, 174
Investment tax credit (ITC), 111, 166–
169
Investment values, 30, 209, 210
ITT Corporation, 50, 208

Kavesh, R. A., 7n.
Key ratios, 255–272
Key trend projections, 14–16
Kisor, Manowm C., 36n.
Klein, L., 7n.
Kroger, 276
Kroger Partnership, Ltd., 151

Lags, 16–18
Largay, James A., III, 149n.
LaSalle Machine Tool, Inc., 163
Last-in, first-out (LIFO) method, 89–99
  LIFO cost layers, 92
  LIFO pools, 92–93, 178–179
  LIFO reserves, 94–95, 188, 261
Lawyer's Title Insurance Corporation,
  155
Leads, 16–18
Lease(s), 122–123, 157–160, 195–200,
  218, 260
Leasehold(s), 191
Leasehold improvements, 191
Leasing subsidiaries, 159–160
Leverage, 280–281
  [See also Capitalization; Debt; Loan(s)]
Levine, S. N., 7n.
Levy. H., 228n.
Liability(ies):
  absent, 46
  cash flows and, 141–142
  current, 141, 189–190
  for deferred taxes, 180–181
  intermediate, 194–202
  off-balance-sheet, 194–201
  for pensions, 76–78, 181–182
  reserves as, 58–59
Life insurance, cash value of, 186
Liquidating values, 210
Litigation:
  contingent liability for, 201
  in income statement analysis, 47
  reserves for, 62
Loan(s):
  valuation accounts for, 65–66
  working-capital position and, 216–217
  (See also Debt; Leverage)
Loan loss reserves, 60
Location of sales, 272
Lockheed Corporation, 69–70
Long-term assets, 191–192
Losses:
  actuarial, 81–82

Losses (Cont.);
  allocation of, 68–69
  asset value analysis and, 211–212
  on company's securities, 53–54
  divisional, 163–164
  of financial companies, 54–55
  operating, 170–172
  on restructurings, 66–70
  of subsidiaries, 162–164
  translation adjustments and, 71
  (See also Capital losses of financial
    companies)

McCormick & Company, Inc., 151
Macroforecasting, 11–12
Management information system, 31–32
Manufacturers Hanover Bank, 125
Marion Laboratories, Inc., 210
Market, equity ratio at, 250
Market multipliers, 235
Market ratios, 235
Marketable securities, 61–62, 192
Maytag Company, 97–98
Mead Corporation, 197–198
Merger value of assets, 206
Messner, Van A., 36n.
Mine-development expense, 123
Minimum value model, 232
Mining companies, amortization, 119–122
Mobil Corporation, 178
Molodovsky, Nicholas, 238n.
Molodovsky effect, 238–239
Montgomery Ward, 178
Moore, Geoffrey H., 6n.
Mortgage methods, 107
Mortgage valuation accounts, 65–66

National car rental, 50
National income, depreciation charges
  and, 117
National product, depreciation charges
  and, 117
Near-term forecasts, 5–7, 10
Net income, deduction of minority
  interest from, 154
Net operating losses, 170–172
New York Times, 25n.
Noncurrent assets, 190–194
Nondurable goods expenditures, 12–13
Norby, William C., 88n.
Normal stock method, 95
Norton Company, 94

Off-balance-sheet financing, 189
Off-balance-sheet liabilities, 194–201
Oil companies:
  amortization charges of, 119–122
  special tax status of, 174–175
Operating activities, 128
Operating income, 42–46
Operating leases, 122–123, 199–200
  asset value analysis and, 213
  balance sheet and, 195
  industry analysis and, 274–275
  interest component of, 198
  key ratios and, 260
Operating losses, 170–172
Operations:
  cash flows from, 138–142
  discontinued, 51
Options, allowance for, 231–232
Outliers, 278

Payout ratios, 248, 265
Pension assets, balance sheet and, 186
Pension Benefit Guaranty Corporation, 186
Pension plans, 76–82, 202, 213, 260–261
Per-share adjustments, 224–234
Philip Morris Companies, Inc., 208
Physical reserves, 267–269
Plant, property, and equipment, 190–191
Platt, R. B., 7n.
Political factors, economy and, 19
Portfolio(s) depreciation, 107–108
Possessions tax credit, 170
Postemployment benefits, 82–84
  (*See also* Pension plans)
Preferred stocks, 189–190, 203, 212
Premium over exercise price, 232
Prepaid expenses, 141, 193
Price(s):
  current, key ratios and, 263
  exercise, premium over, 232
  of stocks, 286–289
Price-earnings ratios, 235–239
Price Waterhouse & Co., 117n.
Prior period adjustments, 48
Product-financing arrangements, 201–202
Production, 270–271
Production costs, 178
Profit(s), inventory, 86–88
Profitability, 264, 276–278
Profitability ratios, 239–245, 276

Progress ratios, 265
Projections, 6–19
Purchase(s) of stocks, 220–221
Purity Bakeries, 163n.

Quarterly demand forecasts, 6
Quick ratio, 215–216

Rate adjustments, reserve for, 65
Ratio(s), 253, 278–289
  (*See also* specific ratios)
Ratio analysis, 223–254
Real estate industry, 150–151
Real Estate Investment Trusts (REITs), 174
Realization principle, 34
Receivables, 186–188
Related party transactions, 201
Relevance of accounting, 32
Reliability of accounting, 32
Renegotiation, 47
Renegotiation reserves, 62
Representational faithfulness, 32
Research and development, 123–124
Reserves, 57–60
  balance sheet, 59, 187–188
  in high-risk industries, 61
  for insurance, 63
  LIFO, 94–95, 188, 261
  loan loss, 60
  loan and mortgage portfolios, 65–66
  for marketable securities, 61–62
  oil, 121
  against other investments, 62
  physical, 121, 267–270
  for rate adjustments, 65
  for renegotiation and litigation, 62
  for unearned finance charges, 64
  for unexpired subscriptions, 64–65
Resorts International, Inc., 61–62
Restatements in income analysis, 48
Restructurings, 66–70
Retail method, 96
Return on capital, 108–109, 133, 240–243, 278–281
Return on equity, 210, 243–244
Revenues and cash flows, 138–140
Rights adjustment, 228
Risk, 61, 185
Robert Morris Associates, 141n., 215
Rohm & Haas Company, 255, 258–267
Royalties on oil, 121–122

Safety, asset as measure of, 206–207
Safeway, 276
Sales:
  of assets, 48–50
  concentration and location of, 272
  installment, 177
  per share, 233
  of stocks, 220–221
Sarnat, Marshall, 228n.
Savings and loan companies, special tax
  status of, 173
Schlumberger, Dowell, 156
Schlumberger Ltd., 156, 221
Scholes, Myron, 232
Seagram Company, Ltd., 192
Sears, Roebuck and Company, 159
Sears, Roebuck acceptance, 159
Securities, 61–62, 192, 206–207, 212
  (*See also* specific types of securities)
Securities and Exchange Commission
  (SEC), 24, 108
Security analysis, economic analysis and,
  10–18
Seed, Allen, III, 132n.
Senior charges, 251–252
Settlements, pension, 82
Sharpe, William F., 232n.
Sinking funds, 107, 189–190
Stability, 247–248, 265
Standard cost method for inventory
  valuation, 95
Stock(s), 44–45, 220–221, 286–289
  [*See also* Common stock(s); Preferred
  stocks]
Stock conversions, 228
Stock rights, 228
Stock splits, 227
Straight-line depreciation, 105, 113–114
Subsidiaries (*see* Affiliates)
Sum-of-the-years' digits, 105, 106
Supermarkets General, 281
Surplus, direct entries to, 46

Tangible factors, key ratios and, 239
Tax adjustments in income analysis, 47
Tax anticipation notes, 190

Tax forgiveness in income analysis, 47
Tax rates, 166, 259n.
Tax Reform Act of 1986, 166–167, 182,
  259n.
  depreciation methods and, 105–106
  foreign remittances under, 170
  interest expense under, 170
  LIFO calculation and, 93
  minimum tax under, 166
  operating losses under, 180
  production costs under, 178
  special tax status under, 173–175
  tax rates under, 259n.
Teledyne, Inc., 221
10-K report, 74
Tonka Corporation, 189, 196–197
Translation adjustments, 70–76
Treasury stock method, 231
Trend(s), key, projections of, 14–16
Turnover ratios, 264

Unearned finance charges, 64
Unearned premium reserves, 63
Unexpired subscriptions, 64–65
Union Carbide, 238
U.S. Department of Commerce, 90
United Technologies Corporation, 76
Units-of-production method, 106, 114
Universal Leaf Tobacco Company, Inc.,
  155–156

Valuation accounts, 58, 65–66
Value Line Industrial Composite,
  151–152
Value Line Investment Survey, 36,
  132

Warrants, allowance for, 231–232
Washington Post, 221
Wharton Econometric Model, 4
Working capital, adjustments arising
  from, 73–76
Working-capital position, 214–217
Write-downs, 66–67, 116, 178

Young, R. M., 7n.